Au

CW00555670

Australia's War, 1914–18

edited by Joan Beaumont

ALLEN & UNWIN

First published in 1995 by
Allen & Unwin
9 Atchison Street
St Leonards NSW 2065
Australia
Phone: (61 2) 9901 4088
Fax: (61 2) 9906 2218
E-mail: frontdesk@allen-unwin.com.au

National Library of Australia
Cataloguing-in-Publication entry:

Australia's war, 1914–1918.

    Includes index.
    ISBN 1 86373 461 9.

    1. World War, 1914–1918—Australia.
    I. Beaumont, Joan.

940.40994

Cover photograph with kind permission from the Australian War Memorial
(negative no. E1223). Cover background image with kind permission from
the Imperial War Museum, London.

Index compiled by Robert Hyslop
Set in 10/11 Times by DOCUPRO, Sydney

10 9 8 7 6 5 4 3 2

Contents

Tables and figures

Tables

Figures

Maps

Acknowledgments

This book arose out of our experience of teaching the history of Australia during the First World War at Deakin University. This revealed the need for a study in one volume of the various aspects of Australia's involvement in that conflict: where Australians fought and why; the impact of the war on domestic politics, society and economy; the changes wrought in Australia's place in and attitudes towards the world; and the evolution of that potent element of national mythology, the Anzac legend.

Many people at Deakin contributed to the development of this book: especially, Frances Baensch, Ian Fox, Alison Littler, Anthony Lynch and Penny Williams. Colleagues throughout Australia read drafts and offered encouragement and advice: Peter Edwards, Raymond Evans, Jeffrey Grey, Roy Hay, Ken Inglis, John McQuilton, Judith Smart, and Garry Woodard. Finally, we owe thanks to our long-suffering families, especially our children, Diana, Caroline and Julia Beaumont; Sonia and Nadine Maclean; and Robin and Leigh Vial.

Abbreviations

AIF	Australian Imperial Force
AWNL	Australian Women's National League
AWM	Australian War Memorial
AWSC	Australian Women's Services Corps
BHP	Broken Hill Proprietary Company Ltd
GDP	Gross Domestic Product
CHG	Collins House Group
CSL	Commonwealth Shipping Line
GNE	Gross National Expenditure
IWW	Industrial Workers of the World
OBU	One Big Union
SIP	Sisterhood for International Peace
WCTU	Women's Christian Temperance Union
WPA	Women's Peace Army
BHAS	Broken Hill Associated Smelters

Contributors

Joan Beaumont is a Reader in History in the School of Australian and International Studies, Faculty of Arts, Deakin University. She is the author of *Gull Force: Survival and Leadership in Captivity, 1941–45* (Allen & Unwin, 1988, 1990), *Comrades in Arms, British Aid to Russia, 1941–45* (Davis-Poynter, 1980) as well as articles on various aspects of the British and Australian experience of the Second World War and the treatment of prisoners of war.

Marnie Haig-Muir is a Lecturer in Social and Economic History and Development Studies in the School of Australian and International Studies, Deakin University. Her doctoral thesis was entitled 'Crisis in Clio's Family: A Study of the Discipline of Australian Economic History, 1918–65'. Her publications include 'Percy Gerald Stewart' in *Australian Dictionary of Biography,* vol. 12, and 'Economic History: A Client?' Working Papers in Economic History, no. 148, ANU, 1991.

David Lowe is Lecturer at the Sir Robert Menzies Centre for Australian Studies, London, on leave from the School of Australian and International Studies, Deakin University. His 1990 doctoral thesis was entitled 'Australia, South-East Asia and the Cold War, 1948–54'. He is currently working on a biography of Percy Spender, the former Australian Minister for External Affairs.

Pam Maclean is a Lecturer in History in the School of Australian and International Studies, Deakin University. Her research interests include German–Jewish relations during the First World War and Australian–Jewish history. She has published articles in the above areas, on Australian refugee policy and in women's studies.

Chronology of the war

1914

28 July	Austria declares war on Serbia.
29 July	Dominion governments advised by London that war is imminent.
31 July	Labor leader Andrew Fisher declares at Colac that Australians will defend Britain 'to our last man and our last shilling'.
3 August	Australian Government offers to place the vessels of the Royal Australian Navy under the control of the Admiralty and to raise a force of 20 000 troops in event of war.
4 August	Britain declares war on Germany.
6 August	British Government accepts Australian offer of troops.
4 August	Royal Commission on food supply appointed. Membership: Alfred Deakin, Dugald Thomson and George Knibbs.
23 August	Japan enters the war on the side of the Allies.
30 August	New Zealand forces seize Samoa.
5 September	Labor Party wins federal general election. Andrew Fisher becomes prime minister.
11–17 September	Australian Naval and Military Expeditionary Force captures German New Guinea.
28–29 October	War Precautions Act passed.
29 October	Turkey enters war on the side of the Central Powers.

1 November	First contingent of the First AIF leaves Australia.
9 November	HMAS *Sydney* engages the German light cruiser *Emden* and causes it to run aground near the Cocos Islands.
3 December	First AIF arrives in Egypt.

1915

3 February	Turkish attack on Suez Canal repelled.
9 March	Blast furnace 'blown-in' at new BHP steelworks, Newcastle.
25 April	Landings on the Gallipoli peninsula.
7 May	Cunard liner the *Lusitania* sinks off the Irish coast after being torpedoed without warning by a German submarine. More than 1400 people, including US citizens, drown.
8 May	Ellis Ashmead-Bartlett's account of the Gallipoli landing published in Australia.
18 May	The commander of the First AIF, Major General Sir William Bridges, dies of wounds inflicted at Anzac Cove on 15 May.
19 May	Private John Simpson killed at Gallipoli. Turkish offensive at Anzac.
24 May	Enemy Contracts Annulment Act.
21 June	Recruiting campaign launched in Victoria.
14 July	Embargo on gold exports imposed.
6 August	British landing at Suvla Bay.
6–8 August	Attack at Lone Pine.
7 August	Attack at the Nek.
6–15 September	'War Census' taken.
11 September	Universal Service League established.
12 October	British nurse Edith Cavell shot by German firing squad in Belgium for harbouring Belgians of military age and helping British and French soldiers to escape across Dutch border.
26 October	Fisher resigns to become high commissioner in London. 'Billy' Hughes becomes prime minister.
30 October	*The Songs of a Sentimental Bloke* by C. J. Dennis published.
4 November	Premiers' conference agrees to abandon referendum to amend the constitution to give the

	Commonwealth government the power to regulate prices.
19–20 December	Withdrawal from Gallipoli peninsula.

1916

6 January	British Parliament votes for conscription.
16 January	Hughes leaves for London.
21 February	German attack at Verdun begins.
3 March	Hughes arrives in London.
14 March	First unit of the Australian Flying Corps prepares to leave for the front.
27 March	Six o'clock closing of hotels introduced in South Australia. By the end of 1916 all States except Queensland had followed suit.
27 April	News reaches Australia of rebellion in Dublin proclaiming an Irish Republic.
12 May	Irish rebels executed.
30–31 May	Battle of Jutland in the North Sea.
14–17 June	Hughes attends the Economic Conference in Paris.
1 July	Battle of the Somme begins.
19 July	Australian 5th Division committed to attack at Fromelles.
23 July	Attempt to capture Pozières begins.
31 July	Hughes returns to Australia from Britain.
3 August	Roger Casement, former British diplomat, hanged for role in Irish rebellion.
30 August	Hughes announces intention to hold referendum on conscription.
4 September	Hughes and supporters expelled from NSW branch of the Labor Party.
14 September	Second reading of referendum bill in Parliament. Frank Tudor, Minister for Trade and Customs, resigns from Cabinet.
15 September	First use of tanks on the Somme.
23 September	Arrests begin of members of the IWW on charges of treason or arson.
2 October	Hughes's Government calls up unmarried men between 21 and 35 for military service within Australia.
27 October	Federal Treasurer, W. G. Higgs, Vice-President of the Executive Council, Albert Gardiner, and honorary Cabinet Minister, Senator E. J. Russell,

	resign in protest at Hughes's orders to interrogate men at polling booths.
28 October	First conscription referendum.
14 November	Hughes and supporters leave the federal Labor Party.
22 November	Men called up early in October allowed to go home.
23 November	Hughes remains prime minister as leader of National Labor Party.
27 November	Imperial wheat purchase concluded.
4 December	Federal Labor Party votes to expel all members who support conscription.

1917

9 January	National Party established through coalition of Liberals and Hughes's National Labor Party.
17 February	National Government sworn in.
16 March	Russian Czar abdicates.
6 April	United States declares war on Germany.
9 April	British 3rd Army attacks at Arras.
11 April	First Bullecourt.
3 May	Second Bullecourt begins.
4 May	French Army mutinies.
5 May	General election resulting in victory for Hughes's National Party.
7 June	Battle of Messines begins.
31 July	Third battle of Ypres begins.
2 August	Strike begins in NSW railways and tramways.
4 September	Adela Pankhurst jailed for three months in Melbourne in response to her role in the Melbourne food riots of August–September.
20 September	Battle of Menin Road.
26 September	Battle of Polygon Wood.
4 October	Attack on Broodseinde Ridge.
12 October	Attack on town of Passchendaele.
31 October	Charge of Light Horse at Beersheba.
1 November	Five Australian divisions grouped into an Australian Corps under General William Birdwood.
7 November	Bolsheviks (Communists) take power in Russia. Hughes announces second referendum on conscription.
29 November	Hughes pelted with egg and involved in a fist fight at Warwick, Queensland, an incident

	which precipitates the establishment of the Commonwealth Police Force.
9 December	British troops capture Jerusalem.
20 December	Second conscription referendum.

1918

8 January	Hughes resigns. Asked to form new administration.
9 January	President Woodrow Wilson announces his Fourteen Points in a speech to the US Congress.
3 March	Soviet Russian Government signs Treaty of Brest-Litovsk with Germany, thus formalising the withdrawal of Russia from the war.
21 March	German offensive at Arras.
12 April	Governor-General's recruiting conference.
1 June	General John Monash takes command of the Australian Corps.
4 July	Australian troops capture Hamel.
8 August	Allied offensive at Amiens—'the black day of the German army'.
18 September	Attack on the Hindenburg line.
1 October	Damascus captured.
30 October	Turkey sues for armistice.
31 October	Germany sues for armistice.
3 November	Austria signs armistice with Allies.
11 November	Armistice signed with Germany at 11 a.m.

1919

18 January	Paris Peace Conference begins.
28 June	Paris Peace Conference concludes with signing of the Treaty of Versailles.
23 August	Hughes returns to Australia.

Introduction
Joan Beaumont

Why study Australia's experience of war? There are few countries in the world where an historian would feel obliged to pose that question. As many commentators have observed, there is a paradox in Australia's national history. Australian society is essentially an anti-militaristic one. Australians traditionally have shown little reverence for military institutions. They have been suspicious of militarism, distrustful of the claims of the state on its citizens for compulsory military service and often ambivalent about their country's contribution to the wars of the twentieth century.

Yet, war has been profoundly significant in shaping Australian public culture and popular perceptions about the national character and identity. The First World War generated the powerful legend of Anzac. For many decades this celebration of the supposed qualities of the Australian serviceman of the war of 1914–18 almost defined the Australian character—or, at least, the character of white Australian males. Of the national holidays celebrated annually, Anzac Day is widely recognised to have been a more effective focus for national pride than Australia Day. Even three-quarters of a century after the landing at Gallipoli, Anzac retains significant emotional power and political utility, as was evident in the ritualistic commemoration, by the media and political leaders, of the seventy-fifth anniversary of the landing at Anzac Cove in 1990.

The First World War also had a lasting legacy in Australian political culture. The bitterness which accompanied the conscription referenda of 1916 and 1917 ensured that conscription for overseas service would always be contentious thereafter. Although a Labor government was able to introduce it in 1943 when the sense of national peril was acute, the divisive debate about conscription for Vietnam twenty years later revealed how deeply embedded in political culture were the attitudes of the 1916–17 debate. Conscription in the 1990s seems unthinkable.

The First World War is therefore a central part of Australian historical consciousness and worthy of study for this reason. In addition, this conflict demands attention because it played a role in shaping Australian political, social and economic institutions. The degree to which it did this, it should be said, is debatable. Given the scale of the conflict and the appalling toll it exacted in death and human suffering, it is tempting to assume that the war was an agent of major change. This sense is reinforced by the fact that in Australia the First World War witnessed political turbulence and class conflict on a scale almost unique in the nation's history. Surely a conflict which generated such divisiveness and caused the deaths of over 58 000 men from a population of less than five million *must* have had profound and lasting impact on Australian politics and society.

Such an interpretation of the impact of the First World War on Australia is consistent with a dominant model of the relationship between war and social change, that was expounded in 1974 by the influential British social historian, Arthur Marwick.[1]

In recent years, however, Marwick's assumption that war is a major determinant of change has been qualified by both British and Australian historians. Historians are now more inclined to stress the elements of continuity between the prewar and postwar worlds, as much as the elements of disruption. Traumatic though the First World War obviously was in terms of personal grief, in many respects, it is argued, it did not cause change but rather accelerated existing social, economic and political developments and exacerbated already entrenched divisions within society.

Yet it would obviously be idiosyncratic to allow the pendulum to swing to the other extreme, and to assert that the Great War, as it was then called, had no impact on Australian society. Clearly it was a towering experience in the national history, and the course of Australia's development would have been different had it not occurred. The split in the Labor Party in 1916, for example, had its roots in a pre-existing divergence between the industrial and political wings of the labour movement. Yet it is difficult to imagine the split having occurred with such bitterness and rancour—and at the time it did—had not the insatiable demands of the war accentuated the confrontationist and dictatorial aspects of Prime Minister 'Billy' Hughes's personality and persuaded him that conscription for overseas service was a political and military necessity. Similarly, the legend of Anzac, as many authors have observed, was deeply embedded in the late nineteenth-century values of egalitarianism, mateship and the importance of the bush in defining the Australian character; but without the First World War and the Gallipoli campaign, with its especially fortuitous combination of the qualities required for the creation of legends, Australian national mythology would have developed in a different way.

It is one of the purposes of this book to examine systematically the problematic question of the impact of war on Australia. This is one of two companion volumes, the first concerned with the war of 1914–18; the second with the war of 1939–45. In this volume our analysis will be focused on the major aspects of the First World War: where Australians fought and why; the tensions and realignments within Australian politics in the period 1914–18; the stresses of the war on Australian society, especially on women and those whom wartime hysteria cast in the role of the 'enemy' at home; the impact of the war on the country's economy; the role played by Australia in international diplomacy; and finally, the creation and influence of the Anzac legend. These themes have, of course, been explored discretely in a growing number of monographs. It is the purpose of this book, however, to bring them together in a single volume.

Our primary audience is the tertiary student, whose need for a comprehensive text on Australia in the First World War has long been unmet. We aim also to reach the general reader whose understanding of the Australian experience of war has been scarcely illuminated by the barrage of film and television miniseries of the 1980s which, as classic examples of 'faction', have perpetuated the more uncritical, if comforting, myths about Australia's past.

A second purpose of this volume is to consider how historians have interpreted Australia's experience of the First World War. As Jeffrey Grey and Peter Dennis have pointed out,[2] Australian writing on the First World War, though extensive, has been unbalanced. For many years the historiography of the war was dominated by the monumental official history, the work, to a considerable degree, of the war correspondent, C. E. W. Bean. His 'democratic history', as it is sometimes called because of its emphasis on tactical history rather than grand strategy and high command (though these are not entirely neglected by Bean), had a profound influence on later Australian writing about the war. Not only was Bean's celebration of the digger often accepted uncritically by popular writers, but his accounts of the battles of Gallipoli and the Western Front have remained primary sources for later academic scholars. Even historians concerned to subject the experience of war and the Anzac legend to a radical critique have sometimes owed much to the writings of Bean.

Bean established a tradition of writing which was essentially narrative, rather than analytical, and inclined to see the infantrymen as being more worthy of attention than the generals. Only in the 1970s and 1980s did biographies of major Australian commanders begin to emerge in any numbers.[3] This was a reflection not only of Bean's influence, and the lack of any tradition of an officer class in Australia comparable to that in Europe. It was also an indication of a sense among historians that Australian commanders, being subordinate to British commanders throughout the war, were in some ways uncomfortable reminders of Australia's colonial and dependent status. The fact that Australia also had very little influence on decision-making in London and Paris reinforced the reticence on the part of historians to consider matters of grand strategy.

Within the democratic tradition of First World War historiography, there was a further imbalance in the amount of attention given to Gallipoli at the expense of the battles of the Western Front. Just as in popular consciousness Gallipoli has a resonance which Amiens, Hamel, Fromelles, Bullecourt and even Passchendaele and Pozières do not, so in the campaign histories of the war there is a preoccupation with 1915. The reasons for this anomaly—an anomaly because almost 87 per cent of Australian deaths were suffered on fronts other than Gallipoli—are complex; but they are obviously linked to the extraordinary capacity of Gallipoli to seize the imagination of military historians (British as well as Australian), and to that intriguing process whereby the campaign became internationally identified with the Anzacs, despite the fact that they were outnumbered three to one on the peninsula by other Allied forces. The imbalance in Bean's official narrative of the war—he devoted two weighty volumes to the eight-month campaign at Gallipoli and four to the remaining three years of the war—also contributed to this distortion.

Australian academics discovered the First World War in the 1960s, no doubt because the issue of conscription, and indeed of war and Australian national identity itself, had acquired a new salience during the Vietnam War. A profoundly influential address by Ken Inglis at the ANZAAS conference of 1964, later published in *Meanjin*, triggered a vigorous debate about the Anzac tradition. At Melbourne University, meanwhile, Lloyd Robson subjected the First Australian Imperial Force (AIF) to critical scrutiny for the first time—an enterprise so implicitly challenging to the semi-sacred status that Anzac had by then acquired that Robson received death threats.

The growth of academic interest in this and subsequent decades has progressively redressed the imbalances in the historiography of the war. In line with overseas developments, social, political and women's historians have begun to 'colonise' military history, shifting the focus from the battle front, with its inherent dominance of men, to the home front. As this has happened within Australia, the view of a society largely united in its war effort and fused by consensus—a view which was promoted by the official historian of the home front, Sir Ernest Scott, in his 1936 publication *Australia During the War*—has been demolished. Frank Cain, Dan Coward, Raymond Evans, Kevin Fewster and Marilyn Lake[4] are among those who have challenged Scott's consensual paradigm. Their studies of New South Wales, Tasmania and Queensland at war, and of the agencies of censorship and repression established by the Australian state, reveal societies 'riven by class, ethnic and ideological divisions, rather than ones united by the forces of nationalism or imperialism, the necessity of war sacrifice or the will for victory'.[5]

With these developments the study of the First World War has acquired greater depth and sophistication. Yet compared to the richness of, say, British writing on the First World War, Australian historiography remains comparatively sparse and narrow. Where, for example, are studies of the demographic legacy of the war to match the seminal work of J. M. Winter in Britain?[6] Where are the systematic analyses of the impact of war on the Australian economy, especially on particular sectors of the economy? Where is a detailed analysis of the socioeconomic base of the AIF, an analysis of how this changed as the war progressed and of how casualties were distributed across class, age and the soldiers' place of origin?[7] And where, especially, are the studies comparing Australia to other nations? A number of historians have observed over the past twenty-five years that the sense of Australians' uniqueness which is integral to the Anzac legend has rarely if ever been tested against the experience and performance of other armies. Yet even limited study of this question suggests that behaviour that is often portrayed as distinctively Australian was characteristic of many other armies, and was perhaps as much a functional response to the stresses of war as a peculiarly Australian phenomenon.

Such comments are not gratuitously negative. Rather they are made with the intention of highlighting the richness of the subject of a nation's experience of war, and to encourage future generations of historians to devote their efforts to studying aspects of Australia's experience that have thus far been neglected.

Notes

1 Arthur Marwick, *War and Social Change in the Twentieth Century: A Comparative Study of Britain, France, Germany, Russia and the United States*, Macmillan, London, 1974.

2 Peter Dennis and Jeffrey Grey, 'Australian and New Zealand Writing on the First World War', in Jürgen Rohwer (ed.) *Neue Forschungen zum Ersten Weltkrieg*, Bernard & Graefe Verlag, Koblenz, 1985, pp. 1–8.

3 A. J. Hill wrote a biography of the Australian commander of the Desert Mounted Corps, General Sir Henry 'Harry' Chauvel (*Chauvel of the Light Horse*, Melbourne University Press, Melbourne, 1978). C. Coultard-Clark in the following year wrote a biography of Major General Sir William Throsby Bridges, the commander of the AIF killed at Gallipoli (*A Heritage of Spirit*, Melbourne University Press, Melbourne, 1979), and followed this in 1988 with *No Australian Need Apply: The Troubled Career of Lieutenant-General Gordon Legge*, Allen & Unwin, Sydney. Monash was the subject of two major works in the 1980s: the fine biography by Geoffrey Serle, *John Monash* (Melbourne University Press, Melbourne, 1982) and the study of his development as a military commander by P. A. Pedersen, *Monash as Military Commander*, Melbourne University Press, Melbourne, 1985. Pedersen, Hill and Coultard-Clark contributed chapters (on Monash, Chauvel and Bridges respectively) to David Horner (ed.) *The Commanders: Australian military leadership in the twentieth century*, Allen & Unwin, Sydney, 1984, which also included chapters on the staff officer, General Sir Brudenell White (Guy Verney) and Vice-Admiral Sir William Creswell (Stephen D. Webster).

4 See the select bibliography at the end of this book for references.

5 Raymond Evans, *Loyalty and Disloyalty: Social conflict on the Queensland homefront*, Queensland University Press, St Lucia, 1987, p. 2.

6 J. M. Winter, *The Great War and the British People*, Macmillan, London, 1985.

7 An example in Britain of such research is Ian Beckett, 'The British Army, 1914–1918: The Illusion of Change', in John Turner (ed.) *Britain and the First World War*, Unwin Hyman, London, 1988, pp. 99–116.

1   Australia's war

Joan Beaumont

In terms of human suffering the First World War was the most traumatic conflict in Australia's history. From a population of less than five million, an army of almost 417 000 men was raised between 1914 and 1918; over 330 000 of them served overseas.[1] 58 132 servicemen died and 156 228 were gassed, wounded or taken prisoner of war.[2] In the Second World War, in contrast, although there was the unprecedented psychological trauma of Australia's being threatened and attacked, the death rate was significantly less: 27 073 service personnel were killed in action or died of wounds, when the population was just over seven million.[3]

Reasons for Australia's involvement in the war

Inevitably, studies of the First World War begin with the question of why Australia was involved in this appallingly costly conflict. Why were so many men willing to fight and die on battlefields which were thousands of kilometres distant, in Europe and the Middle East?

The answer to the first question is, on one level, simple. Australia was involved in the First World War because it had no choice but to be. In 1914 it was a British colony, not a sovereign state. Although the Australian Government had gained control at the time of federation in 1901 over what the Constitution called 'external affairs' in the decade before 1914, this had been taken to mean only relationships between Australia and Britain. Contacts with other countries outside the empire were controlled by London. In

1

1914, therefore, when Britain declared war, it did so on behalf of the whole empire.

Yet, being legally at war was not the same as supporting it enthusiastically. Australia had no choice but to follow Britain into war in 1914, but it did have a choice about its level of participation and the nature of its involvement. The more interesting and problematic question, therefore, is why the Australian Government and so many of its people embraced the war so uncritically. Why did they feel themselves intimately involved in a conflict which was essentially about the challenge of a newly industrialised Germany to the European status quo, and about the international ramifications of the ethnic tensions that were tearing apart the autocratic Austro-Hungarian Empire? Why did Australians not chafe at the decision to involve them in a war being made in London? Why did Australian politicians rush to prove that their parties were deeply committed to the cause of war? In August 1914, when the tension in Europe was reaching crisis point, there was a general election in Australia. The Prime Minister, Joseph Cook, campaigning in Horsham on 31 July, stressed that 'all our resources in Australia are in the Empire and for the Empire, and for the preservation and security of the Empire'. The leader of the Labor Opposition, Andrew Fisher, declared at Colac on the same day (in a statement that entered Australian folklore) that 'Australians will stand beside our own to help and defend her [Britain] to our last man and our last shilling'.[4]

Shortly before war broke out the Australian Government had offered Britain a force of 20 000 troops. It agreed also to put the small Australian Navy, created only in 1909, under the control of the Royal Navy. Meanwhile, the prospect of war brought massive crowds into the streets of the major cities, and the news of war's declaration was greeted with public enthusiasm so unrestrained that in Melbourne it degenerated into rioting and violence. These instances of public euphoria, of course, cannot be taken as being representative of the views of all Australians. There were clearly many individuals who had reservations about the war, which sprang either from political conviction or private dread. Historians of the 1990s no longer accept the judgment of the official historian, Ernest Scott, who, writing from a pro-imperial and Anglophilic perspective in 1936, maintained that there was 'no group which did not approve' of Australia's involvement.[5] Yet, it is equally clear that such Australians were in the minority in August 1914—at least in terms of public criticism of the war. The views of Christian pacifists, and those of members of the radical Left, who denounced the conflict as a sordid struggle between rival capitalist powers intent on commercial and industrial domination of the world, were drowned in the deluge of enthusiasm for the war pouring from the press, the churches, the universities and the schools.

Traditionally historians have explained this enthusiastic response of Australians to the outbreak of war in a number of ways. Firstly, there was the deep attachment to the British Empire, which operated on both the emotional and pragmatic levels. To quote L. L. Robson, for many Australians imperialism 'had all the depth and comprehensiveness of religion'.[6] Britain, the centre of the empire, former home to the vast majority of immigrants and the source of Australia's cultural and political traditions, commanded a profound loyalty and affection, in the middle classes especially. Australians of the late twentieth century may find such an attachment incomprehensible, and certainly difficult to reconcile with any modern notion of nationalism and national interests. But as Avner Offer has said, 'nations have passions as well as interests',[7] and to Australians of 1914 there was no conflict between their dual loyalties. They were, as an earlier prime minister, Alfred Deakin, put it in his celebrated phrase, 'independent Australian Britons', conscious of their own distinctive identity but also basking in the prestige and reflected glory that being part of the British Empire gave them. There are few clearer reflections of this than the name chosen by the first commanding officer of the Australian troops sent overseas in 1914, Major General William Bridges, for the expeditionary force, the Australian Imperial Force (AIF).

How universal such imperial sentiments were within Australian society has been debated. There is considerable evidence that in the late nineteenth century and at the time of the Boer War of 1899–1902, the working classes were generally less euphoric about empire than the middle classes. But in the decade before 1914 working-class children had been subjected to a barrage of imperial propaganda in the school curricula, and the stridently anti-British tone of the nationalism of the *Bulletin* and the radical Left in the late nineteenth century had been muted. In any case, a central element in the Labor political agenda which had emerged in the 1890s and after federation was the preservation of white Australia from the threat of cheap Asian labour. The British connection offered even those who, like Irish Catholics, remained resistant to uncritical Anglophilia, the comfort of being secure within a wider white, Anglo-Saxon race.

The link with Britain also offered Australians the advantage of a supposedly credible defence policy. In the years after federation, Australians of all political complexions had become anxious, and at times hysterical, about the growing power of Japan in the region and German penetration of the south-west Pacific. In Papua, which Australia had inherited from Britain in 1902, they actually shared a border with the New Guinea outpost of the German empire.

Realising the impossibility of adequately defending their regional interests, even with the system of compulsory military service that had been introduced in 1911, Australians saw their salvation in the Royal Navy. The key to imperial defence was mutual help: the notion that if Australia helped Britain, no matter where the challenge to its interests might arise, then Britain would in turn support Australia against regional threats. In fact, in the years immediately preceding the First World War, the Australian Government had been cautious about giving practical substance to this theory. At the Imperial Conference of 1911 it had seemed that Australia and Canada would come only grudgingly to Britain's aid in the event of a European conflict; but all this was swept away in the flood of support for Britain in 1914. Were the 'mother country' to be defeated by Germany, Australians feared, they would be left vulnerable to the dictates of an expansionist German empire.

To these concerns were added many other reasons for enthusiasm about the outbreak of war. Widespread within the Australian community at this time, as within the European world, was a belief in pseudo-scientific theories about the biological struggle for survival among the races of the world. War was seen as a purifying and regenerative force in society. It was therefore welcomed by some as an opportunity for Australians to prove that they, as offshoots of the Old World, had not degenerated as a result of living in the antipodean climate. They would at last have the chance to prove themselves in war, the greatest of all games. The *Sydney Morning Herald* trumpeted on 6 August 1914 that the war would be Australia's 'baptism of fire'. The Protestant churches' leadership meanwhile adopted the line that the war was, literally, a God-given opportunity to bring the nations of the world, especially Australia, back to paths of righteousness through the experience of suffering.[8]

These, it should be stressed, were public views. It is more difficult to assess what motivated those thousands of individuals who volunteered for military service in the first months of the war. Within weeks the contingent of 20 000 men that the Australian Government had promised Britain had been filled and many thousands more volunteers had been rejected as being unable to meet the rigorous standards of physical fitness. What motivated these men to rush to war?

As Richard White has pointed out, we cannot assume that the publicly articulated reasons for Australia welcoming the war were the same as the private motives that inspired Australians to enlist. 'Australians did not necessarily join the war for the same reasons Australia did.'[9] There is a danger, moreover, in assuming that values such as love of empire and patriotic duty, which were propagated through public institutions which embodied middle-class values, had the same resonance among the working classes. They *may* have, given that many within the working class are known to have been politically conservative, but we cannot take it for granted. Did working men volunteer because of their loyalty to Britain or hatred of the Germans? Or were they motivated by a complex mixture of more prosaic considerations? The outbreak of war led to widespread unemployment in industries that were adversely affected by the disruption of international trade. In the Australian countryside 1914 was also a year of drought. Obviously some men were attracted to the army by the promise of regular work and good pay. Receiving six shillings a day, Australian soldiers were the best paid of any army in the world. In 1914 the wage of a rural labourer was perhaps only half of this. Such research as has been done on the rural districts of Australia during the war suggests that this acted as an economic incentive to enlist. Rural labourers (if not farmers who had greater security of employment) were quicker to respond to the call for volunteers than their urban counterparts.[10]

In addition to economic motives, Australians, as Bill Gammage suggests, volunteered for 'a thousand particular and personal reasons'.[11] Many men seem to have been motivated to enlist by the desire to travel, to escape unhappy domestic circumstances, or in the case of recent British immigrants, by the wish to get a free trip home; 400 000 immigrants had arrived from Britain in the ten years before the war.[12] Other Australian volunteers seem to have been inspired by a sense of adventure, by the illusion that war was a romantic and exciting variant on sport, and by the belief that it would be over before Christmas.

Obviously these were motivations which faded as the war progressed and the full brutality of its nature became apparent. Then other motives seem to have inspired volunteers: community pressure, fear of social ostracism as the pressure to enlist every able-bodied man grew, concern to replace those killed in the carnage at Gallipoli or on the Western Front, war hysteria or a desire to avenge friends or family members who had died in action.

We shall never know the relative weight of these motives in the individual decision to enlist. The evidence about men's motivation is fragmentary and problematic. Letters and diaries were usually written after men had volunteered; like memoirs, they were composed with a specific audience in mind and were rarely a reliable indication of a man's innermost thoughts. In any case, written evidence is never fully comprehensive and is inherently biased towards the more literate classes. Oral evidence collected retrospectively, on the other hand, is distorted by the almost inescapable human need to impose order, coherence and above all, significance, on the traumatic events of the past. Trivial motivation is likely to be underplayed when the war is recalled fifty years later; more serious notions of 'duty' may be given priority.[13]

What we do know of Australians' reasons for enlistment suggests that they were very similar to the motives of New Zealanders and English Canadians (the Dominion soldiers whose experience of the war most closely paralleled that of the Australians).[14] Although the Canadian experience was distinctive in that there was a significant French minority who resisted volunteering, a Canadian author has described reactions to the war in a way which almost mirrors the traditional accounts of how Australians responded:

> The declaration of war brought a flood of volunteers . . . The patterns of this feeling for the safety of the empire were deeply etched in the English Canadian consciousness by the school curricula, an Anglophilia that pervaded the popular culture, and large numbers of recent immigrants from the British Isles. Not all those who enlisted did so purely to serve the empire. Large numbers of recent immigrants saw enlistment as a means of getting back home to Great Britain free in return for service in a war that would soon be over. Farmers' sons and unemployed workers found a more relaxed regime or surer wage in the army. As recruiting continued more recalcitrant Canadians 'volunteered' for service in the context of phenomenal social pressure to enlist.[15]

In contrast to these similarities of motivation, there seems to have been little in the Australian response to the war that resembled the almost moral fervour which gripped some Europeans in August 1914. German accounts of the war describe middle-class students and writers greeting the conflict with rapture, seeing in it an opportunity to escape modernity—to flee from an alienating industrial society and rigidly structured social order into a sphere where true community and classless fraternity were possible. For many educated Europeans the early days of August 1914 were remembered as the 'most deeply lived days' of their lives, 'days that would never be forgotten or repeated'. Many German and British volunteers also recalled later that they could not rationally explain their decision to enlist. In retrospect, the euphoria with which the war was greeted seemed a form of collective madness, an outbreak of mass unreason, an uncontrolled release of the suppressed tensions which half a century of industrialisation and prolonged peace had built up within European society.[16]

Of course, the Europeans who articulated feelings such as these were not typical of their societies—any more than J. D. Burns, the head boy at Scotch College, Melbourne, who wrote the famous patriotic poem, 'The Bugles of England', was typical of Australian society.[17] But the absence of any response of the European kind on the part of any Australians is notable. It illustrates how the Australians' response to the war, like their experience of it, was conditioned by their distinctive social organisation. Australia was not the classless society which the promoter of the Anzac legend and official historian, C. E. W. Bean, later liked to portray, but it was certainly much freer of the rigid social hierarchies and the oppressive industrial urbanisation that characterised some early twentieth-century European societies.

The character of the AIF

If we cannot be certain as to why Australians volunteered to serve in the First World War, at least we can reach more empirically-based conclusions about who these volunteers were. The First AIF generated a vast amount of statistical records. For each man who volunteered, there is evidence of his socioeconomic background, his age, marital status, religion, place of residence at the time of enlistment, and his military record. From these it is possible to create a social and demographic profile of the AIF itself. Such a task was first attempted in the early 1970s by L. L. Robson. Sampling 0.5 per cent of the vast number of attestation papers which Australian soldiers completed on enlisting, he concluded that 42 per cent of the AIF were previously workers in industry and labourers; 17 per cent were workers in primary production; 12 per cent were workers in commerce; and 9 per cent were transport workers. Only 10 per cent fell into the professional or clerical classes and 10 per cent came from other or unknown occupations. Predictably New South Wales and Victoria, the more populous States, provided the most recruits, 37 and 29 per cent respectively. Queensland provided 12 per cent, South Australia 9 per cent, Western Australia 9 per cent and Tasmania 4 per cent. Significantly, 18 per cent of the AIF had been born in Great Britain. Most volunteers were between the ages of 18 and 34, and of these 38 per cent were between 20 and 24 years of age. The vast majority (82 per cent) of the force was single.[18]

Given the methodological limits within which Robson was working, his conclusions about the AIF are recognised to have been generally sound. (An exception may be the age profile since that of those killed in the war, at least, was somewhat older.) But there is much about the AIF which Robson's sample did not tell us. He did not, for example, attempt to relate the structure of the AIF to that of the wider Australian population. The methodological difficulties in the way of doing this were formidable, especially as the nearest census dated from 1911, at least three years before AIF volunteers enlisted. Nor was Robson able, because of his sampling technique, to ask some of the more fascinating questions about the AIF. What was the life expectancy of the Australian soldier in battle? Did the middle classes suffer disproportionately high casualties, as research suggests was the case in the British Army? How many of those who enlisted at the start of the war survived till November 1918? Were there any correlations between the experience of volunteers from particular regions and the political attitudes which their relatives at home manifested during the war? Is it possible to link the casualties suffered in, say, the battle of the Somme or the third battle of Ypres with regional voting patterns in the conscription referenda of 1916 and 1917? The answers to such questions about the nature of the AIF can be gained only from a computerised database of all AIF records, a resource which has become available to historians in the 1990s. With the aid of this database,[19] it will also be possible to test more fully the links between employment patterns and enlistment, and to establish whether, as was the case in Britain,[20] certain socioeconomic groups were more likely to enlist at one particular stage of the war than at others.

Australian troops in action, 1914–15

The vast majority of those Australians who volunteered in the first rush of enthusiasm in August 1914 left Australia for the Middle East three months later. In the interim, a small contingent of Australians was sent to occupy northern New Guinea, then a German colony. The presence of German radio stations there, and on other Pacific islands, together with the excellent harbour on the island of New Britain, was believed to offer the German Navy significant strategic advantages. The Australian and New Zealand governments were therefore urged by the British Government on 6 August to eliminate this threat 'as a great and urgent Imperial service'.[21] The Australian force completed its conquest of New Guinea by 17 September; the New Zealanders, meanwhile, occupied German Samoa.

As the men involved in these operations realised—most of them later volunteered for the AIF[22]—this campaign was a sideshow. The real war was in Europe where the British and French forces were halting the initial German advance into France and Belgium and were settling into the stalemate of trench warfare that would dominate the conflict in Western Europe until 1918. When the first contingent of the AIF, together with a force of New Zealanders, left Western Australia on 1 November, they therefore expected that they would go to France. Instead they were disembarked in Egypt a month later. There was briefly a plan on the part of the British Government to divert them to South Africa. The pro-German Boer section of the population there had launched a rebellion in response to the news that South Africa was to occupy German South–West Africa (now Namibia) under British orders. Bridges, on learning of this, suggested that he would 'sacrifice' the New Zealanders if this would allow the Australian forces to proceed as originally planned. However, the whole operation lapsed when the South African Government proved able to contain the rebellion with its own forces.[23]

The decision to send the Anzacs (as they became known early in 1915) to Egypt was partly a pragmatic one, partly a strategic one. By late 1914 the great camps on Salisbury Plain in Britain, to which troops, including those from the Dominions,[24] were sent for training, were overcrowded, short of equipment and unable to accommodate the Australian and New Zealand forces. Moreover, on 29 October 1914 Turkey entered the war on the side of the Central Powers. There was now a serious threat to British interests in the Middle East and to the Suez canal—that lifeline to British imperial networks in Asia and the Pacific—a threat that became real when the Turks unsuccessfully attacked the canal in February 1915.

The four and a half months that the AIF spent in Egypt was devoted to training and reorganisation as new contingents of men joined the original units. The interest of this period for historians[25] lies not in these military concerns but in the off-duty activities of the Australians. These quickly established, in the minds of their British commanders especially, a lasting stereotype of Australian soldiers. Although a great deal of mythology surrounds their behaviour, it is clear that their attitude towards formal military discipline was, at best, casual. It manifested itself most obviously in their reluctance to salute officers. At the same time their behaviour towards the Egyptian population was arrogant, racially intolerant and on occasions violent. On the night of Good Friday 1915 the tension between the local population and the colonial troops exploded in the so-called Wassa riot, when the red-light district of Cairo was ransacked and set alight by Australians and New Zealanders aggrieved at the bad drink and 'diseased' Egyptian prostitutes supplied to them. This riot, and a similar one which followed in July 1915, were excused by some at the time (and by some later historians[26]) as the natural response of Australians to the frustrations of training in the desert when they expected to be in combat. But these incidents were more than larrikinism, that exuberant, mischievous and almost endearing disrespect for authority which has become a central element in the Anzac legend. They were vandalism—and as Bill Gammage, a historian generally very sympathetic to the mystique of Anzac, concedes, they were evidence of 'some of the worst aspects of Australian character'.[27]

The Gallipoli campaign

Problems of discipline in Cairo were soon overtaken by events. In the following two weeks the Australian and New Zealand forces in Egypt set sail for action, the landing on the Gallipoli peninsula on 25 April 1915. Of all the campaigns in which Australians were involved in the First World War, this has attracted the greatest amount of popular and academic attention. This is not only because it proved to be the crucible from which the potent Anzac legend was forged, but because the amphibious landing on Gallipoli was, and remains, a deeply controversial strategic operation. It arose from a larger plan, enthusiastically promoted by the First Lord of the Admiralty, Winston Churchill, in London, to eliminate Turkey from the war by sending a force of the Royal Navy through the Dardanelles into the Sea of Marmara from where it could threaten Constantinople. With Turkey eliminated from the war, it was hoped, the Allies could bring the Balkans into the conflict on their side, secure British lines of communication with India and other imperial outposts, and gain access to the Black Sea ports of Russia, thereby allowing the Russians to export their wheat and gain urgently needed foreign exchange.

The problem with this ambitious plan was that, if it were to have any chance of success, it required both surprise and intense preparation, as amphibious operations are recognised to be amongst the most difficult operations in warfare. Both of these elements were lacking in the case of the Gallipoli campaign. The attempt by the British and French navies to force the Dardanelles on 18 March was abandoned after more than a third of the force was sunk or put out of action. (Most of these losses were caused by mines, a reflection of the often forgotten fact that the navies of Europe in the First World War were as tactically paralysed as were the armies on the Western Front by their inability to counter new technology—in the navies' case, mines, torpedoes and submarines.)[28] With the failure of this operation, and the massive build-up of naval forces around the islands of Lemnos and Mudros, the Turks could not fail to be aware of the imminence of the invasion of the peninsula.

The Anzac landing was only one of three on 25 April. The others, of which later generations of Australians have often remained studiously unaware, were by British and French troops, at the tip of the peninsula at Cape Helles, and on the Asian side of the Dardanelles. These operations were intended to clear the shoreline

Gallipoli, 1915

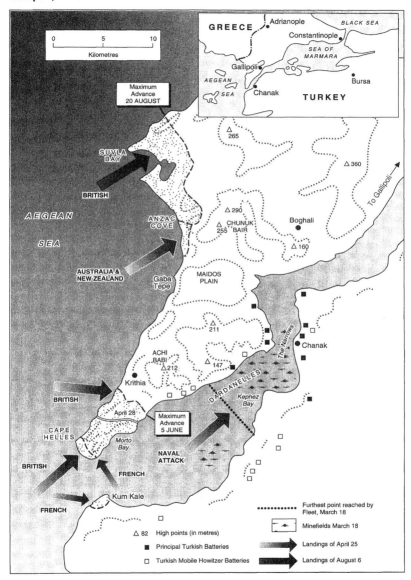

Source: Adapted from Martin Gilbert, *Recent History Atlas*, Weidenfeld & Nicolson, London, 1966, p. 33.

on either side of the strait of Turkish troops and artillery, thus allowing the naval forces to renew their assault on Constantinople unopposed. The Dominion troops, landing further north at Gaba Tepe, were intended to advance across the Gallipoli peninsula and cut the road running down to its tip.

The story of the landing at Anzac Cove has been recorded in great detail in many other places:[29] the error of navigation which resulted in the Anzacs being put ashore a mile further north than intended, the unexpectedly steep terrain the Anzacs then faced, the rallying of the Turkish defences by the young Lieutenant Colonel Mustafa Kemal, and the decision by the British commander, General Ian Hamilton, not to evacuate the force on the first night but to hold onto a precariously small beachhead by digging in. After the initial days, the situation at Anzac Cove settled into a stalemate. An increasingly intricate network of trenches confined within a small area around the cove gave those forces defending their positions an almost insuperable advantage over any attacking force.

On 19 May the Turks attempted to overrun the Anzac positions and were repulsed with such massive loss of life that a truce had to be declared in order to allow the burial of the innumerable bodies, which posed a serious health problem. Three months later, after a period of relative calm, the Allies themselves made an unsuccessful effort to break the deadlock. While a new landing was attempted on 6 August by British troops at Suvla Bay, north of Anzac Cove, the Australians and New Zealanders launched offensives against the heights commanding Anzac. These attempts to attack the Turks at the Nek, Lone Pine and Chunuk Bair proved immensely costly. Most of what remained of the Australian lst Brigade, for example, was lost at Lone Pine and some of the units had every officer killed or wounded.[30] These attacks were also futile, and the campaign once again settled into a stalemate. Finally in December, when it was clear that Allied forces, already weakened by casualties and disease, would suffer gravely in the winter conditions, and that there was no possibility of achieving the Allies' strategic objective, it was decided to withdraw the force. The evacuation on the night of 19–20 December is universally recognised to have been the most impressive part of the whole Gallipoli campaign. Through a variety of subterfuges the Turks were kept completely deceived, and no casualties were suffered by the withdrawing forces.

In many ways the Gallipoli campaign was the sideshow that its critics claimed. Not only was it a failure, but it is debatable what would have been achieved by Turkey's withdrawal from the war. Turkey was, after all, a minor ally of the Central Powers and the German Army, which had to be defeated if the Allies were to win the war, demonstrated a formidable capacity in the following three years to hold the Allied armies in France and on the Eastern Front at bay. Moreover, of the casualties that Allied forces suffered during the war, only a small proportion were incurred at Gallipoli. Of the nearly 60 000 Australian deaths, for example, 8141 were suffered in this campaign.[31] It should also be remembered that the Australian troops were always significantly outnumbered in this campaign by British, French and Indian forces.

Yet, as Trevor Wilson has pointed out, 'There will always be a dichotomy between how military actions appear when they are judged by their contribution (or lack thereof) to strategy and when they are seen in terms of the conduct and experiences of the participants. In the case of Gallipoli this dichotomy was to prove particularly marked.'[32] Despite the strategic failure of the campaign, it quickly became one of the quintessential expressions of heroism in Australian mythology; and despite the predominance of troops of other nationalities, the campaign became irrevocably identified with the Anzacs. Whereas for the British the most potent images of the First World War came from the Western Front—the men going over the top on the first day of the Somme, the mud of Passchendaele—for Australians the most graphic images of the war are, arguably, those of 1915—young men frozen in the moment of death by the bullet's blow as they dashed across the treacherous No Man's Land at the Nek or Lone Pine.

The reasons for the potency of the Anzac legend will be considered in chapter 6. Many of them are rooted in the fact that Gallipoli was Australia's first mass experience of modern war (so few Australians were lost in the Boer War that it scarcely scarred the national consciousness) and that this experience was quickly integrated into already existing Australian traditions and values. At this point, however, it is worth observing that for many commentators, British as well as Australian, there was—and remains—something unique about Anzac Cove. Its appallingly difficult topography, its steep gullies and escarpments from which the Turks were able to keep the Australians and New Zealanders constantly under fire, the crowding of so many men and such suffering into such a confined area, the imminence of danger and death at all times, the logistical nightmares (food and water had to to be brought in by sea)—all these elements combined to give Anzac Cove a particular fascination and an almost hallowed quality.

For the Australian troops involved at Gallipoli, the first experience of war is usually said to have had several enduring effects. It imbued in them a self-confidence, and a conviction, often bordering on arrogance, that they had proved themselves as good as, if not better than, other soldiers. The fulsome publicity given to their exploits by the war correspondents, Ellis Ashmead-Bartlett and

C. E. W. Bean, was an element in this process. In addition to this, the sense of their own superiority was instilled in Australians by their negative impressions of the British at Gallipoli. Although there were inevitably individual British officers and men who commanded Australian affection and respect, the general perception of the British command in this campaign was one of ineptitude. The chaotic management of the whole campaign made such a view understandable.[33] (The very fact that the British were so inefficient at the higher strategic level may be one reason why the Australian performance, at the tactical level, appeared to be so impressive.) Furthermore, the abortive Suvla Bay landing entered Australian mythology as a 'tea party' in which the British 10th and 11th Divisions dawdled while Australians were massacred above Anzac. According to popular tradition, British operational incompetence and reluctance to push inland after landing at Suvla Bay meant that the Australian attack on the Sari Bair ridge was left unsupported, with the disastrous results already noted. This, it should be said, is a view held not only by Australians but by British historians, such as John Terraine, who has described Suvla Bay as a 'fiasco', in which 'inexperienced, half-trained New Army divisions [were] commanded by elderly "dugout" generals who knew nothing of modern war'.[34]

In fact, recent research by an Australian historian suggests that such a view is fallacious. Despite what the commander of the Anzac troops, Lieutenant General William Birdwood, may have thought, the Suvla Bay landing was never intended to assist the attacks at Anzac; its main objective, in the initial stage, was the capture and retention of the bay as a base for future operations and supplying the Anzac force *after* it had captured the ridge. Although there were some British soldiers seen 'lolling about the beaches or bathing'[35] at Suvla Bay on 8 August, the real reasons for the failure of the British force to advance on that day were lack of water, the troops' exhaustion, their disorientation as a result of navigational errors in their landing (as Anzac showed, scarcely a British failing!), and the resistance of the Turks.[36] The myth of the 'tea party', however, has proved enduring, as its repetition in the work of John Terraine and the popular film of 1981, *Gallipoli*, demonstrates.

The Western Front, 1916

After its withdrawal from Gallipoli, the AIF underwent a three-month period of reorganisation and expansion in Egypt. The news of the landing at Anzac Cove had led to a massive increase in enlistments and a surge of recruitment efforts on the part of government authorities in Australia. In July 1915, 36 575 men volunteered, nearly six times as many as in April. This level was never again reached during the war, but enlistment remained generally high in late 1915 and early 1916.[37] This was due in part to the efforts of the indomitable W. M. 'Billy' Hughes, who replaced Andrew Fisher as the Labor Prime Minister in October 1915. Hughes, with a temperament that became increasingly authoritarian as the war progressed, did not hesitate to exploit the emergency wartime powers of his government in any way that would maximise Australia's commitment of manpower to the war effort. After conducting a 'War Census', which supposedly revealed that there were 600 000 fit men available for military service, Hughes promised the British Government 50 000 troops in addition to the 9500 reinforcements required each month to maintain the units overseas.

All this meant an expansion of the AIF from the two divisions of 1915 (the 1st had been joined by the 2nd Division in July) into a much larger force, of five divisions in 1916. In addition there was an Anzac Mounted Division (of Mounted Rifles and Light Horse Brigades) in the Middle East. From March 1916 the five infantry divisions were progressively committed to the Western Front in France.

The experiences of Australians in France, and the bitterness which these generated because of the apparently senseless loss of life, can only be fully understood within the wider context of the First World War. By mid-1916 the belligerents on both sides of the conflict in the west were trapped in a tactical and strategic stalemate which no army had the ability to break. The impasse was the result of a number of developments in military technology in the late nineteenth century and reflected the fact that the First World War occurred, as Paul Kennedy puts it, 'at a very particular period in the history of military technology and transport'. The industrial revolution had given armies, using complex railway systems, the ability to bring masses of men, equipment and ammunition to the rear of the battlefield; but it had not yet created the means (that is, trucks and transport aircraft) to convey these items beyond the railheads at a fast rate. Moreover, the development of rapid-firing guns (machine-guns and artillery) had given defending forces immeasurable advantages over those who were attacking, by making it almost impossible for infantry and cavalry to survive on top of the ground. To quote Kennedy again:

> The fire-power revolution meant that troops had to dig deep to survive; the transport conundrum meant that the more that defensive trench systems could be built up on an elaborate scale
> . . . the more difficult it was to penetrate them. If one attempted

to punch a hole through the first line by prolonged bombardments,
one surrendered the element of surprise and allowed the enemy to
reinforce the second and third line of trenches. Any advance took
the troops farther and farther away from their logistical supplies
and rear commanders . . . [w]hichever side moved forward had put
itself *immediately* at a disadvantage.[38]

Not until the latter years of the war did technology produce the
equipment, in the form of more accurate artillery, aircraft and tanks,
which could break this impasse. Nor, even more crucially, was it
until 1918 that the Allied armies developed, in the light of the
previous years' failures, the tactics and techniques needed to use
these new weapon systems in a way that effectively eliminated
enemy defences and allowed the infantry to advance without suffering horrendous casualties.[39]

Whether the French and British commanders on the Western
Front were excessively unimaginative in their attempts to break the
tactical impasse that faced them in the interim has been a matter
for fierce debate. Whatever the merits of the case on either side, it
is clear that when the Australians arrived in France, the Allied
commanders believed that their only strategic option was mass
frontal assaults on the opposing enemy trenches, which aimed
explicitly at attrition, or the 'wearing down' of enemy forces.

The Australians therefore were involved repeatedly in 1916–17
in attacks which followed a predictable pattern. A massive artillery
bombardment, intended to annihilate enemy defences and destroy
the barbed-wire barricades, preceded the infantry advance across the
No Man's Land between opposing trenches. This attack, if it were
not halted entirely by machine-gun fire, made only limited gains.
An inevitable German counterattack ensued, resulting in further
heavy casualties for the attacking force and often the loss of the
bitterly contested territory. After days, weeks or even months of
blood-letting the stalemate resumed with the position of trench lines
altered to a relatively insignificant degree—and very rarely
advanced a distance that seemed commensurate with the massive
casualties incurred in gaining it.

The first Australian experience of this terrible, destructive warfare came in July 1916. Faced with the need to relieve the pressure
on the French Army, which since February had been almost bled
white by the battle for Verdun, the British commander-in-chief,
General Douglas Haig, decided to launch a major offensive against
German positions around the River Somme. Australian troops were
not involved in the infamous opening stages of the attack, when on
the first day 57 470 casualties were suffered by the British (of which
18 000 were killed)—'probably the greatest single catastrophe of

the whole War', to quote Terraine.[40] Australians, however, were soon drawn into the battle of attrition. On 19 July the 5th Division was committed to an attack at Fromelles. The attack was intended to be a feint to divert German troops from the main battle further along the line, but it cost 5533 Australian casualties in only 24 hours. To put this into perspective, this was almost a quarter of *all* casualties suffered in the eight-month Gallipoli campaign. Although it is Gallipoli that has dominated Australian popular memory of the war, the Somme was in many ways the Australians' baptism of fire. For the first time they met the intense concentrations of heavy artillery, barbed wire and machine-gun fire that, together with poison gas and flamethrowers, were the characteristic features of war on the Western Front, and which Gallipoli, for all its discomforts and dangers, had not possessed.

Apart from its being the initiation of Australians to the Western Front, Fromelles had the distinction, at least in the eyes of Australian historians, of exacerbating Australian distrust of the British and their commanders. Universally agreed to have been poorly planned and executed, and to have achieved remarkably little, Fromelles was also misrepresented in official communiqués in a way that disillusioned Australians—'deliberate lying', Bean called it.[41] In addition, Australian officers were deeply critical of the British command and Australian troops felt let down by the British 61st Division whose supporting attacks had failed. In fact, the British troops were probably unjustly pilloried. They were undermanned, only recently arrived from Britain and 'demonstrably unsuited for battle';[42] and the Australian commander of the 5th Division, Lieutenant General James McCay, was arguably to blame, at least in part, for the disaster at Fromelles. Although he has been defended by some writers,[43] Jeffrey Grey and Peter Pedersen hold him equally responsible, with the British commander of the XI Corps, Lieutenant General Richard Haking, for the failure at Fromelles. Grey concludes, challenging popular mythology, that the whole Somme campaign demonstrated that 'Australian generals were as good at killing Australian troops as were British generals'.[44]

Four days after Fromelles, on 23 July 1916, the Australian 1st Division was committed to what proved to be the most costly battle for Australians yet: the attempt to capture one of the German strong points on the Somme at Pozières. Although previous attempts by British troops to capture the hamlet had failed, the Australians initially succeeded in capturing their objectives; only to then be subjected to a ferocious German artillery bombardment. In the weeks that followed, as the Australians suffered horrific casualties, the 2nd and 4th Divisions were drawn into the battle, until early in September the Australian forces were relieved. By this time

The Somme campaign, 1 July–18 November 1916

Source: Martin Gilbert, *First World War Atlas*, Weidenfeld & Nicolson, London, 1970, p. 12.

23 000 men had been lost. Again comparisons with Gallipoli are instructive. The total casualties for that campaign of nearly eight months were only about 2000 more than for the 45 days of the Somme. As Bean said, with his remarkable facility for immortalising the Australian experience, the Windmill site at Pozières was 'more densely sown with Australian sacrifice than any other place on earth'.[45]

The dead lay sometimes in batches of ten or twelve together [he recorded in his diary on 31 July] . . . There was not a soul in sight; only the powdered grey earth. No sign of any trenches of ours. All as still and dead and deserted as an ash heap . . . I turned back and followed a goat-track path. There were only blackened dead and occasionally bits of men and torn bits of limbs unrecognisably along it. I wandered on for five minutes without seeing a sign of anybody till I came to a gradually improving trench, quite deserted, peopled only by dead men, half buried, some sitting upright with bandaged heads, apparently little hurt except for the bandaged wound; others lying half covered in little holes they had scratched in the trench side . . . I didn't want to go through Pozières again. I have seen it once now.[46]

It should not be forgotten, however, that in the five months that the Somme battle continued relentlessly, the British suffered 415 000 casualties, the French 195 000. How many the Germans lost will never be known but it is possible that they suffered even more heavily.[47] Early in 1917 they took the decision to retreat into a new defensive line, the Hindenburg line, a strategic defeat which reflected the fact, often forgotten in the railing against the 'futility' of the loss of life of the Somme, that the German Army suffered appalling attrition in 1916.

As mentioned earlier, it is impossible at this stage of research into the war, to trace precisely the effect of the terrible casualties of 1916 on specific Australian regions and socioeconomic groups. Yet, in general it is obvious that they had a profound impact on Australian society and politics. Whereas the news of the Gallipoli campaign had triggered a great surge of enlistment, Fromelles and Pozières had no similar effect. On the contrary, enlistment which had been 10 656 in May 1916 remained between 6000 and 6600 in June, July and August. Of course, given the complexity of enlistment patterns and motivation, and the fact that the decline in enlistment had been a gradual one since early 1916, a direct correlation between the Somme and war weariness cannot be proven. Obviously, by mid-1916 the pool of 'eligible' men on whom the AIF could draw was diminishing after the high rates of enlistment in mid-1915; and we do not yet know what proportion of each new cohort of 20-year-olds volunteered for service in the latter years of the war.

The constant drain on manpower caused by the losses in mid-1916 encouraged Prime Minister Hughes in mid-1916 to attempt to introduce conscription: 32 500 recruits were needed for the AIF in September, he told Parliament on 30 August, and 16 500 a month thereafter.[48] Whether this level of recruitment was, in fact, necessary, or whether the figures were inflated by British and military authorities in an effort to strengthen the case for conscription has been debated.[49] Hughes almost certainly had reached the decision that conscription was necessary, for a mixture of political as well as military reasons, while he was in Britain in the first half of 1916 and was able to observe the comparative ease with which compulsory military service had been introduced there.

The referendum which his Government held on 28 October 1916 to give it the mandate for conscription proved to be profoundly divisive, as will be seen in chapter 2. For reasons which will be explored there, the vote for conscription lost by a narrow margin. In its aftermath, enlistment, which had swelled to 11 520 in October in anticipation of a 'Yes' vote and in response to the government's precipitately calling up all men between 21 and 35 for home defence, dropped to 2617, the lowest level of any month of the war. In 1917 monthly enlistment never rose above 4989 (in March).

The Western Front, 1917

In military terms, 1917 was, if it is possible to imagine, a worse year for the Allies. Its first half was dominated by the catastrophic French offensive in Champagne in April under General Robert Nivelle. Sold to British politicians especially as the means of achieving the decisive victory which would end the war, it fell far short of these grand hopes. Although the French made significant gains (significant at least in terms of the Western Front), the death toll and the disappointment of the inflated expectations were such that in May the French Army mutinied. Discipline was eventually restored, at the cost of many fewer executions than is commonly thought (there were 55), but the French Army was never the same again.

In order to support Nivelle's offensive the British high command agreed to launch a simultaneous attack against the Hindenburg line in the region of Arras. Australians were involved in diversionary attacks at Bullecourt in April and May 1917. In the first of these, some use was made of tanks, the new weapon that was being introduced in an attempt to break the tactical deadlock by providing mobile and armoured protection for troops crossing No Man's Land. The tanks, however, were primitive models and had had no time to practise coordination with the infantry. The attack failed and the Australian infantry, after fighting their way into the German lines, were eventually forced to withdraw at the cost of about 3000 casualties, many of whom were taken prisoner. Three weeks later, on the orders of the British commander, General Hubert Gough, the attack was renewed over the same ground—and, in view of the failure of tanks in First Bullecourt, the Allies reverted to the now traditional tactics of relying on massive artillery bombardment against heavily defended German positions. In fact, the Australians did capture part of the German lines and (much more unusual on the Western Front) managed to hold it for nearly a year. But again it was at the heavy cost of 7000 casualties.

As with many campaigns on the Western Front, controversy and mythology surrounds Bullecourt. It is generally agreed that First Bullecourt was a disaster, proceeded with by Gough in the face of protests by Birdwood and his Australian chief of staff, Brudenell White, and against all evidence that the artillery bombardment had not significantly weakened the German defences. Second Bullecourt, likewise, is presented by John Laffin, a writer who even in the 1990s uncritically endorses the Anzac legend,[50] as the battle which

> finally destroyed any confidence the Diggers might still have had in the British High Command. It seemed to all the Australians, from divisional commanders down to private soldiers, that the British generals did not appreciate the strength of the German defence . . . the Diggers had to overcome not only the dogged German enemy but the shortcomings of the British High Command.[51]

In this Laffin echoes the interpretation of Bean, as do so many Australian historians of the First World War. It is clear, from the work of less chauvinistic historians, however, that the responsibility for failure at Bullecourt must be shared more widely. While the British high command was deeply at fault in ordering a second attack over ground that was very favourable to the defending Germans, there were 'serious weaknesses in Australian staff work that contributed to the slaughter of Australians'.[52]

The next major battle in which Australians were involved, the attack at Messines on 7 June 1917, is generally agreed to have been a masterpiece of planning. The British commander of the Second Army, General Herbert Plumer, was one of the better British generals of the First World War and Major General John Monash, who was commanding the well-trained Australian 3rd Division under him, has been universally praised for his meticulous planning of campaigns and attention to detail. Messines, which began with a massive bombardment of three and a half million shells and a spectacular detonation of mines under the German lines, was at long last a major victory for the AIF, though even this was bought at the price of heavy casualties.

This was followed in September and October by several more successful actions on the Australians' part in the third battle of

British offensives in Flanders, June–November 1917

Legend:
- Allied front line 6 June
- Allied front line 14 June
- Allied front line 31 July
- Allied front line 4 October
- Allied front line 11 November

0 1 2 3 4 5
Kilometres

Forest of Houthulst

To Roulers

From Furnes

Steenbeck R.

Langemarck
Poelcapelle

Boesinghe   Pilckem
Elverdinghe   St. Julien   Passchendaele

Gravenstafel

From Poperinghe   Brielen   St. Jean   Zonnebeke

Frezenberg

Potijze

YPRES   Serre   Becelaere

Zillebeke   Gheluvelt

Dickebusch   Verbrandenmolen   MENIN ROAD

St. Eloi   Zandvoorde   Kruiseecke
Vierstraat

Kemmel   Wytschaete   Oosttaverne
Houtem   Wervicq

Canal

Messines   Comines
Warnetone   Lys R.
Wulverghem   From Armentières

Source: Arthur Banks, *A Military Atlas of the First World War*, Heinemann, London, 1975, p. 173.

Ypres. This was Haig's grandiose attempt to break through the German lines and advance to the Belgian coast and the Dutch border. Within weeks of its beginning on 31 July it was bedevilled by appalling weather, the wettest August for thirty years. With some respite from the rain the Australian forces were able to make considerable gains at Menin Road and Polygon Wood in September and, in October, at Broodseinde Ridge, 'the greatest A.I.F. success yet', in the words of Geoffrey Serle.[53] But elation turned to ashes. Believing the Germans defences to be about to collapse and ignoring the advice of some of his senior commanders, Haig insisted on continuing the campaign. The weather broke, and Passchendaele turned into a nightmare of mud and swamp, exacerbated by the shelling of the intricate system of drainage and dykes which had earlier reclaimed the land. Soldiers and guns floundered in the quagmire, sometimes up to their waists in mud, riddled with machine-gun fire and occasionally even drowning. When this, the most controversial of British campaigns had finally ended, the Australians had suffered 38 000 casualties. The total for the whole year was 76 836. For 1916, in contrast, it had been 42 270.[54]

These losses triggered a new political crisis in Australia. Convinced that Australia could not maintain its war effort at existing levels without conscription, Hughes again decided to put this question to the electorate. The second referendum campaign from 7 November to 20 December was if anything more divisive than that of 1916; the margin for 'No' was larger. In contrast to 1916, there was no discernible impact of the political turmoil on voluntary enlistment. It continued its steady decline throughout 1917, reaching a nadir for the year of 2247 in December.

The Western Front, 1918

Fortunately, then, for Australia's war effort and internal political fabric, 1918 proved to be the year in which the Allies finally gained victory—though this was far from apparent in its early months. On 21 March 1918 the German Army launched its last major offensive, aimed at seizing a decisive victory before the slow build-up of troops from the United States, which had joined the war on the Allies' side in April 1917, could swing the balance irrevocably against Germany. At first the Germans had remarkable success, opening up a gap of some 64 kilometres in the British line around the region of the 1916 Somme battle. It was a crisis such as had not faced the Allies since late in 1914 and Australian troops were brought in to help stem the tide of the German advance. This they did, so Serle maintains in one of his rare chauvinistic moments, with a 'glorious Australian self-conceit in the face of the defeatism of so many British stragglers'.[55] In fact their role in this battle is recognised[56] to have been exaggerated by the troops and by Australian commanders such as Monash (who was never known for his self-effacement). It is generally agreed that the German offensive was already losing steam, that the AIF was not the first to stem the

The Western Front, 1918

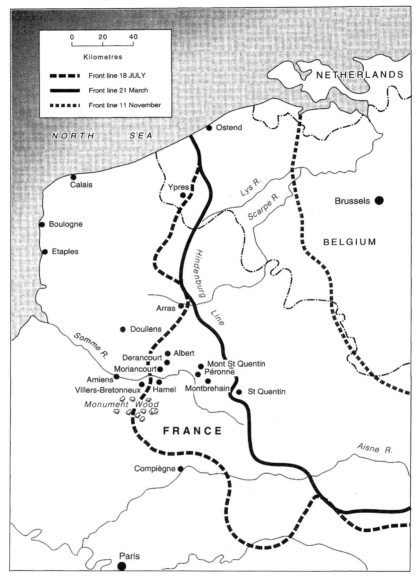

Source: Adapted from Jeffrey Grey, *A Military History of Australia*, Cambridge University Press, Melbourne, 1990, p. 110.

offensive, and that the British Army had not, in fact, lost control of the situation.

Yet, if the Australians' role has been overstated, it is widely agreed that in this, and later battles in 1918, they made a significant contribution to the final Allied victory. From April to November 1918 the stalemate of the previous three and a half years gradually gave way to open warfare. Increasingly the Allied forces developed tactics of 'peaceful penetration' and 'aggressive patrolling': that is, the use of small units, operating mainly at night, to probe out enemy weaknesses, gain ground and take prisoners for purposes of acquiring information. At these kinds of tactics Australians were recognised to be competent. As Kennedy has said, these tactics required intensive training, a much less hierarchical set of relationships between officers, NCOs and rankers and an emphasis on unit cohesion and mutual support—qualities which were more naturally found in forces with 'social backgrounds [which] did not cramp individualism (like the formidable Australian Corps)'.[57]

At the level of command, too, the Australian reputation grew with the appointment in May 1918 of Monash to the most senior position yet held by an Australian in France, the command of the Australian Corps (which had been created in November 1917 by the grouping together of the five Australian divisions, then under the command of Birdwood). Monash's first operation as Corps Commander, the capture of the Hamel spur on 4 July 1918, was brilliantly successful. Described by a leading British military historian as the 'perfect battle', it demonstrated how infantry, artillery, tanks and aircraft could be used in combination to achieve the results which had so long escaped strategists on the Western Front. This success was possible partly because of technological advances in weaponry and communications. Monash exploited these to great effect, but he was not as original as some of his supporters might claim: many of the tactical innovations which he implemented had already been developed more widely among the Allied armies. Monash also typically exaggerated the long-term effects of Hamel on the morale of the Allied high command. The battle is nonetheless thought[58] to have been brilliantly planned and to have established Monash's reputation as an outstanding Allied commander.

This was confirmed by the next major operation in which the Australian forces were involved on the Western Front, the spectacularly successful offensive which began on 8 August 1918 at Amiens. Again there has been some debate about how much credit should be given to Monash and to the Australian troops for the planning and execution of this battle.[59] Australians have celebrated it as the occasion on which the AIF spearheaded the Allied advance which culminated in Germany's defeat—and there is no doubt that the advance on 8 August was, as Bean put it, 'the most bloodless ever made by Australian infantry in a great battle'.[60] Within nine hours nearly 8000 German prisoners were taken for the loss of 2450 men. The British commander of the Fourth Army, General Henry Rawlinson, was very complimentary about the performance of the Australian troops and Monash's staff on this occasion. Yet it should be remembered that Amiens was not exclusively an Australian victory, and that in Canadian mythology it is remembered as 'chiefly a Canadian battle' in which the Canadian Corps was 'the decisive instrument' of victory.[61]

In the weeks that followed Amiens, the Australian Corps pushed on against the crumbling German forces, attacking at Mont St Quentin, Péronne and against the Hindenburg line. These were the greatest moments for the AIF in France, the weeks when superior command, a lavish supply of resources and years of experience and training combined to produce a formidable fighting force and the elation of victory. However, even troops at the peak of their performance have limits to their endurance and on 5 October the Australian forces were withdrawn from the battle for rest. Five weeks later, on 11 November 1918, the war on the Western Front finally came to an end when the German Army capitulated.

Other Australian contributions to the war

The land battle in France was the great maw which devoured by far the majority of Australian lives lost in the First World War. However, it should not obscure the fact that Australian troops were engaged in other theatres of the conflict. After the withdrawal from Gallipoli in December 1915 the Australian Light Horse remained in the Middle East, where it made a major contribution to the war against Turkey. Originally confined to the defence of the Suez Canal, the British forces under the command of General Archibald Murray began the reconquest of Sinai in 1916. In the following year, with the arrival of General Edmund Allenby, the Allied forces pushed on into Palestine, capturing Gaza in November and Jerusalem in December 1917. The occupation of Lebanon and Syria followed in 1918, resulting in the Turks suing for peace on 30 October 1918.

Although this campaign exacted a toll of Australian lives that was infinitesimal compared to other theatres of war—the total number of deaths was 1394—the Middle East campaign is significant for at least two reasons. In contrast to the demoralising stalemate on the Western Front, it was a theatre in which the war remained mobile. The most dramatic demonstrations of this were the famous charge at Beersheba in October 1917, when the mounted infantry raced across nearly five kilometres of open ground against an entrenched enemy position of artillery, machine-guns and aircraft, and the 'Great Ride' into Damascus in September 1918.[62] This mobility on horseback, coupled with the fact that the Australians were confronted in the desert with a struggle for survival similar to that posed by the Australian outback—scorching heat, desperate shortages of water, a harsh terrain that demanded immense adaptability and resourcefulness—ensured the Light Horse a natural place in the bushman-soldier mythology of Anzac.[63] (Indeed this had already been secured at Gallipoli where the Light Horse, dismounted, had been committed to the suicidal charge at the Nek.)

Palestine is also notable because it was the first theatre in which an Australian gained command at the corps level. In June 1917 General Henry ('Harry') Chauvel was appointed commander of the Desert Mounted Corps. This was not an exclusively Australian corps, given the small numbers of Australian troops in the Middle East, but included British, New Zealand and Indian troops.

Australia's naval forces also spent the war in a multinational force. As already mentioned, the Royal Australian Navy, which was barely three years old, was placed under the command of its British counterpart at the beginning of the war. In the four years that followed, it served in every ocean of the world on a variety of duties. An early, and very famous, engagement for the navy occurred in November 1914, when the HMAS *Sydney*, which was part of the force escorting the first contingent of the AIF to the Middle East, destroyed the German raider *Emden*, in the vicinity of the Cocos Islands. In the following year, on the day of the landing at Anzac, an Australian submarine, the *AE2*, made a remarkable passage through the Dardanelles before it was disabled and captured by the Turks. Thereafter the naval war was largely one of patrolling the oceans in an effort to deny passage to the enemy, of escorting British merchantmen threatened by enemy submarines, and of hunting German raiders and commercial shipping. Though much of this work was repetitive and unglamorous, it played an integral role in maintaining Britain's naval supremacy and protecting its trade links, which were vital to the Allied forces' surviving the war.[64]

In contrast to the RAN, Australians who served in the national air forces in the Middle East and France retained a separate national identity. Their numbers were small (less than 3000) but they were organised in four recognisably Australian squadrons which comprised, the Australian Flying Corps. Consistent with aerial warfare practice at this time, their role was primarily to support the embattled infantry below, strafing and bombing enemy aircraft, and flying close-observation and contact patrols during battles. In the opinion of the commander of the Royal Flying Corps in France, the Australians 'showed the most remarkable aptitude for flying and air-fighting'.[65] The fact that they retained their own national force, moreover, gave them advantages, in terms of experience of command and administration, over the airmen from another Dominion, Canada, who were integrated into British air forces.[66]

The problem of Australian command

This raises a question which must be considered before concluding this review of Australia's role in the First World War: whether there is any merit in the argument, which was prevalent during and after the war, that Australians should have had greater control over their own forces. From 1916 on there was some agitation, on the part of Hughes and others, for the British high command to create an Anzac army, by combining all Australian and New Zealand forces. The Canadians had insisted on the creation of a national corps as soon as two of their divisions arrived in France.

The British War Office, however, resisted the proposal. As we have seen, it was not until late in 1917 that an Australian Corps was formed. Even then it remained under a British general,[67] Birdwood, who had commanded the AIF since its evacuation from Gallipoli. Although Birdwood was favoured by Hughes in 1916 to command the proposed Anzac Army, he seems to have viewed his leadership of an Australian force largely in careerist terms. He did little to assist Australians to gain senior command and staff experience and was, in Grey's opinion, 'a poor choice as a commander of a national force'.[68] Not until Monash's appointment in May 1918 was the Australian Corps commanded by an Australian, as were all but one of its five divisions.[69]

The inability of the Australian Government to secure a national army under national command has sometimes been seen as a liability for Australia. The implication in some accounts of the First World War is that the interests of Australian troops were thereby jeopardised. Australians, it is claimed, were used as shock troops and employed in 'innumerable difficult and hazardous engagements'.[70] Had they been commanded by Australians, it is implied, they would not have been 'sacrificed' in the way they were by a thoughtless and incompetent British command.

These views had their roots in the distrust of the British which many Australian soldiers felt during the war, but would Australian command of the AIF have made a significant difference to casualty rates? One of the reasons why Australian troops suffered such a high death rate was because the AIF had an unusually high ratio of combat to administrative troops. Relying on the British Army for many support services the AIF, like the Canadian forces, had much more 'teeth' than 'tail'.

What also needs to be acknowledged is that the terrible slaughter on the Western Front was not entirely—perhaps not even largely—the result of British military incompetence. Although there were undoubtedly instances where this was the case, as we have seen, the stalemate in France was the product of a technological and tactical impasse in which commanders of all nationalities, including the often vaunted Germans, found themselves trapped. To assume that Australian commanders would have somehow been able in the early years of the war to quarantine their soldiers from this appalling juggernaut of modern industrial warfare is naive and basically ignorant of the realities of this conflict.

Moreover, it ignores the fact that Australian commanders had no monopoly on command skills. There is no natural correlation between military competence and nationality. Although Monash and some other Australian divisional commanders were competent, other Australian military leaders, as we have seen, shared with their British superiors some of the responsibility for military disasters. Furthermore, Monash came to very senior command at a time when he, like commanders of all nationalities, was able to exploit the technological breakthroughs of 1916–18 and to capitalise on the tactical lessons learned so painfully from the slaughter of 1915–17.[71] Moreover, Monash had the particular benefit of training a division in England in 1916 when the lessons of the disastrous campaigns of that year became clear, at no cost to his formation or his own reputation.

Conclusion

Speculating about what might have been the fate of the AIF had it been commanded by Australians is, of course, ultimately unproductive. What shaped Australia's experience of the First World War were the events on the Western Front and Gallipoli, as they actually unfolded in 1915–18. What mattered, from the perspective of the impact of the war on Australian society, were the losses, grief and trauma that this reality produced. The precise effect of the nearly 60 000 deaths suffered in the war on Australian family patterns and structures has yet to be explored. Obviously, there can have been few families that were not in some way affected by death and suffering. The strength of the rituals associated with Anzac during and after the war demonstrated the profoundly traumatic impact of this grief on Australian public and private life. But can we go beyond these self-evident conclusions? Historians such as Russel Ward would argue that

> many, probably most, of [those killed in the war] were among the very best, bravest and most idealistic of their generation: men who might have given a lead to their countrymen in many walks of life, had they lived. It is not surprising that, without them, Australian life for the next twenty years was much more staid, cautious and conformist than during the first twenty years of the Commonwealth.[72]

Perhaps so. Research on the British experience of the First World War to some extent validates the notion that there was a 'lost generation' of a leadership elite as a result of the war—at least in the sense that the middle and upper middle classes, in *relative* terms, suffered more than the working classes who were shielded from conscription to a certain degree by their working in reserved occupations or by being so unfit that they failed their medical tests for military service. Yet, so little detailed research has been done on enlistment patterns and the demographic implications of the First World War in Australia that it cannot be assumed that these conclusions are valid for the AIF; and whereas in Britain's case, clearly brilliant young men like the poet Wilfred Owen were lost in the war, it is difficult to point to a similarly distinguished Australian who was killed in 1914–18. In any case, as has been pointed out by David Cannadine,[73] the logic of writers arguing like Ward may be flawed. Horrendous though the death toll of the First World War was, the majority of men who served did actually return from the war; and if there was in any sense a 'lost' elite of Australians, it would have been comparatively young in the 1920s and 1930s, possibly too young to have made a significant difference to the calibre of the cultural and political life in the interwar years.

This is not to deny that the impact of the war of 1914–18 on Australian individuals, society and politics was profound and lasting, as we shall see in subsequent chapters of this book. It is simply to say that our understanding of its impact is as yet incomplete and limited.

Notes

1 Alan D. Gilbert, John Robertson, and Roslyn Russell, 'Computing Military History: A Research Report on the First AIF Project', *War & Society*, vol. 7, no. 1, 1989, p. 106.

2 135 684 were wounded; 16 487 gassed and 4057 taken prisoner of

war (Jeffrey Grey, *A Military History of Australia*, Cambridge University Press, Melbourne, 1990, p. 118).

3 Wray Vamplew, *Australians: Historical Statistics*, Fairfax, Syme & Weldon Associates, Broadway, NSW, 1987, p. 415.

4 Both quoted in Neville Meaney, *Australia and the World: A Documentary History from the 1870s to the 1970s*, Longman Cheshire, Melbourne, 1985, p. 217.

5 Ernest Scott, *Australia During the War*, vol. XI, of *The Official History of Australia in the War of 1914–1918*, Angus & Robertson, 1936, p. 23. For a sustained critique of the view that Australians were uncritically enthusiastic in their support for the war see E. M. Andrews, *The Anzac Illusion: Anglo-Australian Relations during World War 1*, Cambridge University Press, Melbourne, 1933, pp. 40–6.

6 L. L. Robson, *The First A.I.F.: A Study of its Recruitment, 1914–1918*, Melbourne University Press, Melbourne, 1982, p. 16.

7 Avner Offer, *The First World War: An Agrarian Interpretation*, Clarendon Press, Oxford, 1989, p. 1.

8 See Michael McKernan, *The Australian People and the Great War*, Nelson, Melbourne, 1980, ch. 2.

9 Richard White, 'Motives for joining up: Self-sacrifice, self-interest and social class, 1914–18', *Journal of the Australian War Memorial*, no. 9, 1986, p. 6.

10 John McQuilton, 'A shire at war: Yackandandah, 1914–18', *Journal of the Australian War Memorial*, no. 11, 1987, p. 4.

11 Bill Gammage, *The Broken Years: Australian Soldiers in the Great War*, Penguin, Ringwood, 1975 (first published, 1974), p. 10.

12 Ian Turner, '1914–19' in Frank Crowley (ed.) *A New History of Australia*, Heinemann, Melbourne, 1984 (first published, 1974), p. 314.

13 *Citizen to Soldier: Australians before the Great War: Recollections of Members of the First A.I.F.* (Melbourne University Press, Melbourne, 1977), as its title suggests, is a study of the attitudes of First World War soldiers by J. N. I. Dawes and L. L. Robson. Based on interviews with 216 respondents, it seems unaware of the inherent subjectivity and distortions contained in oral evidence.

14 For New Zealand, see Paul Baker, *King and Country Call: New Zealanders, Conscription and the Great War*, Auckland University Press, Auckland, 1988.

15 Daphne Read (ed.) *The Great War and Canadian Society: An oral history*, New Hogtown Press, Toronto, 1978, p. 89. On the Canadian response to the war, see also R. Matthew Bray, ' "Fighting as an Ally": The English-Canadian Patriotic Response to the Great War', *Canadian Historical Review*, vol. 61, no. 2, 1980, pp. 141–68.

16 A good introduction to this subject is in Eric Leed, *No Man's Land: Combat & Identity in World War I*, Cambridge University Press, Cambridge, 1979, ch. 2.

17 Eric J. Leed, 'Class and Disillusionment in World War I', *Journal of Modern History*, vol. 50, 1978, pp. 680–99.

18 L. L. Robson, 'The origin and character of the First A.I.F., 1914–18:

some statistical evidence', *Historical Studies*, vol. 15, no. 61, 1973, pp. 738–9.

19 For a discussion of the research potential of Australian Defence Force Academy's AIF database project, see Gilbert *et al.*, 'Computing Military History'.

20 Ian Beckett, 'The British Army, 1914–18: The Illusion of Change', in John Turner (ed.) *Britain and the First World War*, Unwin Hyman, London, 1988, pp. 99–116.

21 Quoted in Grey, *Military History*, p. 89.

22 Michael Piggott, 'Stonewalling in German New Guinea', *Journal of the Australian War Memorial*, no. 12, 1988, p. 3.

23 Chris Coulthard-Clark, 'Taking the NZ from ANZAC', *Australian*, 25–26 April 1992, p. 18; N. G. Garson, 'South Africa and World War I', *Journal of Imperial and Commonwealth History*, vol. VIII, no. 1, 1979, pp. 69–70.

24 The Dominions were the white, self-governing divisions of the British Empire: in 1914, Australia, Canada, New Zealand and South Africa.

25 For example, Suzanne Brugger, *Australians and Egypt, 1914–1919*, Melbourne University Press, Melbourne, 1980; Gammage, *Broken Years*, pp. 36–41.

26 Russel Ward's account of the first riot in *A Nation for a Continent: the history of Australia, 1901–1975*, Heinemann, Richmond, 1983, implies that there was nothing especially surprising, or reprehensible, about the Australians' behaviour.

27 Gammage, *Broken Years*, p. 40. In defence of the Australians however, it might be observed that the British and New Zealand troops in Egypt were also guilty of racist behaviour.

28 A perceptive analysis of this problem may be found in Paul Kennedy, 'Military Effectiveness in the First World War', in Allan R. Millett and Williamson Murray (eds), *Military Effectiveness*, vol. 1, Allen & Unwin, Boston, 1988, pp. 330–3.

29 A good introductory account is contained in Grey, *Military History*; a detailed account in John Robertson, *Anzac and Empire: The Tragedy and Glory of Gallipoli*, Hamlyn, Port Melbourne, 1990.

30 Grey, *Military History*, p. 99.

31 ibid.

32 Trevor Wilson, *The Myriad Faces of War: Britain and the Great War, 1914–1918*, Polity Press, Cambridge, 1986, p. 137.

33 Effective descriptions of British mismanagement, especially in the care of the wounded at Gallipoli, can be found in Robertson, *Anzac and Empire*, ch. 31, and Andrews, *Anzac Illusion*, pp. 53–4.

34 John Terraine, *The First World War, 1914–18*, Papermac, London, 1984 (first published 1965), pp. 80–1.

35 This is a quotation from the official British historian, Major Aspinall-Oglander, a staff officer at Gallipoli who, for self-interested reasons, was critical of the commanders at Suvla Bay.

36 For a full analysis see Robin Prior, 'The Suvla Bay tea-party: A reassessment', *Journal of the Australian War Memorial*, no. 7, 1985, pp. 25–34.

37 Vamplew, *Australians,* p. 412, gives full details of enlistment by month and State.
38 Kennedy, 'Military Effectiveness', p. 333.
39 The importance to the Allies of changes in artillery techniques and the development of new 'true' weapon systems, with interlocking roles assigned to tanks, aeroplanes, artillery, infantry and various forms of communications is explained in Robin Prior and Trevor Wilson, *Command on the Western Front: The Military Career of Sir Henry Rawlinson 1914–18,* Blackwell, Oxford, 1992, especially ch. 27.
40 Terraine, *First World War,* p. 116.
41 Quoted in Peter Charlton, *Pozières: Australians on the Somme, 1916,* Methuen Haynes, Sydney, 1986, p. 116.
42 ibid. p. 112.
43 See, for example, John Laffin in *Western Front, 1916–1917: The Price of Honour,* Time-Life Books, Surry Hills, NSW, 1987, p. 23; Geoffrey Serle, McCay entry in *Australian Dictionary of Biography,* vol. 10, Melbourne University Press, Melbourne, 1986. Charlton is generally uncritical of McCay.
44 Grey, *Military History,* p. 104; P. A. Pedersen, 'The AIF on the Western Front: The Role of Training and Command', in M. McKernan and M. Browne (eds) *Australia: Two Centuries of War & Peace,* Australian War Memorial in association with Allen & Unwin Australia, Canberra, 1988, p. 172.
45 *Anzac to Amiens,* Australian War Memorial, Canberra, 1961 (first published 1946), p. 264.
46 Quoted in Denis Winter (ed.) *Making the Legend: The War Writings of C. E. W. Bean,* University of Queensland Press, St Lucia, 1992, p. 101.
47 Terraine, *First World War,* p. 122.
48 L. L. Robson, *Australia and the Great War,* Macmillan, South Melbourne, 1969, p. 15.
49 Charlton, *Pozières,* pp. 281–2.
50 See, for example, his absurd claim in the Special 75th Anniversary Edition of the *Australian* magazine, 7–8 August 1993: 'The soldierly reputation of the Diggers of the Australian Imperial Force rivals that of any army in the entire 3500 years' recorded history of warfare—such is the consensus among military historians and generals'.
51 Laffin, *Western Front 1916–17,* p. 135.
52 E. M. Andrews and B. G. Jordan, 'Second Bullecourt revisited: The Australians in France, 3 May 1917', *Journal of the Australian War Memorial,* no. 15, 1989, p. 43. See also Grey, *Military History,* p. 106. David Horner is a little more qualified in his criticism of the Australian command (*Australian* magazine, 7–8 August 1993, p. 11).
53 Geoffrey Serle, *John Monash: A Biography,* Melbourne University Press, Melbourne, 1982, p. 296.
54 Vamplew, *Australians,* p. 414.
55 Serle, *Monash,* pp. 312–13.
56 ibid. pp. 315–16; Pedersen, 'The First AIF', p. 184, and Grey, *Military History,* p. 108.

57 *Military Effectiveness*, pp. 334–5.

58 For example, Eric Andrews 'Hamel: winning a battle', *Journal of the Australian War Memorial*, no. 18, 1991, pp. 5–12. Geoffrey Serle quotes the high praise of J. F. C. Fuller ('the perfect battle') and Hubert Essame, two leading British military historians, for Monash's conduct of Hamel (*Monash*, p. 335).

59 For a thoughtful discussion of this question see Serle, *Monash*, pp. 337–59.

60 *The Australian Imperial Force in France During the Allied Offensive, 1918*, vol. VI of *The Official History of Australia in the War of 1914–1918*, Angus & Robertson, Sydney, 1942, p. 544.

61 Brereton Greenhous, ' ". . . It was Chiefly a Canadian Battle": The Decision at Amiens, 8–11 August 1918', *Canadian Defence Quarterly*, Autumn 1988, pp. 73–80.

62 A useful account of the war in the Middle East is Ian Jones, *The Australian Light Horse*, Time-Life Books, Surry Hills, NSW, 1987.

63 See, for example, the comment by Bill Gammage, quoted ibid. p. 162.

64 The Time-Life series again provides a useful survey of the RAN's involvement in the war: Alun Evans, *Royal Australian Navy*, Surry Hills, NSW, 1988.

65 General Sir John Salmond, quoted in John Laffin, *Western Front, 1917–1918: The Cost of Victory*, Time-Life Books, Surry Hills, NSW, 1988, p. 97.

66 Grey, *Military History*, p. 118.

67 As indeed was the Canadian Corps for much of the war.

68 Grey, *Military History*, p. 108.

69 Thomas Glasgow commanded the lst Division; Charles Rosenthal, the 2nd; John Gellibrand, the 3rd; and Talbot Hobbs, the 5th. Major General Ewan Sinclair-MacLagan, commanding the 4th, was a British officer who had been in Australia at the outbreak of the war and who served with Australians throughout it.

70 Gordon Greenwood, *Australia: A Social and Political History*, Angus & Robertson, Sydney, 1955, p. 266.

71 As Paddy Griffith shows, by 1918 even the much-maligned British army had developed new tactical skills that gave it the battlefield mobility that had been impossible under the conditions of the earlier years of the war, *Battle Tactics of the Western Front: The British Army's Art of Attack, 1916–18* Yale University Press, New Haven & London, 1994.

72 Ward, *A Nation for a Continent*, pp. 125–6.

73 David Cannadine, 'War and Death, Grief and Mourning in Modern Britain', in Joachim Whaley, *Mirrors of Mortality: Studies in the Social History of Death*, St Martin's Press, New York, 1981, pp. 198–200.

2   The politics of a divided society
Joan Beaumont

In histories of the First World War Australia is commonly described as a 'divided society'. This reflects the fact that in October 1916 and December 1917 the fabric of Australian politics and society was torn apart by the two referenda that the Federal government held in an effort to gain a mandate to introduce conscription for overseas military service. During the bitter and divisive campaign of 1916 the Labor Party split in a way that ensured that it would remain in the political wilderness federally for more than a decade. Concurrently, there was a resurgence of deep sectarianism between the Protestant and Catholic sections of the Australian population which continued to affect Australian political life for many years.

Given the cataclysmic nature of the First World War in so many other respects, it is tempting to see these divisions as being caused by the war, and specifically by the issue of conscription. The consensus among contemporary historians, however, is that the tensions which the conscription referenda revealed were already deep within Australian society and that the seeds of the 'divided society' were planted not in 1915–16 but in the decade before the war.

Australian politics before 1914

Any study of Australian politics during the First World War must therefore begin in the prewar period. In the fourteen years after federation Federal and State politics were in transition: a pattern of fluid coalitions between conservatives, liberals and the relatively new Labor Party was giving way to a form of party politics more recognisably modern. None of the political parties could form a national government in its own right. The Labor Party and the liberal protectionist group under Alfred Deakin, however, embraced similar policies of social reform, and were able to form a loose coalition which for most of the first decade dominated the federal political scene.

A wave of social legislation followed which established the right of workers to organise and to enjoy a reasonable standard of living and working conditions, created an arbitration system to set wages, established the principle that governments should set the standards to be followed by private employers, and formed institutions, such as the Commonwealth Bank, to provide government with a regulatory role in the economy.

By 1909, however, this system was breaking down as Labor became more powerful electorally and grew disenchanted with the slowing pace of social reform which they attributed to the liberals' squeamishness about centralised state power. The liberals merged with the conservatives to form the Liberal Party, which gained power federally in 1909. Labor assumed office in its own right in 1910, only to lose power to the Liberals in 1913. As we saw in chapter 1, when war broke out the question of which of these two political parties should govern Australia was before the electorate.

The evolution of Labor into a party of government generated considerable tension between the industrial and political wings of the labour movement. The organisational machinery of the Labor Party gave great weight to trade unions. These were largely responsible for the formulation, at annual conferences, of the policies which Members of Parliament were expected to promote. However, given the pragmatic nature of parliamentary politics and the domination of the State upper houses by conservative forces, Labor parliamentarians were restricted in their ability to implement these policies. It was a constant accusation levelled at Labor politicians by the industrial wing that they sold out to the system once elected.

In dispute between the political and the industrial wings were two main issues: was the Labor Party a truly socialist party? And could it become a 'national', as opposed to a more narrowly based 'class', movement? Within the parliamentary wing of the labour movement some had accepted the pragmatic position that it had to present itself as a 'national' as opposed to a specifically trade union party. It had to reconcile practical politics with the demands of ideology and appeal to the middle-class electorate, concerned with respectability and moderation, as well as to its working-class base.[1]

These disputes within the labour movement were fuelled by a related debate as to whether political or industrial action offered the best means of achieving Labor's aims in the area of wages and working conditions. Some within the unions, influenced by contemporary radical movements in Europe and the United States, especially syndicalism and its American offspring of 1905, the Industrial Workers of the World (IWW or 'Wobblies'), aimed at transferring the control of the means of production to the unions, through direct action culminating in a general strike. Although the IWW attracted only a small formal membership in Australia, its influence was disproportionately great, as was that of the One Big Union movement which advocated the integration of all trade unions into one great union embracing the whole of the working class.

The militancy of many unionists was fuelled by major industrial disputes in 1908–9, most notably with BHP and in the coalmines of NSW. The unions were defeated, owing to the intransigence of the employers backed by a NSW State government that was willing to pass punitive legislation against the strikers. The strikes precipitated an open breach between union advocates of militant action and those in favour of pragmatism. Significantly for the future of Labor politics, 'Billy' Hughes, who was then President of the Waterside Workers' federation as well as a federal Labor parliamentarian, emerged clearly as being committed to limited objectives and averse to strike action.[2]

Given these tensions within the labour movement on the eve of war, many historians believe that the Labor party had a deep potential to split even before the stresses of exercising power in wartime and the conscription referenda assailed it. As Ian Turner has said:

> The fight between the industrial and political wings of the labour movement had threatened on several occasions between 1900 and 1914 to split the Labor Party. When the split came in 1916 and again in 1919, it was the direct consequence of the new character the Labor parliamentarians sought to give the party as it moved from cross-benches or opposition to government.[3]

This interpretation conflicts with that of Ernest Scott, who attributed Labor's split of 1916 to the divisions between 'the many who were for, and the few who were against, the war'.[4] Hughes himself, however, seems to have held a view closer to Turner's. Writing to Keith Murdoch in the aftermath of the first conscription referendum, he said:

> The Labor Party is now split into two camps, and can never come together again. Do not think that the referendum is the cause of this—it is only the occasion for it. The seeds of disintegration

were there. The Syndicalist element has grown until it has quite diverted the development of the movement from the lines along which it had been prospering this quarter of a century—I am confident that if the split had not come now it could not have been delayed for more than a few months at most.[5]

The early years of the war

The pressures on the Labor Party were accentuated by the fact that when war began it was in power in three of the six States (New South Wales, Western Australia and Tasmania) and, from September 1914, at the federal level also. Much to the surprise of the Liberal Prime Minister, Cook, the election campaign that was in full swing when war broke out resulted on 5 September in a clear victory for Labor. Possibly because it had a better public image on defence matters, thanks to its advocacy of compulsory military service for home defence some years earlier, Labor gained a majority not only in the lower house but also in the Senate where it won 31 of the 36 seats. The new government was headed by a Scottish immigrant, Andrew Fisher, who had been prime minister briefly on two previous occasions. The real power, however, in the Labor cabinet was Hughes, who held the portfolio of Attorney-General.

Born in Wales, Hughes was an extraordinarily dominant and energetic personality. Diminutive and rat-like in appearance, partially deaf and irascible, he was immensely able, murderously witty, unscrupulous, sardonic and opportunistic. He was also fervently committed to prosecuting the war. As we saw in chapter 1, within weeks of the conflict beginning the Labor government had not only raised the first contingents of the First AIF but had set in place the legal and administrative framework they thought necessary for maintaining the war effort. Within the shortest possible time allowed by parliamentary procedures, the Government passed the War Precautions Act. This conferred on the Federal government far-reaching and arbitrary powers to restrict civil liberties. On the grounds that the Government had to be able to take executive action for the defence of the Commonwealth, the act gave it the power to legalise censorship, control the newspapers, penalise the spreading of 'reports likely to cause disaffection or alarm', and prosecute anyone who took a public position that might assist the enemy or prejudice recruiting. The act also legalised wide-ranging restrictions on aliens. These, as we shall see in chapter 3, were to have devastating implications for many Australians of German extraction.

Given that the War Precautions Act was to prove ultimately very controversial, and that in the last three years of the war it was used in an essentially dictatorial manner by Hughes, it is significant that its initial passage through Parliament was unopposed. The Liberal Opposition was, as Scott puts it, 'completely compliant'[6]—as were Labor Members of Parliament. This compliance reflected the widespread public support for the war at this time. Even on the left of the labour movement, where many individuals must have had at least private reservations, there was little overt dissent. Socialists were generally confused by the collapse of international opposition to the war. Their European counterparts, for all their earlier commitment to international working-class solidarity against war, had declared for their countries, right or wrong. Only a few militant Australian groups, most notably the IWW, articulated any opposition to the war, the latter calling for a general strike and urging workers not to 'go to Hell in order to give piratical, plutocractic parasites a bigger slice of Heaven'.[7]

Using the powers conferred on it by the War Precautions Act the Labor government moved rapidly to establish a system of censorship in the latter months of 1914. Restrictions were placed on the right to publish information relating to the movement of Australian armed forces. Incitement of disloyalty to the imperial cause by any means was outlawed, as was the publication of information that might interfere with recruitment. The censor was given unfettered powers to enter premises where it was suspected that illegal material was being published. The distribution of censored material was banned and publishers were not permitted to indicate on published material that censorship had occurred. Censorship was applied not only to written material, but also to photographs and cartoons. Newspaper interviews with returned servicemen were carefully scrutinised before being published. Accounts of military operations were similarly subjected to rigorous censorship. Extensive powers were also delegated to military security organisations and State police to spy on citizens and organisations suspected of subversive activities.

Censorship is an intrinsic part of any war in an age of mass communications, as is an extension of state power in response to the demands of military mobilisation. The censorship regime imposed in Australia from 1914, however, was especially intrusive and partisan. Progressively it was used by the Hughes Government not only to restrict the publication of sensitive military information but to muzzle any opposition to conscription, or indeed any reporting in the press of opinions embarrassing or threatening to the Government.

This extraordinary suppression of civil liberties requires explanation. Kevin Fewster has argued[8] that it can only be understood in terms of what the Italian political theorist, Gramsci, would call a hegemonic control of society by the state, the state being defined not simply as the obvious government instrumentalities (courts, legislature, military, police forces and bureaucracy) but as a system of social relations. Within these there develops a consensus to promote what the dominant economic class defines as the national interest, even though this in fact may reflect its sectional interests. Through its control of formal state organisations and institutions of private life—schools, churches and the family structures—this dominant class is able to gain acceptance of its values as the values of wider society. It informs 'with its spirit all taste, morality, customs, religious and political principles, and all social relations, particularly in their intellectual and moral connotations' (to quote from Gramsci's definition of hegemony). Thus, even groups which have economic interests opposed to those of the dominant class can become assimilated into hegemonic values.

Censorship in Australia during the war was an integral part of hegemonic state control, not simply because it was a state instrumentality but because it was staffed by personnel who shared the dominant class's values: people of middle-class professional backgrounds who were all strongly patriotic. Moreover, thanks to the successful imposition by this class of its definition of 'the national interest' on the wider society, many Australians were willing to tolerate, in the name of the war effort, essentially authoritarian measures.

The theory of hegemonic control of society helps to explain the common phenomenon whereby radical political parties become more moderate when in government—the 'selling out' of which Labor parliamentarians, as we have seen, were accused even before the war began. However, it is clear that even under Hughes's increasing authoritarianism, the hegemonic control of Australian society during the First World War was not complete. As Raymond Evans says of Queensland, which elected a radical reforming government in 1915 that under the leadership of T. J. Ryan became fiercely critical of Hughes, 'loyalists did not entirely monopolise social discourse'.[9] As we shall see later, the conscription referenda *were* lost, despite the Federal government's ruthless exploitation of all the state agencies at its disposal. Moreover, although some members of the Labor Party, like Hughes, William Holman, the NSW Premier, and George Pearce, the Minister for Defence, did (in Fewster's terms) become 'absorbed into the ruling class', others, like Ryan, were not. In fact, as the description of Australia as a 'divided society' implies, there were many who remained strongly resistant to values of the dominant class. Confronted with their opposition the state, as we shall see below, eventually resorted to force in an effort to confirm its control.

The opposition of those Australians who resisted the values of the dominant class focused, even before the conscription crisis began, on economic issues. As chapter 4 explains, the onset of war had a severe effect on the Australian economy, linked closely as it was to international trade, especially in the primary commodities. Unemployment rose firstly in those industries dependent upon exports, then more widely. Real wages declined and prices rose, a potentially explosive mixture. The cause of the continuing rise in prices has been debated. Drought and the inflationary pressures in the economy were contributing factors; but radical elements in the labour movement saw the problem as being caused by 'the hogs of society, the exploiting rascals of the people's every day food [who] are trading on misfortune and making the poor pay the bill'.[10] Employers seemed intent on seizing the opportunity of the war to set aside existing industrial awards and to allow the market to set wages. The question of who was bearing the economic burden of the war rapidly became a divisive political issue.

All this at first gave Labor a widened electoral appeal. Although in the Victorian election of December 1914 it gained only 18 of the 58 lower house seats, in South Australia a Labor government under Crawford Vaughan was elected with a comfortable majority in March 1915. More spectacularly, in the Queensland election of May 1915, the engaging and dynamic Ryan defeated the Liberal government which had been in power since 1905. Ryan immediately launched a program of radical legislation which gave women the right to stand for Parliament; established state insurance, banking and business enterprises to compete with private counterparts; introduced price control in the vulnerable sugar industry; and created what was described as 'the most advanced arbitration system in Australia'. Ryan's program, as Turner said in 1965, was 'government intervention in the economy on a scale which had not previously been seen, and which (except for the years of World War II) has not since been equalled'.[11] Moreover, it was a program implemented in close cooperation with the unions.

Ryan's Government, however, was not typical of Labor governments in pressing ahead with radical social reform while the war crisis escalated. In other States and at the federal level there was a growing preoccupation with winning the war, whatever the implications of this for the fulfilment of Labor policy. Increasingly the division between the political and industrial wings of Labor widened. Two issues, in particular, served to inflame it: the regulation of prices;and the movement to introduce conscription.

Regulating prices was a political minefield. Attempts on the part of State parliaments to pass price-control legislation early in the war were blocked by conservative upper houses. The Commonwealth government, on the other hand, did not have the necessary powers to control prices, and attempts to give it such had been rejected by popular vote twice already, in 1911 and 1913. In June 1915, the Fisher government, under instructions from the federal Labor conference, agreed to hold a referendum on 11 December, seeking a mandate for increased Commonwealth powers in seven areas, including trade and commerce, industrial matters and the nationalisation of monopolies.

For Labor supporters this referendum acquired an enormous emotional as well as political significance. It became a litmus test of 'the ability and desire of Labor governments to effect change'.[12] For their conservative opponents, however, it epitomised the willingness of Labor to force divisive party legislation on the country when the maximum unity was required for the war effort. Business groups also opposed it on the grounds of government interference in free enterprise.

Eventually, in what proved to be an immensely significant decision, the Federal government reneged on the commitment to hold a referendum. On 26 October 1915, Fisher, who was weary of politics, resigned as prime minister to become high commissioner in London, and was replaced by Hughes. Already doubting the wisdom of holding the referendum on constitutional reform and doubtful about its chances of success, Hughes seized the opportunity presented to him at a premiers' conference in September to drop it. Ryan and other State politicians were concerned at the erosion of State powers by the Commonwealth and the loss of incentive and capacity at the State level to implement their own programs of social reform.[13] They therefore agreed to abandon the referendum in return for introducing legislation into their respective parliaments to transfer the required powers to the Commonwealth for the duration of the war and twelve months thereafter.

Hughes's decision to abandon the referendum was ratified retrospectively by the Labor federal caucus; but this was in a late-night meeting where members were given the minimum time to consider the implications of the decision. The labour movement outside Parliament was outraged. Believing, correctly, that there was no chance of the upper houses in most States agreeing to the transfer of powers,[14] they saw Hughes's decision as a capitulation to business and the interests of the dominant economic class. As the labour paper, the *Australian Worker* said, in a passage which dramatically evokes the sense of class conflict at this time:

> The issue [of prices] has been shifted from the polling booths where the people prevail, to the non-elective, property-elective branches of the State Legislatures, where the trusts and Combines,

the food-monopolists, the sweaters of industry, and the whole vile crowd of Capitalistic Huns have made their citadels.[15]

Although the Federal government in 1916 did exploit the War Precautions Act to tackle the question of price control, the damage inflicted by its failure to hold the prices referendum is generally thought to have been profound. Turner believes that '[t]he opposition to Hughes, which had until now been only a minority of the party, became the majority'.[16] Ross McMullin, in his centennial history of the Labor Party, claims that Hughes 'antagonized almost the entire labour movement'.[17] Even Hughes's biographer, L. F. Fitzhardinge, concedes that the left wing of the party 'never forgave Hughes for this "betrayal". This, rather than conscription, sealed his alienation from them.'[18]

The year 1916 saw the union movement turning from political to industrial action, with 1.7 million days being lost to strikes in key industries, such as the waterside workers, metal miners, coalminers and shearers. Much of the industrial unrest was in defiance of the union leadership, and reflected the influence of the advocates of direct action among rank-and-file trade unionists.[19]

The conscription crisis

Fuelling this industrial situation, and giving it ultimately the power to 'blow the Labor Party to shreds',[20] was the issue of conscription for overseas military service. As we saw in chapter 1, enlistments for the AIF remained generally high in 1915, thanks in part to the euphoria generated by Gallipoli but also to the intense recruiting drives launched in mid-1915. Notwithstanding this, a movement in favour of conscription began to gather momentum. Spearheading this was the Universal Service League, a group formed initially in Sydney in September, and then spreading nationally. Attracting a wide range of support, including the Catholic Archbishop of Sydney, Dr Michael Kelly, Holman and some of his cabinet, the League was motivated in part by the concern that voluntary enlistment would rob the country of its physically fittest young men, resulting in a process of 'unnatural selection'.

The War Census which the Labor government conducted in September 1915 provided much grist to the mill of the advocates of compulsion. Conceived as a means of collating accurate details about the nation's resources, both in men and wealth, it revealed that there were still nearly 60 000 'fit' men in Australia between 18 and 44 years of age. Recruiting committees dedicated themselves to the task of contacting these men, ascertaining, by house-to-house visitations if necessary, what were their reasons for not volunteering. 'Shirkers' became the object of profound disdain and moral outrage. They were portrayed as selfish and unmanly, and were subjected to immense public pressure, including being given white feathers, the infamous symbols of cowardice. In November 1915 the recruiting committees were encouraged by the authorities to ask every 'eligible' the following questions:

1   Are you prepared to enlist now? If your answer is Yes, you will be given a fortnight's notice before being called up.
2   Are you prepared to enlist at a later date? If so, name the date.
3   If you are not prepared to enlist, state the reasons why.[21]

Predictably, this campaign met with a reaction which even Scott, who was concerned to gloss over the divisions within Australia, called 'bitter'.[22] The more inquisitorial the efforts of the recruiting committees became, the more the opponents of conscription themselves began to mobilise. As early as July 1915 various elements of the union movement declared themselves to be against compulsion. In September the Trades Hall Council in Melbourne and a conference of Victorian unions did likewise, and shortly after, at the instigation of the IWW, which had initiated an Anti-Conscription League, the NSW Labor Council carried a motion rejecting conscription unless there were at the same time a conscription of wealth. (The War Census had shown that half the wealth was owned by less than 3 per cent of the population and two-thirds of it by the top 5 per cent.)[23]

The marshalling of the forces for and against conscription continued in the first half of 1916 while Hughes was overseas. As we shall see in chapter 5, Hughes left Australia on 15 January 1916 to confer with the British Government, and returned more than six months later. In his absence a specially convened interstate congress of unions, representing 97 organisations and almost half of Australia's unionists, declared 'its undying hostility to conscription of life and labour'.[24] Labor Party conferences in NSW, Queensland and Victoria decided that any Member of Parliament supporting conscription would be denied endorsement. Anti-Conscription Leagues launched a series of public meetings, at which there were violent confrontations between the opponents of conscription and enlisted soldiers.

On the pro-conscriptionist side the Australian Natives' Association, an influential and nationalistic friendly society, declared itself in favour of conscription in March, while the Government began to exploit its instruments of political control. Opponents of conscription were prosecuted under the War Precautions Act for prejudicing recruiting and the press, which in any case was overwhelmingly pro-conscription, was heavily censored. The lines were already sharply drawn for battle before Hughes returned in July convinced by his experience overseas that Australia had no option but to introduce conscription as Britain had in January 1916.

Hughes was on record as having said in 1915 that 'in no circumstances' would he agree 'to send men out of this country to fight against their will'.[25] What now led him to change his mind? Historians[26] suggest that it was not simply his single-minded focus on winning the war, nor his conviction after the horrific casualties of the Somme battles of July 1916 that the diggers of the AIF, for whom he had formed a deep emotional attachment while visiting France, must have adequate reinforcement. There were also wider political considerations. As chapter 5 will show, a consistent theme of Hughes's foreign policy was his passion to maintain White Australia against a Japanese threat. His experience in Britain suggested that unless Australia maintained an unqualified commitment to the war, it might not carry its full weight in peace discussions where matters of vital national interest would be at stake. With Britain, and New Zealand also, now committed to conscription, Australia too must submit to compulsion.

Compulsion in itself posed no ethical dilemmas for Hughes. As he, and other supporters of conscription pointed out, compulsion was inherent in unionism. The working movement accepted that the individual's rights at times had to be subordinated to the common good. The argument was now simply being translated to the realm of national defence, where all sections of society had to stand together for the defence of Australia. As Stuart Macintyre says, 'The effect of the war was to augment the nationalist orientation of Hughes's collectivist creed at the expense of any vestigial concern for the class from which he sprang'.[27]

The Federal government had the power under the War Precautions Act to introduce conscription by executive regulation, or it could have introduced legislation into the Parliament. Both manoeuvres, however, had the potential to split the Labor Party. Had Hughes managed to get conscription through the House of Representatives with the support of the Liberal Opposition, it would in all probability have been rejected in the Labor-dominated Senate. As a result Hughes decided to put the question of conscription to the people in a referendum. His Government, he believed, would thereby be given a mandate direct from the people and its opponents within the party and the labour movement would be neutralised.

The campaign which followed Hughes's announcement on 30 August that a referendum would be held two months later provoked possibly the most bitter and divisive debate in Australian political history. Initially Hughes tried to convert his own party and the union movement to conscription by persuasion; but persuasion was not his natural style and he met with limited success. In Western Australia and South Australia the Labor Party apparatus allowed parliamentarians to vote as their consciences dictated. In Victoria and Queensland, on the other hand, the industrial and political wings were against conscription. Most critically, in NSW, Hughes's own political base, the Labor executive and the Labor Council both rebuffed the Prime Minister's pleas for support

When on 13 September Hughes moved the second reading of the bill for the referendum in Parliament, he did so against the opposition of an articulate section of the federal caucus[28] and a member of his own cabinet, Frank Tudor, resigned in protest. It is symptomatic of the grassroots pressure to which Labor parliamentarians were now being subjected that Tudor resigned, not so much out of personal conviction but because his constituency party had already announced that he would be addressing street meetings called to oppose conscription. Finally, in late September, the NSW executive expelled Hughes from the party and withdrew their endorsement from Holman and other pro-conscriptionist parliamentarians.

Hughes officially opened the referendum campaign on 18 September 1916 with a rally at the Sydney Town Hall. This was attended by a galaxy of public figures whose presence was intended to indicate the widest public support for conscription. The anti-conscriptionist forces launched their counterattack on the same day, at Ballarat in Victoria. Over the next few weeks every imaginable argument, scare tactic and prejudice was given an airing. Rational arguments for and against conscription were submerged under deeply emotional accusations of disloyalty, treachery and racial threat. For both sides conscription became the vehicle for giving voice to much wider concerns and anxieties which reflected a deep social polarisation. As Evans says, in his illuminating account of Queensland during the First World War:

> To the increasingly embattled loyalist, it seemed as though a miasma of disaffection was rising about the pillars of imperial fidelity and war allegiance. As Armageddon ground onwards, the house no longer seemed so united and the pillars were beginning to tremble. Working at the foundations, the pacifist and the revolutionary were clearly detected, advancing the enemy cause. To the pro-war advocate, they were obviously in league with some unknown number of German agents and other threatening aliens, intent upon imperilling the entire social edifice.[29]

As this suggests, the forces proposing conscription saw the campaign in many senses as a moral crusade, to be waged against the forces of disorder and disloyalty. The war, they believed, was a righteous one against a barbaric enemy. Germany was depicted in the lurid cartoons of Norman Lindsay and the Dutchman Raemakers, as a rapacious, slavering ape-like beast which posed a dire threat to humane values. If the Allies were defeated, Australia would be vulnerable, not only to such horrors as had supposedly been visited upon Belgium under German occupation, but also to Asian assaults upon White Australia. As Hughes said: 'We need not fear an influx of coloured labour while the people of Australia hold political power in their hands and while the power of Empire is behind them'.[30] In the face of such threats, the pro-conscriptionists believed all Australians had a duty to fight. A voluntary system was inherently invidious, in that it allowed the best and fittest of Australian men to volunteer leaving Australian racial stock diminished.

The anti-conscriptionists based their case on arguments which again mingled pragmatism, principle, conspiracy theories and racism. Conscription, they argued, was not essential to maintain Australia's five divisions in the field, as its advocates claimed. It would divide the country into warring factions and thus hinder rather than help the war effort it was intended to promote. Voluntarism, in contrast, was more likely to draw the fullest effort out of the country. Indeed, some argued, Australia was already doing more than enough, when its enlistments were compared with, say, Canada.

In addition to this, there were moral arguments against compulsion. How could it be justifiable to force a man to take another man's life? How could matters of conscience become the subject of coercion? A pamphlet published by the *Australian Worker* argued:

> Society may say to the individual: 'You must love this; you must hate that'. But unless the individual feels love or hatred springing from his own convictions and his own feelings, society commands him in vain. He cannot love to order. He cannot hate to order. These passions MUST find their source within his soul . . . The man who is forced to fight is as vilely outraged as the woman who is forced to fondle.[31]

Such arguments had added force when it was acknowledged that many of those voting in favour of compulsion would not themselves be of military age.

The anti-conscriptionist forces also argued a case that reflected the industrial workers' deep sense of economic grievance. Compulsion for military service, it was argued, would be a prelude to industrial conscription and the further erosion of workers' rights and freedoms in the interests of capitalism. It would militarise Australia. Even worse, it would denude the country of its white work force, making it vulnerable to Asian invasion and the infiltration of cheap coloured labour. Radically different though their perspectives were, the anti-conscriptionists shared with their opponents an obsession with White Australia and a willingness to exploit racism. The arrival of 98 Maltese immigrants of military age in September 1916 was seized upon as a dramatic instance of the dangers posed by foreign labour. The hysteria generated by the incident was such that the Government had to divert a further group of Maltese en route to Australia to Noumea rather than allow them to land.

As the battlelines for the referendum were drawn, the case in favour of conscription was apparently in a commanding position. Although it is difficult to establish a precise correlation between attitudes to conscription and class, religion, gender or ethnicity, the pro-conscriptionists were more likely to be middle class. They were able to draw on the resources of the state, the media, and the education system as they established National Referendum Councils in each State. Almost the entire leadership of the Protestant churches, who continued to see the war as a means of national redemption, favoured conscription, as did most academic leaders, the professional classes and most major newspapers, except Labor and Catholic ones. The federal Liberal Opposition and all but one State government (that of Ryan) supported Hughes. The Prime Minister threw himself into campaign for a 'Yes' vote with furious energy. He toured every State, making numerous public speeches, while also galvanising Murdoch in London into organising a campaign to ensure that the soldiers in the AIF voted in favour of conscription.

In addition, Hughes brought to bear all the machinery of censorship and surveillance.[32] Anti-conscriptionist meetings were monitored by detectives recording the words of the speakers with a view to prosecuting them under the War Precautions Act. Anti-conscriptionist literature was vetted: the editors of the metropolitan daily newspapers were persuaded to 'shut down on all resolutions of anti-conscriptionist meetings, as, Hughes claimed, they were generally violent and mostly intended to do harm'.[33] The premises of anti-conscriptionist forces were raided.

The Government also resorted to direct repression of its opponents. In his search for enemies to demonise, Hughes focused on the IWW. As advocates of internationalism, longstanding opponents of the war and promoters of industrial action, they were 'foul parasites [who] have attached themselves to the vitals of labour'. 'You have to go for them with the ferocity of a Bengal tiger', he said.[34] In late September the Government arrested twelve leaders of the movement for supposed treason and arson.[35] This was the culmination of an unrelenting campaign to blur the distinction between being anti-conscription and anti-war and to equate a 'No' vote with disloyalty and subversion. As Hughes said in his last appeal to the electors before the referendum, 'The advocates of the "No" vote include every enemy of Britain open and secret in our midst. They include the violent and the lawless, the criminals who would wreck society and ruin prosperity. Will you dishonour Australia by joining their company?'[36]

Of course, the advocates of 'No' were far from this. They included some activists who were anti-war but these were in the minority. The core of the anti-conscriptionists were members of the working class and the union movement, though they also included middle-class liberals, pacifists and, as we shall see in chapter 3, feminists such as Adela Pankhurst and Vida Goldstein. There was also a strong identification with the anti-conscriptionist cause on the part of many Irish Catholics, who made up 21 per cent of the Australian population at this time.

The anti-conscription movement had the invaluable asset of being in control of the nationwide union network, but with the much greater powers at his disposal Hughes was confident that the pro-conscriptionist case would carry the day. So confident was he that he ordered the call-up for service inside Australia of all unmarried men between the ages of 21 and 35 even before the referendum was held. Men thus called up had their fingerprints taken, a process which confirmed in many minds an impression of authoritarianism on the part of the Government. Moreover, Hughes instructed the returning officers at the polling booths on referendum voting day to interrogate males of military age as to whether they had obeyed the Defence Act and entered camp. (Only 190 869 of the estimated 600 000 eligibles had responded to the call-up.)[37] Their voting papers were to be kept separate if they fell into that category, and it would be decided later whether they would be counted or not. This, in the opinion of Holman, was one of Hughes's greatest blunders.[38] The obviously irregular nature of this ruling provoked the resignation of three further ministers from the Cabinet on the very eve of the referendum. On 28 October the electorate was asked:

Are you in favour of the Government having, in this grave emergency, the same compulsory powers over citizens in regard to requiring their military service, for the term of this war, outside the Commonwealth, as it now has in regard to military service within the Commonwealth?[39]

Within two days it was clear that the result was a victory for the

'No' vote: 1 160 033 against, 1 087 557 in favour. It was a narrow victory, and one which reflected the degree of polarisation within Australia. If only some 36 000 out of an electorate of 2.25 million had voted differently, it would have been a victory for Hughes. Yet, constitutionally the Government required a majority of States, as well as a majority of voters, in favour of conscription. Only three of the six States, Victoria, Tasmania and Western Australia voted thus. NSW, Queensland and South Australia voted against. The AIF returned a majority for the 'Yes' vote, but it was not the sweeping endorsement of conscription that Hughes had hoped for.

The impact of the referendum result on the Labor Party was immediate and dramatic. In all States, except Western Australia, the party expelled parliamentarians who had campaigned in favour of conscription. In NSW Holman took with him a group of pro-conscriptionist Labor members and formed a Nationalist administration with his former conservative opponents. Hughes came under attack at the federal caucus meeting on 14 November. Confronted with a vote of no confidence, he walked out, followed by 23 supporters of the 65 members present.[40] The federal Labor Party was left shattered under the leadership of the uninspiring Tudor.

Hughes remained Prime Minister, heading an interim ministry until he negotiated by January 1917 a merger with the Opposition to form the Nationalist Party. This coalition gave him a majority in the lower house but Labor retained control in the Senate. When various machinations in the following months, including possibly bribery,[41] failed to secure a Senate majority for Hughes, he called a general election on 5 May.

The Nationalists campaigned on the claim that they alone were competent to manage Australia during the war—indeed their other title was the 'Win-the-War party', a description they had taken from a similar group in Britain which had opposed the Government of Asquith in 1916 on the grounds of its ineffectual prosecution of the war. They asserted that Labor had 'blown out its brains' when it expelled Hughes and its followers; and Hughes assured the electorate that he had accepted the popular verdict on conscription.

The result of the election was a decisive victory for the Nationalists: a majority of 33 seats in the Representatives and all of the eighteen seats being contested for the Senate. This, it is generally assumed, meant that the vote against conscription in October 1916 had not been a vote against the war.

1917 and the second conscription referendum

With this crushing defeat for Labor, the Nationalist Government was in a commanding position, but, as Macintyre has pointed out, Hughes's supremacy within it was 'precarious'.[42] Not only were there significant policy differences between him and his conservative coalition partners, but the ex-Labor parliamentarians who supported Hughes were heavily outnumbered within the coalition by former Liberals. Moreover, Labor's parliamentary numbers may have been slashed but it retained a powerful political base: most working-class votes and 44 per cent of the ballot in May 1917. Hughes therefore had to weld together a rather fragile coalition. He could do this only by maintaining an atmosphere of crisis and emergency and by fostering 'the polarization of political life'— something to which his predilection towards secrecy, duplicity and 'reliance on methods of political brinkmanship' inclined him anyway.

The remaining months of 1917 were ones of escalating industrial tension, bitterness in public life, and violence at levels rarely seen in modern Australian politics. Hughes, who in Labor demonology became the 'Judas' leading the 'rats' who had deserted the party, had no qualms about crushing dissident opinion. An Unlawful Associations Act was rushed through Parliament in December 1916 and amended in 1917 to declare organisations like the IWW illegal. It also made membership of them after the declaration of the act punishable by six months' imprisonment and attendance at meetings prima facie evidence of membership. By the end of the year the IWW was effectively destroyed as a political force—a clear instance of the state, confronted with the limitations of indirect means of enforcing its hegemonic control, resorting to force. Over one hundred 'Wobblies' were imprisoned and those who could not prove that they were born in Australia were deported, often to Chile, where they found themselves in a civilian no-man's-land, again harassed by police and threatened with destitution.[43]

The Government also confronted the union movement. In 1917 the industrial action of 1916 continued and intensified. In Queensland, there were 39 strikes, seven less than in the previous year, but they were longer and more acrimonious, with almost double the days lost.[44] In NSW August saw a dispute about the introduction of timecards within the railways (see chapter 4) snowball into a general strike which eventually took in 100 000 workers across many industries and caused the loss of four million days work. The NSW Government, with the support of the Commonwealth government and employer associations, chose to depict the strike as 'an organised attempt to take the reins of government out of the hands of those duly elected by the people to carry on the affairs of the country'.[45] The strike was smashed. Unions were deregistered and their leaders were arrested on charges of conspiracy. Non-union labour was raised to keep essential industries running and strikers were blacklisted and denied their old jobs at the conclusion of the dispute. One of these was Ben Chifley, a Bathurst engine-driver, who was inspired by this 'harsh and oppressive treatment'[46] to embark on the political career that would culminate in his being Australia's prime minister from 1945–49.

It was into this cauldron of unrest that Hughes in November 1917 threw the dynamite of a second referendum on conscription. Throughout the year frenetic efforts had been made by the authorities and committed individuals to increase the number of volunteers. A national network of recruiting committees had been set up in the aftermath of the first referendum; eligible males were interviewed and personally urged to enlist. Women were encouraged to target 'shirkers', importuning them with pleas to volunteer until they finally succumbed.

Prodigious energy and earnestness was poured into these recruiting campaigns. Public meetings, appeals at theatres and ballrooms, the open-air showing of films of the war, recruiting marches collecting volunteers as they marched through country towns, cartoons and exhortations in almost all the major newspapers, the insertion of pleas to enlist in restaurant menus: these were only some of the many devices resorted to.[47] Wounded returned servicemen played a prominent role: one of them, still limping from his wounds, was Captain Stanley Bruce, later to become Australia's prime minister in 1924.

Yet despite all this, recruitment remained at levels which the Government believed were inadequate to replace the appalling losses suffered by the AIF at Bullecourt, Messines and especially in the third battle of Ypres. Under pressure from his coalition partners, Hughes decided to again put the question of conscription to the electorate.

Predictably the second referendum campaign in November–December 1917 was profoundly divisive, with all the arguments of the previous year being rehearsed again and the invective of treachery on each side reaching new extremes. Typical of the exchanges was the publication by the very able anti-conscriptionist and editor of the *Worker*, H. E. Boote, of 'The lottery of Death'. Conscription, he claimed, would 'reduce its citizens to the level of cannibals drawing lots for an obscene feast'.[48] Even more extreme was a pamphlet, 'The Bucket', which depicted the casualty station at the front thus: 'In the field at the back the dead are lying. The first has no face, the next has bled to death. The corpses are pulled about as the slaughterman pulls his dead sheep. Intestines and pieces of lung are in a bucket outside the tent, so the surgeon may get good practice.'[49] The pro-conscriptionist forces,[50] meanwhile, published what remains perhaps the most notorious polemic of the conscription campaigns: the Anti's Creed.

> I believe the men at the Front should be sacrificed.
> I believe we should turn dog on them.
> I believe that our women should betray the men who are fighting for them.
> I believe in the sanctity of my own life.
> I believe in taking all the benefit and none of the risks.
> I believe it was right to sink the *Lusitania*.[51]
> I believe in murder on the high seas.
> I believe in the I.W.W.
> I believe in the Sinn Fein.
> I believe that Britain should be crushed and humiliated . . .
> I believe in Considine, Fihelly, Ryan, Blackburn, Brookfield, Mannix, and all their works.[52]
> I believe in egg-power rather than man-power.
> I believe in holding up transport and hospital ships.
> I believe in general strikes.
> I believe in burning Australian haystacks.
> I believe in handing Australia over to Germany.
> I believe I'm worm enough to vote 'No'.
> Those who don't believe in the above creed will vote 'Yes'.

As in 1916, the anti-conscriptionists were painted as cowardly, selfish, disloyal to Australia and Britain, sympathetic to the barbaric enemy, destroyers of the social and economic order and allies of the radical IWW. The Creed also, as its title reveals, identified the anti-conscriptionists with Irish Catholicism and, particularly, with the *bête noire* of Hughes, Cardinal Daniel Mannix.

Mannix, from May 1917 Archbishop of Melbourne, had played a relatively minor role in the 1916 referendum campaign,[53] but his intervention riled Hughes. In 1917 he became a far more prominent and controversial advocate of 'No'. In the absence of any charismatic figures in the rump of the Labor Party, Mannix emerged as a spokesman of the working classes, whose economic grievances he articulated. With his considerable powers of oratory, he was able to attract crowds of over 100 000 to anti-conscription rallies. How significant an impact he had on the outcome of the referenda is debatable, but it suited Hughes, now that the IWW had been crushed, to depict Mannix as a bogeyman, responsible for delivering the Catholic vote into the anti-conscriptionist camp.

Throughout the second campaign, the Federal government continued to employ censorship and to manipulate the agencies of surveillance. These now included a new Commonwealth Police

Force which Hughes established after he was hit by an egg in a melee at Warwick in Queensland (hence the reference to 'egg-power' in the Creed).[54] This incident was the culmination of an astounding sequence of events in Brisbane when the Queensland Premier, Ryan, defied Hughes by reading into Hansard a speech against conscription that had been previously mutilated by the censor. His intention was to have 10 000 copies of the speech distributed as pamphlets, but Hughes personally descended upon the printing office at the head of a military force to seize the copies of this and other offending material. Although the whole drama had elements of what Lloyd Robson has called the 'ridiculous',[55] Evans has shown it had the potential to spark a civil war in Brisbane. The city was already wracked with clashes between the hysterical pro- and anti-conscription forces and Ryan's Cabinet considered raising a paramilitary force of unionists to confront the forces under Commonwealth control.[56]

Hughes's dictatorial manner, which this incident manifested, was evident also in his peremptory closing of the rolls for the referendum only two days after it had been announced on 7 November. Thousands of voters were disenfranchised, including many in rural districts who received news of the impending vote only after the rolls had closed.

Yet, for all its heavy-handedness—indeed, perhaps because of it—the Federal government was rebuffed again. The second referendum on 20 December resulted in a stronger vote against conscription: 1 181 747 'No' votes, against 1 015 159 'Yes' votes. This time four states rejected conscription, Victoria joining NSW, Queensland and South Australia in opposition. Only in Western Australia was there a clear majority in favour of conscription with the 'Yes' vote attracting almost twice the number of 'No' votes. In Tasmania, the majority in favour of conscription was very narrow: 379 votes out of an electorate of more than 79 000. In 1916 the majority had been 10 000; this represented the most significant swing away from conscription in Australia.[57] The votes of soldiers overseas also swung away from compulsory service, though again there was a majority for the 'Yes' vote.

Analysing the referenda results

The question that naturally has preoccupied historians is why the two conscription referenda were lost—or, if one views it from the perspective of the anti-conscriptionists, won. Any answer to this question must be multifaceted, and to some degree speculative, at least at the level of the individual voter's motivation. Historians, writing largely in the 1960s and 1970s, when the Vietnam War gave the conscription debates a particular salience, identified birthplace, religion, gender, employment in the rural sector, experience of overseas military service, and affiliation with the trade unions and/or the Labor Party as all being factors influencing the way Australians voted. Australians born in Britain, a number of historians concluded,[58] were more likely to vote 'Yes'. This could help to explain the strong vote in favour of conscription in Western Australia.[59] A majority of soldiers serving overseas also favoured conscription. Bean thought the men in training or in camps actually voted 'Yes' rather than the men on the front.[60] Murdoch suggested that the Light Horse in Egypt and troops training in England secured a 'Yes' majority from the AIF.[61]

As for the vote against conscription, it has been traditional to give the union movement and Irish Catholics prominence in explaining the 'No' vote.[62] Primary producers have also sometimes been cited[63] as opposing conscription, supposedly because they feared losing the labour force essential to farming.

These conclusions were based largely on a study of public documents. A quantitative analysis of conscription voting, carried out by Glen Withers in 1982, has showed the need for some revision of previous views. Migrant groups and women, Withers showed, played a far more significant role in the 'Yes' vote than previously thought. Primary producers also were supporters rather than opponents of conscription.[64]

The role of the Catholics in the vote against conscription has been of particular interest to historians. What motivated Catholics? Were they voting 'No' for specifically Catholic reasons, such as their fear that the brothers of their teaching orders would be conscripted? (There were some grounds for this concern, with the Grand Master of the Loyal Orange Lodge in Melbourne declaring publicly in July 1916 that Catholic separate schools were a greater menace in Australia than German schools!)[65] Were Catholics, as Michael McKernan argues, influenced more by class?[66] Many of them were working class, identified with Labor and sharing the widespread anger at deteriorating working conditions and the economic hardships imposed by the war. Or were Catholics inspired to oppose conscription by their identification with the Irish Republican cause of the Sinn Fein? Not all Australian Catholics were Irish, nor all Irish Australians Catholic, but as Alan Gilbert has said, 'for the majority in each category in 1916 and 1917 Irishness and Catholicity were virtually indistinguishable'.[67] The abortive uprising in Dublin during Easter 1916, which the British suppressed with the ruthless execution of its leaders, caused great indignation in Australia. As Hughes and other pro-conscriptionists claimed at the time, it seems to have converted a number of important Catholics to the anti-conscriptionist cause. In the opinion of some historians, it made the vital difference to the outcome of the 1916 referendum.[68] Gilbert, however, is more cautious. While Irish republicanism generated an atmosphere in which Australian Irish Catholics were insulated from the emotional impact of imperial patriotism, and 'secured for anticonscription some of that fairly small minority of Irish-Catholic voters which would otherwise have endorsed the Government's proposals', '[p]erhaps Ireland's troubles confirmed rather than formed an Irish-Catholic stand'.[69]

There are, of course, dangers in speaking of an 'Irish-Catholic stand' and an 'Irish-Catholic vote'. Despite the impression created by Mannix's high profile, he did not speak for the Catholic Church. During the first referendum campaign, Archbishop Kelly of Sydney personally supported conscription and the public position of the Catholic hierarchy was one of neutrality. Many leading Catholics were embarrassed and alienated by Mannix, to the extent that in March 1917 a delegation waited on Archbishop Carr (at that stage still Archbishop in Melbourne) to protest at Mannix's disloyalty and the damage to the church's interests that he was causing.

In 1917, the Catholic hierarchy did move to an anti-conscriptionist position, in response, it is argued by McKernan, to the obvious popularity of this stance with working-class Catholics and the growth of sectarianism in 1916. The laity, however, remained divided, along lines which generally reflected class. As B. A. Santamaria says, 'a numerically small group of Catholics belonging to the professions and more socially prominent than their fellows . . . were largely assimilated to the dominant groups in Australian society, and . . . vigorously opposed Mannix'.[70]

Whatever the debate about the Irish-Catholic vote, it is incontestable that the involvement of Mannix and Catholics in the conscription crises—together with the strong alignment of the Protestant churches with the government cause—precipitated a revival of sectarianism in Australian public life. In the latter half of the nineteenth century the question of education had fuelled a bitter confrontation between Catholics and Protestants. To a considerable degree this had been ebbing in the years after federation, but the events of 1916–17 inflamed it once again. For years after the war the Catholic Church would not participate in public commemorations of Anzac Day. Nor was it represented at a quintessential expression of national memory of the war, the laying of the foundation stone for the Australian War Memorial in 1929.[71] The striking absence of Christian symbolism from Australian war memorials, in contrast to those of, say, France, is further testimony to the manner in which the war had made religion again a contested area in Australian public life.

The aftermath of the referenda

When putting the question of conscription again to the Australian people in December 1917 Hughes had insisted that he would not continue as prime minister without this mandate. It was, however, only with reluctance that he resigned on 8 January 1918. Almost immediately he was asked to form a new administration by the Governor-General, Sir Ronald Munro-Ferguson, who could countenance neither of the alternative candidates for prime minister: Tudor, or the veteran of Western Australian politics, John Forrest. Hughes's Labor opponents raged and brought a vote of no confidence in Parliament but they did not have the numbers to unseat the Prime Minister.

In most accounts of the war the events of 1918 on the domestic political front are something of an anticlimax. It is almost as if historians, like those involved in the hysteria of 1916–17, have been intellectually and emotionally exhausted by the conscription crisis. But in the aftermath of the second conscription referendum the divisions and tensions in Australian political life continued to be played out. Conscription as a policy option was dead, but the radical elements on the left of politics that had spearheaded the opposition to conscription now turned their attention to a more explicit rejection of the war itself. There had always been opponents of the war within the socialist movement. As early as October 1914 an Australian Peace Alliance had been formed to advocate a negotiated end to the war on the basis of self-determination for all nations and an end to the European balance of power. As chapter 3 will show, there were also bands of committed women who established organisations promoting pacifism or opposition to war on the grounds, partly, that they had a biologically determined mission to defend life. However, until 1917–18 these anti-war elements were in the minority.

The conscription crisis, however, progressively drove the more enthusiastic supporters of the war out of the labour movement and strengthened those elements who opposed the conflict. This was evident at a conference called by the Governor-General in April 1918, at the height of Germany's spring offensive on the Somme, in an effort to increase recruiting. All the parliamentary leaders and some trade unionists attended. The representation of the latter, however, was thin and they stressed that they would not bind their organisations to any decisions taken at the conference. Tudor, Ryan and other Labor parliamentarians continued to support recruiting thereafter but their position was subject to mounting criticism from the rank and file, significant sections of which in the months that followed publicly adopted the position of opposing recruiting and supporting a negotiated peace.

If the tensions within Australian political life eased in the latter part of 1918 it was because the scent of Allied victory relieved some of the pressures on the political system, and because Hughes agreed to meet demands for a review of the War Precautions Act and to release those people imprisoned during the 1917 strike and referendum campaign. Hughes also departed on 26 April for London to attend a meeting of the Imperial War Cabinet in London. He remained in Europe until the end of the Paris Peace Conference in mid-1919. Australian political life was thus spared the tensions that his aggressive personality and confrontationist style of government imposed.

Conclusion

The bitterness and divisions of the First World War had lasting implications for the future of Australian politics. Whereas in April 1916 the Labor Party was holding office nationally and in five of the six States, fifteen months later it was in opposition everywhere but in Queensland. At the federal level it did not regain power until 1929 and then only for a brief period. After a further ten years in opposition John Curtin became prime minister in October 1941, but even then Labor did not command a majority in both houses until 1944. Of the first 80 years after federation Labor held power for only sixteen.

Obviously it would be unreasonable to lay all blame for Labor's long periods in opposition at the door of the First World War. Such is the complexity of political life that many factors—for example, Labor's unlucky timing in coming to power at the onset of the Great Depression, its later catastrophic split in 1954 resulting from the tension between the Catholic and socialist strands of the party—must be taken into account.

However, the war exacerbated Labor's difficulties in a number of ways. It generated an atmosphere of crisis, grief and hysteria which made any reasoned discussion of the economic hardships caused by the conflict exceedingly difficult. The pressures of the war also accentuated the confrontationist and dictatorial elements in Hughes's personality, thus making resolution of the already existing rifts within the labour movement almost impossible.[72]

The split of 1916 also changed the religious composition of the political party. Prior to the conscription debates Catholics made up

21 per cent of federal Labor Members of Parliament; after 1916 they constituted 45 per cent. The 'loose links between the Catholic church and the Labor Party prior to 1914 were forged into a strong, if defensive alliance in 1917'.[73] In the next three decades, as communism became a major force internationally and to a lesser extent domestically, this alignment of many Labor politicians with Catholicism was to create new and ultimately irreconcilable tensions within the party.

The war also gave the conservative opponents of Labor the opportunity and incentive to mobilise more effectively. This was not only at the level of federal politics where the supposed need for surveillance and censorship gave the state greater power and capacity to impose its hegemonic values. In the wider social arena also the middle classes acquired from the war years the skills and incentive to mobilise against what they perceived to be the forces of disorder. As we shall see in chapter 3, women effectively campaigned in favour of temperance. Later, in the 1920s and 1930s the male middle-class response to the challenge of communism and socialism was to create paramilitary organisations. By these means the violence that 1916–17 had introduced into Australian political life continued to permeate politics for at least fifteen years thereafter.

Finally, the First World War provided one of the key elements which kept the Labor Party in the political wilderness federally for so many years: its effective identification by non-Labor parties with the cause of disloyalty. Labor, it should be noted, was not excluded from power in the interwar years at the State level. It formed governments in all States at various times during this period and in Queensland was in office for all but three years between 1915 and 1952. At the federal level, however, it suffered wounding electoral damage because its opponents, as we shall see in the next chapter, were able to develop a new political rhetoric. This characterised Labor, in part, as being incompetent in international affairs. In much the same way that Robert Menzies effectively painted Labor as being untrustworthy in foreign policy in the 1950s and 1960s, so in the 1920s and 1930s Labor was portrayed as incapable of nurturing the vital relationship with Britain. While nationalism was appropriated by the Right of politics, and loyalty became a hegemonic value, Labor retreated into a world of isolationism, pacifism and distrust of supposedly sordid international politics—from which it emerged only with the crisis of another war.

Notes

1 One of the most comprehensive introductions to the tensions within the labour movement is Ian Turner, *Industrial Labour and Politics: The Dynamics of the Labour Movement in Eastern Australia, 1900–1921*, Hale & Iremonger, Sydney, 1979 (first published 1965), pp. 45–67.

2 See Stuart Macintyre, *The Oxford History of Australia*, vol. 4, *1901–1942: The Succeeding Age*, Oxford University Press, Melbourne, 1986, pp. 113–21.

3 Turner, *Industrial Labour*, p. 45.

4 Ernest Scott, *Australia During the War*, vol. XI of *The Official History of Australia in the War of 1914–1918*, Angus & Robertson, 1936, p. 365. A later historian of the Labor Party, in contrast, believes it was Hughes's confrontationist leadership that made the split inevitable (Ross McMullin, *The Light on the Hill: The Australian Labor Party, 1891–1991*, Oxford University Press, Melbourne, 1991, p. 121).

5 Quoted in Malcolm Booker, *The Great Professional: A Study of W. M. Hughes*, McGraw Hill Book Co., Sydney, 1980, p. 203.

6 Scott, *Australia During the War*, p. 53.

7 Quoted in Turner, *Industrial Labour*, p. 71.

8 Kevin Fewster, 'The Operation of State Apparatuses in Times of Crisis: Censorship and Conscription, 1916', *War & Society*, vol. 3, no. 1, 1985, pp. 37–54.

9 Raymond Evans, *Loyalty and Disloyalty: Social Conflict on the Queensland Homefront, 1914–18*, Allen & Unwin, Sydney, 1987, p. 8.

10 W. Wallis in *Labour Call*, 15 July 1915, quoted in Turner, *Industrial Labour*, p. 76.

11 ibid.

12 Marilyn Lake, *A Divided Society: Tasmania during World War I*, Melbourne University Press, Melbourne, 1975, p. 39.

13 L. F. Fitzhardinge, *The Little Digger, 1914–1952: William Morris Hughes: A Political Biography*, vol. II, Angus & Robertson, Sydney, 1979, p. 52.

14 In fact only NSW passed the required legislation. The Legislative Councils in Queensland and South Australia, and the Legislative Assembly in Victoria, rejected the legislation. In Tasmania and Western Australia it was not introduced.

15 Quoted in L. L. Robson, *Australia and the Great War*, Macmillan, South Melbourne, 1969, pp. 55–6.

16 *Industrial Labour*, p. 81. Evans agrees that the abandonment of the prices referendum 'carried important repercussions for anti-war activists throughout Australia' (*Loyalty and Disloyalty*, p. 70).

17 McMullin, *Light on the Hill*, p. 100.

18 Fitzhardinge, *Little Digger*, p. 56.

19 Macintyre, *1901–1942*, p. 163.

20 These are the words of a Labor activist, William Somerville, to Pearce, quoted in McMullin, *Light on the Hill*, p. 107.

21 Scott, *Australia During the War*, p. 311.

22 ibid. p. 312.
23 Evans, *Loyalty and Disloyalty*, p. 85.
24 Quoted in McMullin, *Light on the Hill*, p. 103.
25 Quoted in Scott, *Australia During the War*, p. 337.
26 For example, McMullin, *Light on the Hill*, p. 103; Fitzhardinge, *Little Digger*, pp. 173–4.
27 Macintyre, *1901–42*, p. 161.
28 Fifteen Labor members of the Representatives and twelve Labor senators voted against the bill (Booker, *The Great Professional*, p. 200).
29 Evans, *Loyalty and Disloyalty*, p. 84.
30 Quoted in Lake, *A Divided Society*, p. 74.
31 Quoted in Scott, *Australia During the War*, p. 343.
32 For details of this see Frank Cain, *The Origins of Political Surveillance in Australia*, Angus & Robertson, Sydney, 1983.
33 Quoted in Macintyre, *1901–1942*, p. 165.
34 Quoted in Evans, *Loyalty and Disloyalty*, p. 77
35 For a full account of the suppression of the IWW, see Frank Cain, *The Wobblies at War: a history of the IWW and the Great War in Australia*, Spectrum Publications, Melbourne, 1993, chs 8–11.
36 Quoted in K. S. Inglis, 'Conscription in Peace and War, 1911–1945', in Roy Forward and Bob Reece (eds), *Conscription in Australia*, St Lucia, Queensland University Press, 1968, p. 38.
37 Evans, *Loyalty and Disloyalty*, p. 91. Of the 110 863 declared medically fit, 88 516 had lodged claims for exemption.
38 L. L. Robson, *The First A.I.F.: A Study of its Recruitment, 1914–1918*, Melbourne University Press, Melbourne, 1982 (first published 1970), p. 108.
39 Scott, *Australia During the War*, p. 341.
40 This figure is taken from Scott, *Australia During the War*, p. 365. Booker (*The Great Professional*, p. 205) says Hughes took 24 members of caucus with him: McMullin (*Light on the Hill*, p. 108) says Hughes's National Labor group which he formed after 14 November included 25 'defectors', leaving 46 in the Federal Parliamentary Labor Party.
41 The machinations included the resignation of the Labor Senator Ready and his rapid, behind-the-scenes replacement by John Earle, the Tasmanian Labor leader who had resigned as leader of the state opposition in the aftermath of the 1916 conscription referendum (Lake, *A Divided Society*, pp. 91–2).
42 Macintyre, *1901–42*, p. 168.
43 See Frank Cain, 'The Industrial Workers of the World: Aspects of its suppression in Australia, 1916–1919' *Labour History*, vol. 42, 1982, pp. 54–62.
44 Evans, *Loyalty and Disloyalty*, p. 138.
45 Turner, *Industrial Labour*, p. 146.
46 Quoted in McMullin, *Light on the Hill*, p. 113.
47 The best account is ch. 7 of Robson, *First A.I.F.*
48 Quoted in L. C. Jauncey, *The Story of Conscription in Australia*,

Macmillan, Melbourne, 1968, p. 281. Originally published in 1935, and full of documents from 1916–17, Jauncey's book became something of a gospel of the anti-conscriptionist case.

49 Quoted in Robson, *First A.I.F.*, p. 169.

50 Specifically the Reinforcements Referendum Council.

51 The *Lusitania* was an American passenger ship sunk by German submarines in 1915 with considerable loss of civilian life.

52 Michael Considine was the militant president of the Amalgamated Miners' Association, for a time a member of the Marxist Australian Socialist Party, and from 1917 a federal Member of Parliament. John Fihelly was a Labor member of Queensland Parliament, an outspoken critic of British policy in Ireland and a supporter of Irish dissidents. Maurice Blackburn was a Labor Member of Parliament in Victoria who lost his seat in 1917 because of his pacifism and outspoken opposition to conscription and the war. Jack Brookfield was president of Labor's Volunteer Army.

53 See B. A. Santamaria, *Daniel Mannix: a Biography*, Melbourne University Press, Melbourne, 1984, pp. 80–1.

54 There had in fact been plans for a Commonwealth Police Force under discussion for over a year, but the Warwick incident provided Hughes with the occasion to establish it (Booker, *The Great Professional*, p. 217).

55 Robson, *First A.I.F.*, p. 175.

56 Evans, *Loyalty and Disloyalty*, pp. 107–112.

57 Lake, *A Divided Society*, p. 130.

58 P. M. Gibson, 'The conscription issue in South Australia, 1916–1917', *University Studies in Politics and History*, vol. 4, 1963–64; Inglis, 'Conscription in Peace and War', p. 39; A. R. Pearson, 'Western Australia and the conscription plebiscites of 1916–1917', *RMC Historical Journal*, vol. 3, 1974; F. B. Smith, 'The Conscription Plebiscites in Australia 1916–1917, Victorian Historical Association, Melbourne, 1966.

59 J. R. Robertson, 'The Conscription Issue and the National Movement in Western Australia: June 1916–December 1917', *University Studies in Politics and History*, vol, 3, 1959, p. 45.

60 C. E. W. Bean, *The Australian Imperial Force in France, 1916*, Angus & Robertson, Sydney, 1939, p. 892.

61 Robson, *First A.I.F.*, p. 119.

62 This has been emphasised, for example, by Turner, *Industrial Politics*; Robin Gollan, *Radical and Working Class Politics: A Study of Eastern Australia 1850–1910*, Canberra, 1960; Smith, 'The conscription plebiscites'; Scott, *Australia During the War*; and Jauncey, *Story of Conscription*.

63 For example, by Smith, 'The conscription plebiscites'; Turner, *Industrial Labour*; Inglis, 'Conscription in Peace and War'; J. Alcock, 'Reasons for the rejection of conscription, 1916–17', *Agora*, vol, 7, 1973; P. Bastion, 'The 1916 conscription referendum in New South Wales', *Teaching History*, vol. 5, pt 1, 1917; I. Bertrand, 'The

Victorian vote in the conscription referendums in 1916 and 1917; the case of the Wannon electorate', *Labour History*, no. 26, 1974.

64 Glenn Withers, 'The 1916–1917 conscription referenda: a cliometric re-appraisal', *Historical Studies*, vol. 20, no, 78, 1982, pp. 36–46.

65 Robson, *First A.I.F.*, p. 89.

66 Michael McKernan 'Catholics, conscription, and Archbishop Mannix', *Historical Studies*, vol. 17, no. 68, 1977, p. 300.

67 Alan Gilbert, 'The Conscription Referenda, 1916–17; The impact of the Irish Crisis', *Historical Studies*, vol. 14, no. 53, 1969, p. 54; Robson, *First A.I.F.*, p. 95.

68 K. S. Inglis, 'The Easter Rising and its influence in Australian politics', *Sydney Morning Herald*, 9 April 1966; Robson, *First A.I.F.*, p. 95.

69 Gilbert, 'Conscription Referenda', pp. 71, 67. Santamaria reaches a similar conclusion, the Easter uprising adding the 'element of passion' to an 'already inevitable development' (*Mannix*, p. 77).

70 Santamaria, *Mannix*, pp. 83–4.

71 K. S. Inglis, 'A Sacred Place: The Making of the Australian War Memorial', *War & Society*, vol. 3, no. 2, 1985, p. 109.

72 McMullin believes that under 'a leader of Ryan's tact and ability the party might have avoided a rupture. Hughes' leadership made one inevitable' (*Light on the Hill*, p. 121).

73 D. J. Murphy, 'Religion, Race and Conscription in World War I', *Australian Journal of Politics and History*, vol. XX, no. 2, 1974, p. 161.

3   War and Australian society
Pam Maclean

On the Australian home front the most spectacular impact of the war occurred in the politically and socially divisive campaigns associated with the referenda to allow men to be conscripted for overseas military service. The passions generated by the conscription debates have understandably dominated much of the historical analysis of the impact of the war on the home front, but the question of conscription was only one of a number of issues arising from the war which had ramifications for society as a whole. This chapter will focus generally on the effect that the war had on shaping social relations in Australia, and ask whether the war reinforced existing social values or resulted in significant changes. The situation of women on the home front and the treatment of Germans and other so-called enemy aliens resident in Australia during the war provide useful case studies for such an analysis.

As we have seen earlier, Australian enthusiasm for the war was primarily based on a sense of loyalty to the British Empire, at least as much as on a belief that the security of Australia was directly at risk. In the decade before the outbreak of war State governments, persuaded by fears of a resurgent socialism and pacifism, actively promoted the spread of pro-imperial propaganda in government and non-Catholic private schools, as part of a general intensification of imperial sentiment in both Britain and the Empire. Boys, in particular, were exhorted to prepare themselves to fight in defence of the Empire, and in 1911 a system of compulsory cadet training was introduced for boys from 12 to 18 years of age.[1] The inculcation of imperial values may have been expected to pave the way for wholehearted support for the war.

Nevertheless, the distance of the war from Australian soil and the lack of a sense of immediacy made it difficult to sustain domestic enthusiasm over the longer term. Indeed, it seems that because of their sense of isolation from the theatre of war some of the more entrenched loyalists could never be satisfied that sufficient dedication was being shown on the home front. In mid-1915, for instance, at the peak of a successful recruitment drive, the prominent Melbourne lawyer, Frederic Eggleston, wrote, 'We are still to realise its [the war's] meaning—our life goes on the same, our energies are not stimulated—and we try to make the war as small a part of ourselves as we possibly can'.[2]

Historians disagree on how much of 'a part of ourselves' the war had become, perhaps because questions of support for the war effort became confused with support for conscription. For example, Lloyd Robson commenced his study of recruitment for the AIF with a description of the high level of popular patriotism which, he believed, suffused the Australian home front until the end of 1915. Robson, however, also concluded that opposition to Billy Hughes's attempts to introduce conscription demonstrated that: 'Throughout the whole campaign, *and indeed throughout the war*, people could not be convinced that the threat to them and their families was immediate enough to justify all that governments demanded [my emphasis]'.[3] Ultimately, historiographic evaluation of the direct impact of the war on Australian society has been shaped by the interpretative framework within which historians have written; by their understandings of Australia's prewar traditions, and their analysis of the wider social implications of government policy.

In his pioneering account, *Australia During the War*, published eighteen years after the war ended, Ernest Scott very clearly presented the view that Australians entered the war believing that the enterprise of war was marginal to their national consciousness. According to Scott, the tendency to experience the war as distanced from Australian national life was strengthened by a predisposition in Australian society to regard the prosecution of war as a characteristic of older, European societies, rather than as an intrinsic part of Australia's national tradition. Scott was at pains to distinguish between the history of European states which had achieved nationhood and federation through force, and Australia's own 'peaceful' and democratic traditions:

A comparison between the history of federations in other parts of the world and that of Australia presents a striking illustration of the peaceful progress which had characterised the formation of Australian institutions . . .
But the Australian federal movement did not emanate from

war. It grew without such impulsion. It is true that one motive
which influenced the advocates of the federal cause was that of
defence. But prudent precaution was different from the driving
force of actual war . . . A people whose form of government was
evolved in peace, who had never felt the shock of war upon their
soil, and who were geographically remote from the storm centres
of the earth, were not attuned to the real significance of the
fermentation which was at this time proceeding in Vienna, Berlin,
St Petersburg, Paris, London, Brussels and Belgrade.[4]

Scott's characterisation of Australia as a peaceful society may strike
today's readers as naive, especially in view of the brutal suppression
of the Aborigines; but his assumptions accurately reflect the dominant perception of the majority of Australians at the outbreak of
war: that war was essentially alien to the Australian experience. The
emergence of the Anzac legend (to be discussed in a later chapter)
modified such perceptions by suggesting that Australia's true identity was forged on the battlefields of Gallipoli. Even here, however,
the Australian soldier was distinguished from his European counterparts by his alleged contempt for authority and attachment to
democratic principles.

Fundamental to Scott's analysis is the association of the term
'peaceful' (and implicitly democratic) with the idea of 'progress'
suggesting the contemporary perception that Australian society on
the eve of the war was inexorably improving itself. Such a view
contrasts with the pessimism which characterised many European
nations immediately prior to the war. In countries such as Germany
and France war was welcomed as a way of giving direction to
societies believed to have lost their way. It was anticipated that war,
not peace, would provide the mechanism for social improvement.
An assessment of the experience of the Australian home front
therefore provides an interesting contrast with Europe. In the case
of Australia it is necessary to ask whether, and, to what extent, the
war affected Australians' confidence in prewar assumptions about
their capacity to improve Australian society.

At the turn of the century the basis of progress in Australian
society was believed to lie in two main areas: Australia's ability to
improve the racial capacity of British 'stock' and the capacity of
the Australian political and industrial relations system to generate
social reform.

The historian Carol Bacchi draws attention to the influence in
the late nineteenth century of social Darwinism which was concerned with the question of why some racial groups apparently
succeeded, while others failed. Of particular interest was what
happened to a racial group if it were transplanted into a different

environment. This was relevant because of fears that, in the over-crowded environment of industrial Europe, European racial groups were declining. Great faith was placed in the beneficial potential of Australia's climate and generally superior physical surroundings for overcoming inherited physical and intellectual defects, and for providing a sound base for social improvement.[5] For example, many Australians believed that their participation in the Boer War at the turn of the century demonstrated that they were at least physically the equal of their British forebears, if not superior to them.[6]

On a political level, the early establishment of an industrial arbitration system, the creation of a system of tariff protection, the granting of the vote to women and the introduction of aged pensions, exemplified post-federation reform initiatives. In the early twentieth century, Australia was regarded internationally as a progressive social laboratory. Importantly, the fact that such reforms were achieved through the cooperation of the Labor Party (whose base was the trade union movement) and leading liberals indicated an apparently broad social consensus between the working and middle classes on the direction society should take.[7] This reformist vision of Australian society was presented as intrinsically Australian and therefore as an extension of the values of mateship and egalitarianism which coloured much of the thinking that surrounded the development of late nineteenth-century Australian nationalism, and that contributed to the construction of the Anzac legend.

Although Australia's confident national self-image can be contrasted to the relative insecurity of the European belligerents, this needs to be qualified. Bacchi points to the emergence of self-doubts in Australia in the years immediately preceding the outbreak of war when some social commentators began to suspect that environment and social reform had perhaps not triumphed over genetics. Influenced by overseas paranoia about the degeneration of their populations, critics expressed concerns that insanity, alcoholism, venereal disease and similar indicators of social decline were not under control and still represented real threats to the well-being of Australian society.[8] Once war broke out this type of social anxiety was reflected in calls for social control by those who feared that Australia's capacity to fight was seriously compromised by physical—and, by extension, moral—weakness.

Together with strident propaganda directed against the supposed threat to Australia's eugenic fitness, fears about the racial security of the Australian people undermined socially progressive ideas of reform. Richard White, in contrast to Scott, challenges the view that the reforms of the post-federation period reflected a fundamentally progressive attitude. White emphasises instead the legislators' essential defensiveness when he argues that: 'Protection, not only of local labour and industry from foreign competition, but also of the nation generally from foreign aggression and assaults on its unity or moral purity became a dominant feature of Australian society'.[9] Symptomatic of the hardening climate of opinion was the consolidation of support for the White Australia Policy on all sides of politics.

As suggested earlier, a heightened consciousness of Australian vulnerability also contributed to increasing expressions of support for the British Empire and an emphasis on Australian nationalism within the context of imperial loyalty. A significant manifestation of this trend was the introduction of Empire Day in 1905.[10] Celebrated on 24 May, the anniversary of Queen Victoria's birthday, the Empire Day school holiday provided an ideal opportunity to extol to children the cultural and military superiority of the British Empire, and some historians argue that such rhetoric was crucial in shaping the nature of subsequent response to the outbreak of war.[11] Also important in anticipating potential wartime reactions (in this case sectarian divisiveness) was the major source of opposition to Empire Day, the Catholic Church. Because the symbolism of Empire Day was so strongly imbued with the Anglophilic values of the Protestant elite, it was resisted by Catholics. Indeed, the success of Empire Day prompted the Catholic Church in 1911 to declare an alternative patriotic celebration, an 'Australian Day', also on 24 May, when Catholic children were encouraged to sing 'Advance Australia Fair' and were called upon to 'Place Australia first'.[12]

It is possible to identify two competing threads running through Australian society on the eve of the war, both of which were to shape Australia's response to war. On the one hand, many Australians—particularly those identifying themselves with the values of the labour movement—were still strongly influenced by a view of Australian society, derived from the 1890s, which regarded it as independent, progressive and dynamic. On the other hand, concerns about racial purity and, more generally, Australia's position as a European enclave in a hostile environment, sowed the seeds of self-doubt, and contributed to the increasing influence of racism and a reaffirmation of links with Britain prior to the war. Not only was Australia's reaction to war shaped by these opposing tendencies, but the experience of war influenced which of these orientations had a greater impact on Australian society in the longer term.

Identifying the experience of war on the home front

As Richard White has pointed out, much historical writing about war is obscured by the use of metaphorical language. Terms such as 'the coming of age' of a nation oversimplify the possible diversity of war experience and distract attention from factors including a person's age, gender, class, nationality or regional location which alone, or in combination, may mould their reaction to war. By focusing historical analysis on specific social categories and what White calls the 'changing relations' within these categories, it may be possible to pin down more concretely the actual effects of war.[13]

An analysis of the experiences of specific social groups needs still to take into account the impact of more general national values and ideology, however. During the war there was an interplay between the various claims of patriotism, imperial loyalty, racism, national identity, socialism and feminism—to identify some of the more obvious ideological strands directly affecting the response of specific social groups to the war. These often cut across categories such as class and gender with at times contradictory results.

For example, women from all social classes shared the assumption that women's position in society was determined by their biology, but this assumption manifested itself in different ways. For many middle-class women this became linked to patriotic support for the war with the result that many women participated enthusiastically in auxiliaries to raise money and provide goods for Australian soldiers. These women believed that their ancillary role in support of the war and, in many cases, conscription, was a natural extension of their role as wives and mothers. In more radical, working-class circles, on the other hand, the argument that women were naturally oriented towards nurturing was turned on its head. Some of the most active opponents of conscription were socialist feminists such as Adela Pankhurst, who urged women to oppose the war because its slaughter ran contrary to women's allegedly uniquely life-giving mission. In addition, the decline in living standards on the home front that came as a direct result of the war was taken as evidence of the especially adverse effect of war on women and children, and of the special obligation of women to object to the war.

A further example of the impact of a shared ideology on all walks of society is evident in the emergence of anti-Germanism during the war. Whereas before the war Germans had been viewed as having a common racial and cultural heritage with the British, from 1914 on they were progressively depicted as a hostile race. Anti-German feeling transcended all social groups. Members of the middle class and the working class alike engaged in rabid anti-German activity. Gender, too, influenced the way in which Germans were presented. Women were the targets of propaganda portraying Germans as sub-human rapists.

Just as it is necessary to distinguish between the effects of war on society in general and its impact on specific groups, so too it is important to differentiate between the immediate and longer term impact of war. On the home front the immediate effects of war on people's lives were fairly obvious. Women were left to care for families without the support of their partners, many of whom never returned. Even if soldiers were unmarried their parents suffered financially if their sons were killed and could no longer contribute to the household income.[14] Families had to learn to cope when men returned, often bearing the physical and psychological scars of war. Able-bodied men who did not enlist were subject to constant pressure to do so, regardless of their personal circumstances, while men who wished to enlist but were not able to do so experienced a sense of frustration.

Escalating inflation undermined the wages of those remaining at work. Schoolchildren, meanwhile, participated in any number of activities, from fundraising to carpentry, gardening to poetry writing, all designed to instil a strong sense of patriotism. The theme of self-denial and self-sacrifice permeated their schooling, as did ongoing propaganda stereotyping the 'unspeakable' horrors of the enemy.[15]

What is harder to determine is the more lasting social impact of war. Recently a number of historians have drawn attention to the fact that the war apparently marked the decline of a reformist prewar tradition which was replaced by a far more conservative approach, characterised by the enhanced power of the state and the increasing marginalisation of the labour movement.[16] The degree to which the war was the reason for this shift in emphasis remains open to question.

On the one hand, it is clear from our discussion of the prewar years that the influence of conservative ideas, manifested through renewed enthusiasm for the imperial connection or heightened racism, was growing even before the outbreak of war. Nevertheless, it is also clear that inherently the circumstances of war reinforced the conservative agenda. Where strong government organisation was required and the values of national loyalty and social cohesion were promoted, the result, according to a recent study of Melbourne during the war, was 'a heightened emphasis on leadership, on centralisation, on bureaucracy and on surveillance'.[17] Even Scott draws attention to the emergence of a system of censorship and surveillance during the war which seemed out of keeping with the democratic traditions of Australian society. Developing once again the theme of the alien nature of war in Australian society, he comments that:

Australia had had no experience of the restraints which war conditions imposed upon the liberty of the press, and when the censorship began to operate it seemed to many persons, of whose loyal disposition there could be no question, that an assault was being committed against one of the bulwarks of democracy.[18]

While sympathetic to concerns expressed at the time about the erosion of civil liberties, Scott concluded that censorship and surveillance were necessary to combat the leakage of information about Australia's war effort to Germany.

Subsequent studies of the role of censorship and surveillance in Australia during the First World War have not only questioned the true extent of the sensitivity of the material censored and the effectiveness of the process of censorship, but have also pointed to the abuse of increased state powers for personal political purposes. They question the legitimacy of Hughes's blatant attempts to muzzle the publication of material opposing conscription and his systematic persecution of political and industrial organisations campaigning against conscription.[19]

As chapter 2 showed, the mechanisms legitimising the operation of censorship and surveillance were established shortly after the outbreak of war under the provisions of the War Precautions Act which empowered the Governor-General to make any regulations necessary for the defence of the Commonwealth of Australia. Many of the activities of the censor and the police were in the end counterproductive. Time and resources were wasted pursuing non-existent dangers, and the rumours that emerged in the absence of genuine information were in themselves highly damaging. The strengthening of the authority of the state at the expense of reformism, and the apparent movement of politics to the right, provoked strong reactions. With the deterioration of the war situation after 1915, social divisiveness escalated. There were increasing indications of public unrest as the trade union movement attempted to reassert its influence. The 1917 strike by NSW transport workers was a prime example of the intensification of union militancy that occurred against the background of divisions in the labour movement.

White suggests that the defeat of the conscription referenda demonstrates that Australians were not prepared blindly to accept the Government's authority. He also argues that the results of elections held during the war indicate that there was little change in the prewar balance of party politics and social relationships.[20] Instead, there was a 'rhetorical shift' in the way the labour movement was publicly represented:

Although the Great War itself did not bring about major shifts in class relations, it did have some particular effects. It did not create a mass base for conservatism, but it did provide much of its rhetoric. It conveniently made available a new set of organising concepts and images that could become useful ideological weapons, particularly in defining loyalty, leadership and nationhood. The war also reinforced bourgeois fears about the potential for violent revolution in the working class. Some of the troops had demonstrated their capacity for violence and indiscipline, not only at the front but in riots in Sydney and Cairo. When channelled in politically desirable directions against Turks or Germans in Europe or anti-conscriptionists or trade unionists at home, such working-class violence was accepted, though not without misgivings, but what if it was turned on the middle class itself?[21]

The language used by government figures such as Hughes to portray the labour movement no longer placed it in the mainstream of political life, but represented it as marginal and threatening to Australian values. Whereas the war facilitated efforts to diminish the strength of organised labour, it provided an opportunity for middle-class groups to establish stronger organisational structures. This was particularly true, as will be discussed later, in the case of middle-class women's organisations and the temperance movement.

War, sport and religion

While historians have tended to concentrate on the more general social effects of the war on class and gender relations, or on the less tangible changes in ideology, there has been relatively little attention paid to the impact of war on the everyday life of individuals whose stories are less likely to be documented in the archival records of official organisations. Studies of motives for recruiting highlight the pragmatic attitude of many men whose reasons for enlisting were influenced as much by a desire for economic security or a taste for adventure, as by any deep-seated commitment to the war effort. Although this is not to deny that there were those who joined up out of genuine patriotism, there is no reason to believe that amongst the civilian population at large response to the war would not be equally pragmatic. Research by Michael McKernan, examining the impact of the war on sport and on the church, suggests that many ordinary people were sceptical of calls for civilian self-sacrifice.

McKernan's research also indicates that Eggleston's lament about the indifference of the general populace to the war, noted earlier, was not an isolated expression of concern. Attempts to curtail mass spectator sport during the First World War, because it was believed to distract the public's attention away from the serious business of war, highlighted the anxiety felt by those in authority when confronted by signs of less than total commitment to the war effort. The presence of young men who were apparently eligible for enlistment in the crowds of spectators and on the sporting fields was felt to fly in the face of exhortations for self-sacrifice. While amateur sports generally closed down their competitions for the duration of war, the semi-professional, working-class sports such as Rugby League and, to a lesser extent, Australian Rules Football, whose players were dependent on the income derived from their activities, continued to operate during the war.[22] Parochial, everyday concerns, persisted in the face of pressure to focus attention single-mindedly on the war.

McKernan's research into the role of Australia's churches during the war provides further insights into reactions to war at the grass-roots level.[23] Despite Australia's reputation at the beginning of the twentieth century as an unusually secular society, the part played by the churches in mediating between public life and ordinary people was crucial. Clergy often (but not always) espoused official loyalist sentiments and believed it was their duty to use the churches to promote such views among their parishioners. The reaction of the overwhelming majority of Anglican and other Protestant clergy-men to the war was unquestioning support and affirmation of the divine righteousness of the imperial cause: a reaction that undoubt-edly mirrored the response of many Australians, at least at the outset of war. The Catholic response, as we have seen, was more complex and diverse.[24] The pronouncements of church leaders and their analysis of public opinion are important sources for historians seeking to tap the mood of a diverse group of people. Because most Australians identified in some way or another with one of the denominations, McKernan argues that: 'In a real sense, the nation looked to clergymen to speak for them . . . When church leaders spoke they drew on these submerged identifications and were given a wider hearing than, perhaps, they suspected.'[25]

The majority of the Anglican leadership was drawn from Britain and many of the Australian-born leaders of the other Protestant churches had been educated in that country. Their pronouncements set the tone for the parish clergy and were couched in the language of middle-class rectitude. A Methodist clergyman from Bendigo, Samuel Scholes, encapsulates these sentiments:

> It is not for me just now to discuss the various bearings of the situation in which we find ourselves as an Empire involved, but it is not too much to say that in the most deliberate judgment of those most competent to determine, Britain's attitude is justifiable

not only before the courts of men, but also before the face of
Almighty God.[26]

War was believed to form part of a natural cycle in the history of
nations that allowed for moral renewal. In this way the inexplicable
suffering of war could be rationalised as a mechanism for testing
Christian faith and reforming corrupt society. War was also intended
to be a means of uniting Christians of all denominations and of
pulling together and strengthening congregations. In reality, however, it brought an intensification of sectarian divisions as the
controversies surrounding the conscription referenda escalated.

The clergy's optimism that the war would act as a focus of
religious renewal was only partially realised. Booming attendances
at special church services called to mark the outbreak of war
evaporated as the war dragged on and celebration was replaced by
mourning. Clergy complained about the public's apparent indifference to the important task ahead of them. The editor of a Sydney
Methodist newspaper observed that: 'there is little or no abatement
to the extent of Sunday pleasuring. Sport and amusement still claim
their tens of thousands of ardent devotees. Meanwhile, Sunday
congregations do not show any appreciable improvement.'[27]

Towards the end of the war, when the priest or minister became
increasingly associated with the news of the death of a family
member in battle, indifference to the church turned to dread at the
unwelcome prospect of a visit from the local clergy.

Both in the political and non-political spheres of Australian life
it can therefore be argued that the war acted as a focal point for
conflict over the nature of social relationships. To illustrate this the
chapter concludes with two case studies. The first focuses on the
role of women during the war. The contribution that women could
make to the war effort was shaped by contemporary ideas that a
woman's position in society was biologically determined. Although
the war enabled a number of women to expand their horizons, it
also reinforced pre-existing gender stereotypes. The second case
study describes the treatment of so-called 'enemy aliens', who were
citizens of belligerent countries, or their descendants, resident in
Australia at the outbreak of war. The restriction on the civil liberties
of 'enemy aliens' and the sporadic outbreaks of demonstrations
directed against foreigners underlined the potential for xenophobic
violence present in Australian society.

Women and the war

At the outbreak of war Australian women had achieved the right to vote, but in many other respects Australian society failed to extend equality to women. A significantly smaller, and from the 1890s apparently declining, proportion of women than men participated in the paid work force and female employment was concentrated in the most poorly paid areas.[28] Middle-class women were generally not expected to work and by the early twentieth century the idea that a woman's main role lay in the organisation of home and care of children was gaining in popularity.[29] This trend occurred despite the efforts of Australian feminists from the late nineteenth century to enhance women's role in public life.

To what extent did the onset of war signal substantial changes in the situation of women in Australia? What implications did the absence of men have for women in the economy? Did the war create opportunities for public service that enabled women to redefine traditional roles or did the war merely result in an even more rigorous reinforcement of preconceptions concerning the role of women? The following discussion will suggest that while overall the war appeared to have little impact on the relative position of women, there were circumstances where women challenged accepted expectations about their behaviour and instigated change.

It might be expected that, given the high level of male enlistment into the armed forces, new employment opportunities would be created for women as gaps opened up in the labour market. While there was an expansion in employment of women from 24 per cent of the work force in 1914 to 37 per cent in 1918, women's jobs were not created in great numbers in traditionally blue-collar male areas of employment. During the war manufacturing gained only 4000 new female jobs, despite the loss of 20 000 male jobs.[30] Male employment in construction and mining declined significantly (as described in chapter 4) but this had no impact on levels of female employment in these sectors.[31] Growth in female employment was concentrated in the clothing and textiles, food and printing sectors, the expansion of which related to the need to provision the armed forces. These were already traditionally large employers of female labour and therefore areas of relatively low wages. Increasing numbers of women were, however, employed in the relatively smaller 'commercial' and 'professional' sectors, reflecting a growth in shop assistant positions in department stores and the replacement of male teachers by females. W. A. Sinclair suggests that not only did the movement of unmarried women into these areas of employment arrest the prewar decline in female work force participation, but it indicated that there was greater acceptance of employment of unmarried, middle-class women.[32]

The impact of war on employed women in Australia thus differed markedly from the United Kingdom where a strong growth in female employment was brought about by the need to replace a proportionately greater number of men than was the case in Australia. In the UK female employment was directed towards the replacement of men in heavy industry, including the manufacture of munitions, and was accompanied by a relative increase in wage rates. Australian women did not experience the sense of emancipation that many British women felt when they realised that they could competently undertake work previously believed to be too skilled or arduous for women. Nor did Australian women enjoy the benefits brought to British female workers by the higher wages associated with traditionally male employment.[33] Indeed the impact of wartime inflation on the already relatively low incomes of Australian women workers was a source of grievance which, as will be seen later, precipitated sometimes violent demonstrations organised by socialist feminists.

Australian women were also more restricted than their British sisters in the contribution that they were allowed to make to any area that might have been construed as military service. On the rare occasions that women were engaged on overseas service, for instance, as nursing sisters near the front, Australian authorities had little idea of how to deal with them.

Jan Bassett describes the frustration experienced by Australian women willing to contribute to the war effort in a variety of ways, but refused permission by the Defence Department to do so. Aware that the British Government allowed women to participate in a number of auxiliary roles, Australian women wrote to the Government offering to serve as 'cooks, nurses, ambulance scouts, stretcher bearers, motor-car drivers, interpreters, munitions workers and skilled farm workers'— offers which were invariably rejected except in the area of nursing, which was regarded as an extension of women's 'natural' nurturing role.[34] Even usually conservative women who supported the Government's conscription referenda could not understand why, in the face of a shortage of men to serve, women were not permitted to take a more active role.

Australian nurses were sent as far afield as France, Egypt, Greece and India. Their deployment was characterised by the provision of inadequate and inappropriate equipment and often appalling mismanagement. In Egypt male army medical administrators so successfully undermined the authority of the highly experienced matron-in-chief that she had no option but to return to Australia.[35] Much of the source of such conflict derived from the fact that in the early part of the war Australian army nurses, unlike Canadian and New Zealand nurses, held no army rank. The absence of a formal command structure defining the relationship between the military and army nurses, combined with the misogyny of a number of male army officers, resulted in the nurses being subjected to unwarranted bullying. Many Australian nurses accepted this situation, nevertheless, because they agreed that women and men operated in 'separate spheres' and felt that the imposition of a hierarchical rank system contravened the female nursing ethos of mutual caring. When in May 1916 nurses were required to wear badges of rank in an effort designed to enhance their status, one nurse commented that her badges made her feel 'like an ironmonger's shop'. Another undesired side effect of the adoption of rank was that nurses were now restricted from associating with men of other ranks.[36] Suspicion of female sexuality was reinforced by the automatic discharge of women who married during their period of service (with the result that many marriages remained a secret).

Nurses in the field were required time and again to display levels of ingenuity, competence and independence which belied the popular stereotype of female helplessness. They learnt to give anaesthetics, to administer difficult treatments to severely wounded soldiers, and to cope under bombardment.[37] The reality of their experiences continued to run against the grain of domestic perceptions of the nurturing female who tended injured soldiers from a safe haven behind the lines of battle. Children's playground games, for example, reinforced the gender roles of the aggressive male soldier and the subservient female nurse. In the schoolyard boys playing 'injured' soldiers went 'to hospital . . . on the girl's side'.

The nature of formal uniform and insignia (which had been an important issue for nurses overseas) was also significant on the home front in highlighting the difference between the masculine world of action and the feminine domain of service:

> This was a very male war. The males could wear uniforms, from the Boy Scouts up, the Senior Cadets, the Citizen Forces and of course the Army . . . There were no uniforms for females, not even the Red Cross, so all they could do was make things for men.[38]

While such observations are not completely accurate—there were, in fact, a few examples of women's organisations that adopted uniforms—these were the exceptions and did not make the same impression as male uniforms. Where women's experience at war diverged from conventional expectations, this barely impinged on home-front perceptions.[39]

The failure of the Government to draw fully on the potential of women in the economy or in national service largely reflects the strength of prevailing ideas about the role of women and men in Australian society. Carmel Shute's pioneering analyses of women in the First World War emphasise the pervasive influence of the ideology of motherhood on all levels of Australian society. Shute argues that counterbalancing the celebration of male virility born through the trials of warfare (and manifested in the Anzac legend) was the notion that it was women's primary, and biologically determined, duty to bear children. The focus on women's maternal function not only limited the options which were regarded as appropriate for women, but undermined concepts of sexual equality. The differences between men and women were reinforced by placing greatest value on masculine attributes of strength and physical courage, which were regarded as pivotal in times of war.

Supporters of war, and specifically conscription, appealed to women to encourage men to enlist by referring to a mother's sense of duty. Newspaper comments such as, 'It is such a beautiful sight to see a mother say good-bye proudly to her soldier son', exemplify contemporary beliefs that it was women's supreme contribution to the war to bear sons to serve the higher good.[40] Women were expected to serve only vicariously, through men, not directly. The propaganda material of organisations such as the Australian Women's Service Corps, formed specifically to encourage male enlistment, highlighted maternal duty, but also played on male sexual insecurity. The poem 'The Test' is typical of such material: addressed to 'The Shirker' it seeks to shame men into enlistment:

Those who are God's true mothers, those who are worthy wives,
Think you they value their honour, or only sloth-stained lives?
Will she who is worth the winning,
She who is yet to be won,
Take to her marble bosom, one who has turned from a gun?[41]

While women were not meant to pull the trigger themselves, their role was to induce men to do so.

The image of the caring mother could be employed equally as the basis of appeals against conscription. Anti-conscriptionists very effectively played on women's fears that support for conscription was equivalent to a death sentence for their sons. In another contemporary poem 'Blood Vote', which has been described as the most effective piece of propaganda in the anti-conscription campaign, a mother seeks forgiveness from her son for voting 'Yes' in the earlier conscription referendum:

They put the dagger into my grasp,
It seemed but a pencil then.
I did not know it was a fiend a-gasp
For the priceless blood of men.
They gave me the ballot paper,
The grim death-warrant of doom.

> And I smugly sentenced the men to death
> In that dreadful little room.
> I put it inside the Box of Blood
> Nor thought of the man I'd slain.
> Till at midnight came a 'whelming flood
> God's word and the Brand of Cain.
> O little son! O my little son!
> Pray God for your Mother's soul.
> That the scarlet stain may be white again
> In God's great Judgement Roll.[42]

The emotive tone associated with such appeals to women was complemented by more pragmatic arguments which also drew on popular preconceptions about women's domestic role. Thus male unionists opposed mass conscription quite openly on the grounds that gaps created in the work force would result in the replacement of male workers by females, an appeal both to the preservation of traditional roles and to longstanding fears about being undercut by lower priced labour.[43]

As Joy Damousi says, Shute's work has been invaluable in pointing out how the war 'strengthened and reinforced . . . definitions of gender and the associated assumptions relating to men's and women's fixed positions within society'.[44] Nevertheless, despite these constraints, the war had sometimes quite unintended effects on the role of women. A good example of this is provided by the conservative Australian Women's National League (AWNL). Formed in 1904 to promote 'Loyalty to the Throne and Empire' and to organise women voters against the 'socialist menace', its membership peaked during the war at 54 000 nationally. At the time it constituted the largest non-Labor organisation in Australia. Although the AWNL vehemently opposed notions of sexual equality and encouraged women to exercise political power by influencing the behaviour of their husbands and sons, the scale of its activities during the war demonstrated the organisational competence of women. AWNL members participated in a range of fundraising activities, as well as in the provision of soldiers' 'comforts' such as tobacco, knitted goods and food, a task coordinated through the Red Cross. The AWNL was also actively engaged in recruitment drives and in the pro-conscription campaigns.[45] In other words, the war enabled the AWNL to raise the public and organisational profile of women in the Australian community virtually in contradiction of its own aims and objectives.

The frustration felt by women loyal to the war effort, but inhibited in their ability to make a meaningful contribution, is reflected in a number of letters written to newspapers. Typical are the observations of 'One of Them', published in June 1915: 'Hundreds of intelligent women are wondering whether they might not be doing something more helpful than knitting and making flannel garments'.[46] The main coordinating body for fundraising and the provision and distribution of clothes and comforts for men on the front was the Red Cross. Under the leadership of the wife of the Governor-General, Lady Helen Munro-Ferguson, the Australian Red Cross established an extensive network of branches throughout Australia. Women were organised into a massive effort of sewing and knitting. In addition, the Voluntary Aid Detachment, a subsidiary organisation of the Red Cross, mobilised 10 000 women to assist in the care of returned soldiers. Various Patriotic Funds and the Australian Comforts Fund provided further opportunities for women to contribute to the war effort.[47] And yet, many women agreed with 'One of Them', that involvement with the Red Cross and the Patriotic Funds was a poor substitute for a more direct contribution to the military campaign.

Concerted efforts were made to encourage the Government to mobilise women's organisations in government service by middle-class women who under normal circumstances subscribed to the notion that a woman's place was in the home. The Australian Women's Services Corps (AWSC) was formed in November 1916 in response to the defeat of the first conscription referendum. Comprising mainly middle-class women between the ages of 21 and 45, it offered the services of its members in clerical, nursing and general auxiliary field work, so that men could be freed up to serve at the front. As indicated by the poem 'The Test', quoted earlier, the AWSC in no way sought to undermine women's conventional role. Yet, in the latter years of the war, undeterred by continuing official rejections of its offers to replace men in non-combat roles, the AWSC had organised its membership into an almost paramilitary organisation, complete with modified uniform, drills and swimming lessons. Working-class women also attempted to extend the boundaries of accepted forms of women's service. For example, in 1917 women employed at the Commonwealth Clothing Factory demonstrated their patriotism by forming the Khaki Girls, who at first undertook conventional fundraising activities and support of soldiers, but who then sought to engage more directly in military preparedness through formal drill and training activities.[48]

It was perhaps in the area of the 'moral crusade', however, that women were most directly involved in the successful implementation of social change. The movement to ban or restrict the sale of alcohol, the temperance movement, had been active in Australia from the late 1870s without achieving major successes, but in the context of the social anxiety of the immediate prewar years it had enjoyed a revival of influence. The main support for this movement lay within Protestant church groups who believed that alcohol was the source of both moral and social decay. The fact that many publicans were Catholics, who regarded the temperance campaigns as further evidence of victimisation, provided an additional ingredient to sectarian tensions. While male church leaders were to the forefront of campaigns to control alcohol consumption, women's organisations such as the Women's Christian Temperance Union (WCTU) played a leading role in what proved to be a highly successful wartime campaign to restrict the hours of opening of hotels. The decision to campaign for restricted drinking hours, rather than total abstinence, represented a significant compromise for the temperance movement.

The case against alcohol was buttressed in the early months of the war by reports of drunk and disorderly behaviour in city streets by newly recruited soldiers. Immediate concern about the unacceptable behaviour of troops was extended to a generalised belief that control of drinking was essential for the execution of a militarily efficient operation. A well-ordered, self-disciplined and morally upright home front was a precondition for the successful prosecution of the war. The WCTU embarked on a vigorous campaign of prayer, education, government petition and deputation which, in conjunction with the mobilisation of propaganda from the broader temperance movement, culminated in significant changes to drinking hours' legislation throughout Australia. By 1916 the State governments of South Australia, New South Wales, Victoria and Tasmania had all succumbed to pressure for hotels to close at six o'clock in the evening. Although this did not represent a full realisation of the aims of those seeking to achieve total bans on the sale of alcohol, it certainly reflected a marked increase in influence for the temperance movement and has been interpreted as signifying a shift towards a formalisation of more conservative social values.

Membership of the WCTU, like that of the AWNL, experienced significant growth during the war. Like the AWNL too, membership of the WCTU was drawn from middle-class women who strongly subscribed to the view that women's primary responsibility was to their families. Nevertheless, the war offered such women an unprecedented opportunity to engage in public life—an opportunity which they readily seized upon because in their minds private morality and public good were merged in the service of the imperial cause. If women were not able to fight overseas, they could at least fight 'the enemy within society', a sentiment reflected in a 1915 address to the WCTU by its president, Mrs Downing: 'the truest patriotism consists of engaging in the world-wide war against the drink evil to raise national and personal efficiency and to stop the war by

stopping intoxicating drink'.[49] The militancy of the WCTU
illustrated that, despite the effect the war appeared to have in
reaffirming conservative values about the place of women in society,
the nature of the mobilisation of women in support of the war in
itself represented a shift in women's social role.

The commitment of large numbers of women to the war effort
was impressive. As discussed previously, a smaller, but equally
committed, number of women participated in organised opposition
to the Government's wartime policies. Women's anti-war activities
occurred either within the framework of a plethora of socialist
parties[50] or within the context of exclusively women's groups, such
as the Sisterhood for International Peace (SIP), an organisation
committed to promoting pacifist education in schools, or the
Women's Peace Army (WPA). In the main, dissenting women, like
their patriotic sisters, justified their actions in terms of fulfilment
of a biologically predetermined mission. Warmongering was presented as contrary to women's life-giving and nurturing function.

Gender also affected women's style of participation. In the case
of socialist parties whose membership was predominantly male,
women's involvement was primarily directed towards supporting
their male comrades. Women were engaged in the inevitable round
of fundraising activities or involved in behind-the-scenes party
organisation; they were not encouraged, nor did they necessarily
seek, the public political spotlight.[51]

By contrast, women-only anti-war organisations enabled women
to play an active and public role. While subscribing to the belief
that women were inherently pacifist by nature, organisations such
as the WPA placed women at the forefront of public protest against
the consequences of war. Formed in July 1915 under the leadership
of the feminists, Vida Goldstein and Adela Pankhurst, the WPA not
only campaigned vigorously against the two conscription referenda
but actively promoted general socialist reform. In particular, the
WPA focused attention on the immediate impact the war was having
on women's lives. Among the issues of concern to the WPA was
the plight of women affected by wartime unemployment and rising
prices. The WPA's concerns paralleled those of the conservative
women's organisations. It identified increased violence against
women due to the concentration of soldiers in cities as an important
issue, and hence joined with conservative women's organisations in
supporting six o'clock closing. The WPA also had a common interest
with conservative women in their campaign against the spread of
sexually transmitted diseases by returning overseas soldiers. The
WPA, however, rejected as discriminatory the introduction of what
it regarded as unfair legislation which required mandatory reporting
of those who had contracted venereal disease. It feared that the

legislation would affect almost exclusively female prostitutes, who were vulnerable to arrest on charges of vagrancy and who were unlikely to remain anonymous because of their attendance at public clinics. In contrast, the chances of male 'clients' having to face publicly the consequences of their social activities were remote.[52]

The disruptive potential of organised women in the public sphere was realised by the Women's Peace League, a female off-shoot of the Victorian Socialist Party. Adopting a more militant stance than the WPA, the League, under the leadership of Adela Pankhurst (who had by then severed ties with the WPA) engaged in a series of street marches in Melbourne in August and September 1917. These demonstrations against rising food prices resulted in extensive damage to property and the imprisonment of participants. The level of disruption was justified by Pankhurst in terms of conventional women's concerns for the needs of starving women and children.[53] Given Pankhurst's views on woman's biological mission, it was perhaps appropriate that she married Tom Walsh, an active unionist, on 1 October 1917 in order to foil Hughes's attempts to deport her to Britain.[54]

Recent analysis by Joy Damousi suggests that where women tried to enter the public arena and debate issues in their own right, rather than in the context of women's concerns, they were met with strong, sometimes violent, opposition. Female speakers addressing anti-conscriptionist rallies and sharing the same platform as male opponents to conscription were subjected to physical violence and verbal abuse. Returned soldiers seemed to find the presence of women pacifists particularly threatening to their sense of masculine identity.[55] Radical women who quite openly crossed the boundaries of what was considered appropriate female behaviour were therefore doubly ostracised: firstly, because they undermined the war effort and secondly because they called into question the legitimacy of the male fighting role.

The First World War offered the opportunity to Australian women to mobilise, mainly in support of, but also in opposition to, the conflict. This mobilisation occurred within a framework which built on and reinforced pre-existing ideas about women's 'natural' role as wife and mother. The reluctance to employ women in traditionally male areas, and the pervasiveness of appeals to women's maternal instincts in propaganda material, suggest that the war did far less to alter women's place in Australian society than had been the case in the United Kingdom. Nevertheless, the high public profile adopted by women in campaigns for and against conscription or in the temperance movement, points to women exercising a degree of influence which extended beyond the bounds of previously accepted ideas and paved the way for future change.

What historians debate is how this involvement is to be interpreted—whether it represented a step forwards or backwards.

The treatment of enemy aliens

Chapter IV of Scott's *Australia During the War,* called the 'The Enemy within the Gates', outlines the Government's treatment of Germans resident in Australia during the war. The imprisonment and surveillance of Germans and those of German descent was regarded by Scott as an understandable response by the Government to the potential danger posed by those whose loyalties could not be relied upon. Research more recently undertaken by McKernan, Raymond Evans and Gerhard Fischer has questioned the extent to which Germans posed a genuine threat to Australia's internal security and have suggested that anti-German activities were undertaken as much for propaganda purposes as for legitimate reasons of state. Although the latter should not be discounted entirely, Fischer goes further and is highly critical of what in today's terminology would be regarded as the human rights abuses of many innocent Germans (as well as citizens of other countries at war with the Allies, including those Balkan states that were part of the Austro-Hungarian Empire). Often without the benefit of due process of law, these people were forced out of employment and, in many instances, imprisoned.[56]

The concept of an 'enemy alien' is highly problematic. To assume that all citizens of enemy countries living in Australia were spies or saboteurs was patently absurd. On the other hand, it would have been naive to harbour no suspicions and take no precautions. Historians agree that actions taken to control German officers, army reservists and consular officials immediately after the declaration of war were probably justifiable. The requirement of the War Precautions Act that all German subjects register at local police stations, giving details of occupation and change of address, was also reasonable. This, however, proved to be the thin end of the wedge as the provisions of the War Precautions Act were interpreted with increasing latitude. The protection accorded by naturalisation was removed and Australian citizens born in Germany (and later whose parents, or even grandparents were not Australian born) were subjected to arbitrary search, surveillance and arrest. While the initial actions taken against enemy aliens could be rationalised on grounds of security, subsequent actions, based not on concrete evidence but on rumour, innuendo or the financial insolvency of individual aliens, served a far broader purpose.

As the war went on, the Government encouraged a public campaign against Germans in Australia in order to stir up loyalist emotions. The apparent presence of the 'enemy within the gates' created a sense of the immediacy of the danger to the Australian community that was otherwise difficult to sustain, given the distance from the theatres of war. The focus on the German threat was by no means an isolated example of the internalisation of the enemy into Australian society during the war, although it was arguably the most blatant. As chapter 2 showed, in the context of the conscription controversies, Hughes's campaign against the IWW and other left-wing trade unionists relied heavily on creating the impression of internal disloyalty and potential social danger. Arbitrary deportation of American, British and Irish activists reflected Hughes's ruthless determination to rid Australia of subversive elements at any cost.[57] In a different way we have seen how the temperance movement played on fears relating to the dangers posed by alcohol to mobilise against what it regarded as a grave threat to both society and the war effort. Similarly, venereal disease was projected as seriously endangering society's racial integrity, and therefore as undermining Australia's ability to conduct the war. The insecurities felt by a society at war enhanced its susceptibility to fear campaigns and created an atmosphere in which emotions were readily manipulated.

Evans emphasises that anti-Germanism was not a spontaneous phenomenon but a deliberate strategy adopted by the Government to heighten public support for the war: 'Anti-Germanism actually grew in vehemence as enthusiasm for warfare was *intentionally* mobilised. Painstakingly contrived propaganda and distortive censorship, inducing hatred against the enemy, were vital elements in that mobilisation.'[58] An important feature of the anti-German propaganda was its escalating racism. Prior to the war Germans had been welcome European residents who were believed to share a similar 'Aryan' racial background to the British. From mid-1915 the public was inundated by newspaper articles, novels and films which portrayed the Germans as barbaric and untrustworthy 'Huns'. Indeed, central to the process of discrediting Germans was the creation of the idea that Germans belonged to an alien and inferior race—as opposed to their being, in today's terms, ethnically different from Australians. This built on the longstanding Australian tradition—so well represented in the White Australia Policy—of characterising peoples regarded as threatening to Australia's security in terms of negative racial stereotypes. Thus, a contributor to a Brisbane soldiers' magazine believed he could demonstrate that Germans were not Europeans but Central Asians:

> They are a race alone and apart, interlopers and squatters in Europe . . . The very name 'Ger-man' or 'Alle-man' means 'Wolfman'. . . invented by Germans to inspire terror

('Frightfulness') . . . The Hun love for inhuman atrocities has
been fostered by this savage tribal cult of the wolf and the carrion
raven.[59]

The effect of stereotyping was to dehumanise and degrade its
objects and to reinforce the idea of Australia as a bastion of British
imperial values. Schoolchildren and teachers, bombarded with anti-
German propaganda, were given a ready excuse to legitimise
victimisation of children who somehow did not conform by labelling
them as German sympathisers.[60] The creation of a system of surveillance of enemy aliens combined with a sustained propaganda
campaign had serious consequences for Germans in Australia who
increasingly became the subject of public hostility. Numerous police
raids on innocent Germans were precipitated by anxious neighbours
concocting suspicions out of thin air about non-existent radio trans-
mitters or clandestine meetings, the purpose of which later turned
out to be purely social. Complaints against Germans were also
motivated by jealousy of business success and a desire to eliminate
competition.[61] In addition, trade unionists refused to work with
Germans and other enemy subjects. The result was severe disruption
to German communal life and individual trauma, financial destitution for many Germans and the imprisonment of almost 7000 in the
course of the war. (This included some 2500 Germans captured
outside Australia and subsequently interned in Australia.) At the
conclusion of the war 6150 Germans and other enemy alien nationals were deported.[62]

At the time of the 1911 Census there were 33 381 German-born
residents in Australia. Germans and their descendants were concentrated in rural communities, mainly in Queensland and South
Australia, and to a far lesser extent in Victoria and New South
Wales. The location of Germans away from strategically important
urban centres in itself reduced the likelihood that Germans might
pose a security threat.[63] Nevertheless, through the war 4500 Australian residents were interned, 700 of whom were naturalised British
subjects, and 70 Australian born.[64] There was, if anything, a negative
correlation between numbers interned and areas of strongest German
settlement. The largest proportion of aliens interned relative to
numbers resident was in Western Australia and New South Wales.
Germans concentrated in urban areas were possibly easier to locate
than those scattered in rural locations.[65]

In Western Australia the concentration on the Kalgoorlie gold-
fields of miners of assorted Balkan ethnicity, who were technically
subjects of the Austro-Hungarian Empire, created a ready target for
misplaced patriotic zeal against a group who had no necessary
allegiance to the German cause. The Government and the mine

owners succumbed by late 1915 to increasing pressure from unionists by dismissing and imprisoning a number of migrant workers.
Such actions were based on unfounded fears of anything 'foreign'
and had the bizarre effect of subjecting a significant number of
innocent non-Germans to persecution and impoverishment in the
service of the anti-German cause. The Western Australian experience
represents the most extreme example of the arbitrary basis of arrest
and imprisonment, which in reality seemed to be determined often
as much by the socioeconomic status of its victims, as by the
potential threat they posed.

Social vulnerability seems also to explain why the second
highest rate of arrest of aliens occurred in New South Wales, despite
the comparatively small numbers of Germans living in that State.
Whereas the majority of Germans living in South Australia and
Queensland had migrated many years previously, many Germans in
New South Wales were only recently arrived and employed in
factory and clerical jobs. Once dismissed from employment (which
became increasingly the case in the wake of anti-German hysteria)
and with no means of support, such Germans were required to
submit themselves to 'voluntary' arrest and imprisonment.

In comparison to wage and salary earners, self-employed
German farmers resident in the established German communities in
South Australia and Queensland were cushioned against the likelihood of unemployment, the major reason for imprisonment.
Certainly conspicuous individuals, such as the prominent German
Consul to Brisbane, Eugen Hirschfeld, were imprisoned and
deported. High-profile medical practitioners and readily identifiable
German-born business and community leaders were similarly
interned in order to placate public anxiety. Nevertheless, the majority of Germans living in Australia managed to escape public notice,
apart from sporadic denunciations from neighbours. Fischer suggests
that regional variation in prosecution may also have reflected the
relative enthusiasm and resources available at a local level to
military authorities.

The decision to intern enemy aliens paid scant regard to the
contribution that many had made to the Australian community. If
anything, their incarceration deprived the war effort of their skills,
while at the same time tarnishing the reputation of the system of
justice. In the majority of cases there was no evidence that the
internees were engaged in subversive activities, but they had no
access to due legal process to demonstrate this. Sole discretion to
release the internees rested with the Minister for Defence, who was
obviously in no position to consider each case on its individual
merits.

The detention of enemy aliens necessitated the construction and maintenance of several camps. Few records exist in relation to the smaller camps located in Queensland, Western Australia, Tasmania and Victoria. It is apparent that conditions in the camps in New South Wales varied considerably, depending on size, the individual philosophy of those running the camps and the composition of their inmates.

The worst and largest of the camps, holding at its peak 5000 inmates, was Holdsworthy near Liverpool in New South Wales. At this camp there was incompetent administration and severe problems of overcrowding. The camp housed German soldiers and sailors caught in Australia at the outbreak of war as well as those transported from overseas. Military personnel were mixed in with German civilians from all walks of life and with assorted nationals from the Austro-Hungarian Empire. The mixture of ranks (officers and men), class and ethnic groups was a source of internal unrest amongst the prisoners, and in 1916 a riot occurred amongst the inmates, some of whom were seeking protection from criminal elements in the camp. The camp management appeared to have little idea of how to control an often volatile situation.

In contrast to Holdsworthy, life in smaller camps such as Berrima, located south-west of Sydney, and Trial Bay, in northern New South Wales, was comfortable. The administration of these camps seemed far more lenient and their inmates, while still suffering from boredom and separation from family, were able to engage in a number of constructive cultural and educational activities.[66]

Prevailing stereotypes shaped Australia's treatment of enemy aliens, just as they limited the role women were able to play during the war. Prejudice provoked by fear resulted in actions being taken against Germans which diverted energy and resources away from a productive contribution to the war effort, often for dubious benefit. The divisiveness of such an approach damaged the society which it was intended to assist and undermined the future capacity of society to work on a consensual basis. In responding to war Australian society had difficulty distinguishing between genuine and imagined threats and fell easy prey to emotional manipulation. Given Australia's physical isolation from the war front, perhaps no other response could have been expected.

Notes

1 Raymond Evans, 'The Lowest Common Denominator: Loyalism and Schoolchildren in War-torn Australia 1914–1916' in Lyn Finch, *Young in a Warm Climate: History of Childhood in Australia*, University of Queensland Press, St Lucia (forthcoming); and Maurice French,

' "One People, One Destiny"—A Question of Loyalty: the Origins of Empire Day in New South Wales 1900–1905', *Journal of the Royal Australian Historical Society*, vol. 61, pt. 4, 1975, p. 240.

2 Quoted in Raymond Evans, *Loyalty and Disloyalty: Social Conflict on the Queensland Homefront, 1914–18*, Allen & Unwin, Sydney, 1987, p. 39.

3 L. L. Robson, *The First A.I.F.: A Study of its Recruitment 1914–1918*, Melbourne University Press, Melbourne, 1970, p. 108.

4 Ernest Scott, *Australia During the War*, vol. XI, of *The Official History of Australia in the War of 1914–18*, Angus & Robertson, Sydney, 1936, pp. 4–6.

5 C. J. Bacchi, 'The Nature-Nurture Debate in Australia, 1900–1914', *Historical Studies*, vol. 19, no. 35, 1980, p. 200.

6 Quoted in Richard White, *Inventing Australia: Images and Identity 1688–1980*, George Allen & Unwin, Sydney, 1981, p. 73. White points to the significance of the participation of Australian colonial troops in the Sudan (1885), the Boxer rebellion (1900) and the Boer War (1899–1902).

7 See especially John Docker, 'Can the centre hold? Conceptions of the state 1890–1925' in Sydney Labour History Group, *What Rough Beast? The State and Social Order in Australian History*, George Allen & Unwin, Sydney, 1982, pp. 57–88 for an excellent account of the rise and fall of optimistic consensus on the possibilities of reforming Australian society. Compare with White, *Inventing Australia*, who interprets the post-federation programs as defensive reactions to Australia's perceived vulnerability to economic and racial enemies, pp. 114 ff. .

8 Bacchi, 'Nature-Nuture debate', p. 209.

9 White, *Inventing Australia*, p. 114.

10 Judith Smart, War and the Concept of a New Social Order, PhD thesis, Monash University, 1992, p. 28.

11 Stewart Firth and Janet Hoorn, 'From Empire Day to Cracker Night' in Peter Spearitt & David Walker (eds) *Australian Popular Culture*, George Allen & Unwin, Sydney, 1979, pp. 25–30; Evans, 'The Lowest Common Denominator'.

12 Maurice French, 'The Ambiguity of Empire Day in New South Wales 1901–1921: Imperial Consensus or National Division?', *Australian Journal of Politics and History*, vol. XX1V, no. 1, 1978, pp. 70–1. Also Firth and Hoorn, 'From Empire Day', *passim*.

13 Richard White, 'War and Australian Society', in M. McKernan and M. Browne (eds), *Australia: Two Centuries of War and Peace*, Australian War Memorial in association with Allen & Unwin, Canberra, 1988, pp. 391–7.

14 Personal communication from John McQuilton.

15 Scott, *Australia During the War*, pp. 733–7; Evans, 'The Lowest Common Denominator'.

16 See White, 'War and Australian society', pp. 398–9; Smart, War and the Concept, pp. 34–5; Evans, *Loyalty and Disloyalty*, ch. 2, and Kevin Fewster, 'The Operation of State Apparatuses in Times of

Crisis: Censorship and Conscription', *War & Society*, vol. 3, no. 1, 1985, pp. 37–54.

17 Smart, War and the Concept, p. 34.

18 Scott, *Australia During the War*, p. 58.

19 See especially, Frank Cain, *The Origins of Political Surveillance in Australia*, Angus & Robertson, London, 1983; Fewster, 'The Operation of State Apparatuses', pp. 37–54. Also, Evans, *Loyalty and Disloyalty*; Smart, War and the Concept, *passim*.

20 See also Ian Turner, *Industrial Labour and Politics: The Dynamics of the Labour Movement in Eastern Australia, 1900–1921*, Australian National University, Canberra, 1965, p. 180. Turner suggests that the political split in the Labor Party barely extended beyond the parliamentary party. He points to a revival in Labor electoral fortunes in by-elections held in late 1917 and in the 1918 Queensland and South Australian elections.

21 White, 'War and Australian Society', p. 400.

22 Michael McKernan, 'Sport, war and society: Australia 1914–18' in Richard Cashman and Michael McKernan (eds) *Sport in History: The Making of Modern Sporting History*, University of Queensland Press, St Lucia, 1979, pp. 1–20.

23 Michael McKernan, *Australian Churches at War: Attitudes and Activities of the Major Churches 1914–18*, Catholic Theological Faculty and Australian War Memorial, Sydney and Canberra, 1980. The discussion of the role of the churches follows McKernan's analysis.

24 Robson, *First A.I.F.*, pp. 51–2, 70. In contrast to Mannix, Archbishop Kelly of Sydney officiated at a high mass to commemorate fallen Australian soldiers on Empire Day, 1915 (Firth and Hoorn, 'From Empire Day', p. 29).

25 McKernan, *Australian Churches*, p. 8.

26 Quoted ibid. p. 28.

27 Quoted ibid. p. 65.

28 W. A. Sinclair, 'Women and economic change in Melbourne 1871–1921', *Historical Studies*, vol. 20, no. 79, 1982, pp. 279–80.

29 Kerreen M. Reiger, *The Disenchantment of the Home: Modernizing the Australian Family 1880–1940*, Oxford University Press, Melbourne, 1985.

30 Jennifer Crew, 'Women's wages in Britain and Australia during the First World War', *Labour History*, no. 57, 1989, p. 30.

31 M. Keating, 'Australian Work Force and Employment, 1910–11 to 1960–61', *Australian Economic History Review*, vol. VII, no. 2, 1967, pp. 150–71.

32 Sinclair, 'Women and economic change', pp. 288–90.

33 Crew, 'Women's wages', pp. 22–43.

34 Jan Bassett, 'Ready to serve: Australian women in the Great War', *Journal of the Australian War Memorial*, no. 2, 1983, p. 9.

35 Jan Bassett, *Guns and Brooches. Australian Army Nursing from the Boer War to the Gulf War*, Oxford University Press, Melbourne, 1992, pp. 36–9.

36 Quoted ibid., pp. 55–6.

37 ibid. ch. 3.

38 B. Lewis, *Our War: Australia during World War I*, Melbourne University Press, Melbourne, 1980, pp. 33–9 and p. 85, quoted in Evans, 'The Lowest Common Denominator'. Evans draws on the memoirs of Bryan Lewis's account of his Melbourne childhood during the war.

39 See Evans, 'The Lowest Common Denominator' for the tendency to fantasise in representations of war.

40 *Brisbane Courier*, 12 July 1917, quoted in Carmel Shute, 'Heroines and Heroes: Sexual Mythology in Australia, 1914–1918', *Hecate*, vol. 1, no. 1, 1975, p. 8.

41 Quoted ibid. p. 10.

42 W. R. Winspear quoted in Carmel Shute, 'Blood Votes and the "Bestial Boche"': A Case Study in Propaganda', *Hecate*, vol. 2, no. 2, pp. 12–13.

43 ibid. pp. 13–14.

44 Joy Damousi, 'Marching to different drums: Women's mobilisations 1914–1939' in Kay Saunders and Raymond Evans (eds) *Gender Relations in Australia: Domination and Negotiation*, Harcourt Brace Jovanovich, Sydney, 1992, p. 151.

45 Judith Smart, 'Eva Hughes: Militant Conservative' in Marilyn Lake and Farley Kelly (eds) *Double Time: Women in Victoria—150 Years*, Penguin, Ringwood, 1985, pp. 178–88. 1904 also saw the formation of the Women's Auxiliary of the British Empire League in Sydney which played a crucial role in the successful promotion of Empire Day. See French, 'The Ambiguity of Empire Day', p. 64.

46 Quoted in Bassett, 'Ready to serve', p. 11.

47 Scott, *Australia During the War*, ch. XXI.

48 Bassett, 'Ready to serve', pp. 11–12, 15–16.

49 Quoted in Judith Smart, 'The panacea of prohibition: The reaction of the Women's Christian Temperance Union of Victoria to the Great War' in Sabine Willis (ed.) *Women, Faith & Fetes: Essays in the History of Women and the Church in Australia*, Dove Communications, Melbourne, 1977, p. 176. Discussion on the WCTU is taken from Smart, 'The Panacea', pp. 163—92 and Smart, War and the Concept, ch. 5.

50 These included the Victorian Socialist Party (VSP), the Australian Socialist League (ASL), the Socialist Labor Party (SLP). See Joy Damousi, 'Socialist Women and Gendered Space: The Anti-Conscription and Anti-War Campaigns of 1914–18', *Labour History*, no. 60, 1991, pp. 1–15.

51 ibid. p. 5.

52 See Pat Gowland, 'The Women's Peace Army' in Elizabeth Windschuttle (ed.) *Women, Class and History: Feminist Perspectives on Australia 1788–1978*, Fontana/Collins, np, 1980, pp. 216–34; Judith Smart, 'Feminists, labour women and venereal disease in early twentieth-century Melbourne', *Australian Feminist Studies*, vol. 15, 1992, pp. 25–40, and 'The Great War and the "Scarlet Scourge": Debates about Venereal Diseases in Melbourne During World War I', in J. Smart and A. Wood (eds) *An Anzac Muster: War and Society in*

Australia and New Zealand 1914–18 and 1939–45, Monash Publications in History, no. 14, Monash University, Clayton, 1992, pp. 58–85.

53 Judith Smart, 'Feminists, Food and the Fair Price', *Labour History*, no. 50, May 1986, pp. 113–31.

54 Raymond Evans, '"Tempest Tossed": Political Deportations from Australia and the Great War', in R. Daniels & K. Saunders (eds) *Internment and War, International Perspectives*, Allen & Unwin and Australian War Memorial, (forthcoming).

55 Damousi, 'Socialist women', pp. 10–15.

56 Scott, *Australia During the War*; Michael McKernan, *The Australian People and the Great War*, Nelson, Melbourne, 1980; Evans, *Loyalty and Disloyalty*; Gerhard Fischer, *Enemy Aliens: Internment and the Homefront Experience in Australia 1914–1920*, University of Queensland Press, St Lucia, 1989.

57 Evans, 'Tempest Tossed'.

58 Evans, *Loyalty and Disloyalty*, p. 44.

59 Quoted ibid. p. 55.

60 Evans, 'The Lowest Common Denominator'.

61 McKernan, *Australian People*, pp. 158–9.

62 Evans, '"Tempest Tossed"'.

63 McKernan, *Australian People*, pp. 150–1.

64 Fischer, *Enemy Aliens*, pp. 77–8. A further 2300 civilian 'prisoners of war', Germans captured in South-East Asia and the Pacific by the British, were transported to Australia. Discussion on patterns of internment follows Fischer, ch. 5.

65 Personal communication from John McQuilton.

66 Fischer, *Enemy Aliens*, pt 3.

4 The economy at war
Marnie Haig-Muir

Australia went into the First World War as a small, open economy dependent on exports of primary produce and minerals, with a limited manufacturing sector, and an atypically large tertiary (service) sector. Standards of living were amongst the highest in the world, and income distribution amongst the world's most even. The war did not have a dramatic effect on the Australian economy. Even so, by 1919 the strong feelings of isolation and vulnerability engendered by the war had acted as a catalyst for changes which shaped the nature of longer term economic growth.

A number of highly important economic outcomes resulted from the pressures of war on Australia. The most important include the consolidation of Australian ownership and control of key heavy industries in iron and steel and non-ferrous metals; important shifts within manufacturing industry which increased local capability to make replacements for imported products like textiles, and added new products in more technologically sophisticated areas like chemicals and energy; improved financial institutions, regulatory and allocative frameworks;[1] and a growth of centralised political power at the expense of the States. The combination played a significant role in preparing Australia for later moves toward the greater complexity and maturity more characteristic of an advanced economy.

The nature of the Australian economy

The Australian economy in 1914 was quite unlike other early twentieth-century industrialised nations. In many ways it is doubtful whether Australia was, in fact, 'industrialised' at that time. For example, in 1913 exports of manufactures, including processed primary produce, accounted for only 13 per cent of Australian Gross Domestic Product (GDP)[2] compared with 50 per cent or more in other industrialised countries.[3] The nation had then, and still has in the early 1990s, a small, open economy highly vulnerable to international trade fluctuations, shifts in preferences and/or trade policies of the world's major commodity producers and purchasers.

Early twentieth-century Australia had plentiful land, limited domestic savings and capital, and a work force with living standards higher than most other industrial societies. Investment capital, technologically sophisticated manufactures, producer goods, and, intermittently, labour of certain kinds were imported from Britain—at a price. With a population of about 4.5 million in 1911,[4] concentrated mainly in the south-east of the continent, the domestic market was small, fragmented and highly urbanised. Wool, and, to a lesser extent, wheat and minerals, were produced particularly cheaply and efficiently and formed the bulk of Australia's exports.

In that context it is worth noting Avner Offer's recent work reinterpreting the role of primary sector commodities in the First World War.[5] Offer sees primary commodities, that is, food, industrial raw materials and people, as influencing the war's eventual outcome more than technology or industrial capacity. He argues that British prewar trade policy deliberately interlinked the economies of the United Kingdom and the staple-producing empire countries, particularly the Dominions, in such a way that Britain acquired primary produce at prices that allowed significant domestic capital accumulation. That capital was then invested overseas in the Dominions, India, South America and the United States. In return for buying their primary produce, Britain sold textiles and machinery to countries like Australia. Offer believes that those established trading links and naval dominance of world trade routes gave Britain a crucial economic advantage over Germany, which was blockaded during the First World War.

Certain characteristics of the prewar Australian economy are worth stressing because they help to explain what happened during the war, and why some changes were particularly significant to postwar economic growth. Australia's pattern of economic development, for example, has been quite different from that of other modern urban industrial societies. As a recent work put it, the process did 'not pass in linear fashion through a sequence of stages that can neatly be labelled agricultural, industrial and service-sector dominated'.[6]

Between 1901 and 1914, in terms of average annual percentage changes, GDP grew 4 per cent, population 2 per cent, and real GDP per capita at a rate of 2 per cent.[7] Public sector investment and the private housing sector, two traditional sources of Australian economic growth, boomed in the years immediately preceding the war.

Throughout Australia's history after European settlement the tertiary (service) sector has always been atypically large. By 1913/14 a sectoral breakdown of GDP shows the primary sector (farming and mining) accounting for 28.6 per cent, the secondary (manufacturing) sector for 13.4 per cent, and 'other', mostly tertiary/service sector activities, for 58 per cent. The First World War did not produce major changes in the sectoral division of the Australian economy in terms of GDP. In 1919/20 the equivalent figures were 26.5 per cent (primary sector), 13.5 per cent (secondary) and 60 per cent (tertiary/service).[8] Important economic changes did take place, but these were mainly institutional, shifts within sectors, or qualitative rather than quantitative in nature. Many related to aspects of economic life that are difficult, if not impossible, to count because they involve subjective variables like quality of life, or preference for leisure.

The impression of dominance by the primary sector in the Australian economy is widespread, but inaccurate.[9] Australian agriculture, more particularly, pastoralism, was extensive in nature, highly productive and efficient, with an atypically high capital to labour ratio. Although not export-led, the national economy depended on primary sector exports, especially wool and wheat, for foreign exchange needed to service debts incurred by Australian public and private sector borrowers for imports, dividends, and capital formation.[10] For all but about two decades of the nation's history borrowings have underpinned economic growth and development by filling the gap between the cost of imports and the receipts from exports. Any major disruption to financial markets or shipping inevitably had dire consequences.

Manufacturing industry was almost exclusively based in the cities, principally in the capital port cities where it provided substantial employment. Considerable growth and some diversification took place in the quarter-century preceding the war,[11] but in 1914 most factories were still relatively small and inefficient. Most still merely processed primary produce and raw materials in labour-intensive ways requiring little skill or investment in complex and costly techniques or technology.

In 1913/14 manufacturing accounted for about 20 per cent of employment, but only about 13.4 per cent of GDP. [12] Few products had significant value added to them by the manufacturing process. Production was concentrated in areas like textiles and clothing, food and drink, (simple) metal works, woodworking, vehicles (mostly horse-drawn) and fittings, and processing pastoral and agricultural products. Other, more sophisticated goods were imported, mainly from Britain although recent work suggests that Australian firms were increasingly turning to the United States.[13]

Increasing manufacturing activity and continued labour-shedding by rural industries contributed to permanent changes affecting urban growth, employment, and demand for housing and infrastructure. Between 1911 and 1921 the proportion of the work force in pastoralism decreased by 6.4 per cent, whilst agriculture increased by 18.5 per cent, and manufacturing by 36.9 per cent.[14] Over the same period the percentage of population in urban areas rose from 57.83 per cent to 62.33 per cent—an increase the Commonwealth statistician saw as being closely associated with occupational changes.[15] To put the point another way, between 1911/12 and 1913/14, and 1924/25 and 1926/27, male employment in all rural industries increased by only 4 per cent compared with 38 per cent in manufacturing industry. Significantly, most of that increase occurred in protected industries, at a rate roughly proportional to the tariff level.[16]

The tertiary sector covered a wide range of economic activities, again mainly urban-based, and related to services and their provision. Female employment, only a tiny fraction of the whole, was found mainly in tertiary sector activities, heavily clustered in the low status, lowly paid areas of domestic service and commerce, particularly shop and clerical work.[17]

Attention should be drawn to the disproportionately large role traditionally played by the public sector in Australian economic development. Unlike Britain and the United States, Australian governments—colonial, State and Commonwealth—were major economic actors that owned and operated a range of enterprises, particularly transport, communications and public utilities.

The relatively large size of the public sector is important for two reasons. First, because governments, in this case mainly State governments, required large ongoing injections of foreign capital to continue the construction and operation of enterprises under their control.[18] Public works projects were generally large, costly and long-term. In economists' parlance, the investment needed for them was 'lumpy' with a long gestation period which ensured that the States' funding needs continued unabated into the war period. The States' funding priorities set the scene for serious clashes with the Commonwealth over borrowing activities, especially on the London market.[19]

Second, Australian governments were substantial employers, even in peacetime, and thereby integrally involved as interested parties in questions related to wages, conditions and industrial relations. Wartime growth in the armed forces and government defence industries further increased the public sector's employer role as did war-related pension and benefit schemes.

The impact of war

Once war broke out in 1914 most Australian industries responded quickly and to the best of their somewhat limited capabilities. Overall, the economy's capacity to respond was limited by several internal, or endogenous, factors: structural constraints already discussed; the movement of civilian labour into the armed forces; and the diversion of funding to military expenditure. Three external (exogenous) factors also adversely affected the Australian economy. These were a rapid, substantial and sustained decrease in shipping servicing Australian ports for the duration of the war; the consequent massive disruption to trade; and serious problems related to the supply and use of overseas investment capital. The combination seriously impeded production, economic growth and capital formation. The very fabric of economy and society was strained as local industries and infrastructure struggled to meet the increased and diversified wartime demands.

The primary sector

The terms of trade fell steadily from 1913/14 to 1921/22. Trade was vital to Australia's economy with 42 per cent of national product being traded externally in the period from 1911 to 1913.[20] The vast majority of exports, some 95 per cent, were primary products with wool, wheat and minerals accounting for 71 per cent of the total.[21] During the war Australian exporters faced three main problems: shipping space shortages, seriously diminished market opportunities, and payment difficulties. From a late twentieth-century perspective the vital role of shipping in Australia's economy during the First World War is easily underestimated, but at the time most internal and all external trade then depended on sea transport. Therefore the chronic wartime shipping shortages which cut Australian freight capacity by over 50 per cent were little short of disastrous.

In 1916 shipping problems worsened, endangering sales of a record wheat crop. Before special wartime deals were struck with Britain, Australian government advances to growers for grain could not be recouped until after delivery to the purchasers. In response to the shortage of British ships Hughes, then Prime Minister, took action to give Australia some shipping capacity of its own. Overriding British objections, he bought fifteen small tramp steamers in London for about £2 million, the expenditure of which was approved by the Australian Labor Party as an experiment in state socialism. These ships formed the basis of the ill-fated Commonwealth Shipping Line (CSL).[22]

A number of special primary produce marketing initiatives, generally known as the imperial purchase agreements, were directly linked to shipping problems. Under wartime conditions Australian wheat (worth about £9 per ton in 1918) was far less attractive to Britain, the principal buyer, than wheat from closer sources, like Canada, or a more valuable and/or scarcer commodity such as wool (worth about £144 per ton in 1918).

The Australian Government was in a difficult position. Wheat was perishable, and failure to sell what was surplus to domestic requirements on export markets would glut home markets, drive down local prices and deprive Australia of vital foreign exchange. In addition, wheatgrowers, principally smallholders of limited means, would have their incomes slashed, further eroding already depleted domestic purchasing power.

Dry seasonal conditions in 1914/15 postponed the problem, but the record harvest of 1916 brought matters to a head. With sales threatened, Commonwealth and State governments joined forces to control all aspects of wheat marketing and transport. Arrangements varied from State to State, but in general, grain was pooled and sold by a board on behalf of growers to both local parties' mutual advantage. Large quantities of grain sold to Britain in 1916/17 and 1917/18 were paid for but never delivered, having been destroyed in storage by mice, weevils and weather while awaiting the agreed carriage by British ships.

State intervention in wartime primary produce marketing created an unfortunate precedent. Not realising that the success of those State initiatives had depended on special conditions caused by the war, primary producers' expectations of similar schemes in the future were unrealistically optimistic. As wheat prices dropped below production costs during the 1920s and 1930s, the contentious issues of wheat pools and 'orderly marketing' became high political priorities for rural interest groups.

One political consequence was the disruption of the basically dualistic system described in chapter 2 by the postwar emergence of political groups representing a range of rural interests. The nature of those early agrarian interest groups varied greatly from State to State. For example, while its NSW counterpart was relatively conservative, the Victorian Country Party was, in its early years, both radical and politically independent of other existing parties.

Australia was the world's largest producer of wool, an essential raw material that represented one-third of the nation's exports in value terms in 1914. In 1913/14 Germany bought about 25 per cent of the wool sold through Australian brokers; France and Belgium combined took about 40 per cent. Together, the other major purchasers, Britain, the United States and Japan, bought almost all the remainder. When war broke out European orders were cancelled wholesale. An embargo was placed on all exports to the Central Powers; Belgium and parts of France were battle zones. Without major changes only about one-third of Australian wool production was likely to clear the market, at a reasonable price, until the war ended.

What followed is somewhat confusing and not necessary to follow in detail. Initially, doubts about the war's impact halted sales, thus creating cash flow and credit problems for the whole pastoral industry. Serious downward multiplier effects throughout the economy followed as purchasing power contracted.

Wool export policies were made and remade with bewildering frequency in the early part of the war.[23] Change, when it came, was demand-driven as British demand for wool rose sharply. After some negotiation with Australian brokers about inferior quality wool, an agreement was reached which cleared the market of the 1914/15 clip, although over 200 000 bales remained unshipped in June.[24]

By 1916 the British Government was extremely anxious to ensure continuity of supply and to prevent wool reaching enemy hands. A regulatory body with representatives from all parts of the industry was formed in Australia in 1916 to handle wool marketing. In November an agreement was reached with the British Government whereby the wool would be paid for prior to its transportation. This arrangement was exceptionally favourable to Australia given Germany's move to unrestricted submarine warfare in 1917. As in the case of wheat, shipping problems in 1917–18 caused a huge stockpile of wool to remain in Australia until after the war, although in this case all parties profited handsomely.

Wartime marketing arrangements were also made by the Australian Government for exportable surpluses of other primary products like meat, bacon, dairy produce, jam and dried fruit. In each case, the British Government was either the principal or the sole buyer. The details do not matter here since the wool and wheat industries' experiences illustrate the main issues.

Three other observations concerning the primary sector should be made at this juncture. The first concerns productivity. The combination of ongoing structural change, drought and AIF recruiting cut the rural labour force by 27 per cent over the course of the war.[25] An already atypically high capital to labour ratio in the sector rose even higher as labour-saving technology became more common. Ironically, the improved productivity of capital and land which resulted worked against postwar employment opportunities in the primary sector.

Second, as Kosmos Tsokhas pointed out, British policy during the First World War was driven by military considerations while Australian policy tended to be more economic in emphasis. Tsokhas argues that, as the virtual monopoly producer of wool, a vital raw material, Australia held the whip hand in trade negotiations from about 1915 onwards. Referring to the imperial wool purchases, he claims that the British Government 'only considered giving as much as was demanded and bargained for by the Australians'.[26]

Third, through the imperial purchase agreements the Australian Government propped up traditional export industries and in that way actively assisted the retention of prewar economic structures. At the same time, and despite the declining position of the primary sector in Australia's economy,[27] the war continued, even accelerated, prewar trends towards more intensive land use. Tables 4.1, 4.2 and 4.5 all illustrate that point.

Tables 4.1 and 4.2 show the changes in shares and value of exports in the period spanning the war. The relative decline in wool, minerals and gold in favour of wheat/flour, butter, fruit and 'other', that is, manufactured, goods is clear.

Import figures also illustrate the growing importance of local manufacturing to the Australian wartime economy.

Several movements occurred in the direction of Australia's trade, although it is difficult to say precisely what caused them because in many ways the war speeded up and/or reinforced existing trends.

Percentage decreases, of course, do not imply absolute decreases especially since the same period saw the average annual value of

Table 4.1 Diversification of Australian exports (%)

Period	Wheat/flour	Butter	Meat	Fruit	Wool
1881–90	5.3	0.1	1.2	0.2	54.1
1891–1900	2.9	2.4	4.1	0.3	43.5
1901–13	9.7	4.1	5.1	0.5	34.3
1920/1–1928/29	20.5	5.6	4.6	2.2	42.9

Period	Minerals (excl. gold)	Gold	Other
1881–90	9.6	17.6	7.9
1891–1900	9.5	23.6	7.6
1901–13	14.8	20.6	4.8
1920/1–1928/29	6.6	2.2	7.3

Source: E. A. Boehm, *Twentieth Century Economic Development in Australia*, Longman, Melbourne, 1972, p. 68.

Table 4.2   Exports by value (current) £ million

	Wool	Wheat/flour	Butter	Meat
1913	26.3	9.9	3.6	7.7
1919	42.8	17.1	3.2	8.8
	Fruit/veg	Mining (excl. gold)	'Other'	Total all exports
1913	0.5	12.4	3.8	74.6
1919	1.0	9.8	11.2	106.8

Source: W. Vamplew (ed), *Australians: Historical Statistics*, Fairfax, Syme and Weldon, Broadway, Sydney, 1987, pp. 194–5.

Table 4.3   Imports by value (current) £ million

	Machines/ machinery	Motor vehicles	Stones and minerals[1]	All other[2]
1913	4.4	1.5	1.9	17.3
1919	3.6	1.4	0.9	7.8

Notes: 1 includes partly manufactured metals
2 includes some simple manufactures

Source: Vamplew, *Australians*, p. 197.

Table 4.4   Direction of export trade—value (%)

	United Kingdom	Germany	France	Japan	United States
1899–1913	47.2	7.5	8.5	1.1	4.5
1920/21–1928/29	41.3	4.9	10.3	7.2	7.3

Source: Boehm, *Twentieth Century Economic Development*, p. 91.

total home-produced merchandise exports rise from $98 million to $258 million.[28] What should be observed is the general trend away from Britain in favour of France, Japan and the United States. Between 1886 and 1914/15 British imports to Australia rose in value from £20.5 million to £30.8 million. Over the same time Britain's percentage of total imports declined from 89.3 per cent to 69.9 per cent. In other words, while the value of imports from Britain increased 50 per cent, the total value of Australian imports rose 92.3 per cent.[29]

Declining British influence in the Australian economy is evident, even before the war. Several reasons have been suggested. They include aggressive marketing, especially by Germany and the United States; the unwillingness and/or inability of Britain to adapt and compete; and a growing interest in the United States by some Australian firms.

Australia's reduced dependence on Britain needs to be considered within a broader context of change in the postwar international economy. Serious long-term structural problems experienced by British export industries were particularly important. Trading difficulties encountered by the old British staple industries, especially textiles and machinery, in the more competitive postwar international economy created substantial pressure on empire countries to give British products preferential treatment.

Metals

Minerals, particularly iron, base metals (lead, zinc, copper, tin), and gold were all central to the war effort. Heavy industry barely existed in prewar Australia—a situation which altered swiftly as shipping shortages and the switch of British manufacturers from exports to war production together provided natural protection for the 'infant' Australian steel industry. Wartime demand then fuelled an unexpectedly rapid expansion of domestic steel production to replace British imports.

The Broken Hill Proprietary Company Ltd (BHP) was a major beneficiary of increased protectionism. Already in the process of building a relatively small steel plant at Newcastle when war broke out, BHP took full advantage of the opportunities presented by the changed circumstances. With strong government encouragement, output was increased and diversified far beyond prewar plans as production jumped from 47 000 tons in 1913 to 332 000 tons in 1919. There were substantial linkage effects too.[30] From 1915 backward linkages created a domestic iron ore mining industry to supply basic raw material inputs. Forward linkages are apparent into a range of civil and military engineering, metallurgy and metal industries. After the war ended, newly increased tariff barriers protected the high-cost Australian iron and steel industry from international competition.

In the case of base metals, the situation was more complicated. During the late nineteenth century control of Australian smelting industries had passed out of British hands as Germany became technologically dominant throughout the world. By 1914 several large German firms virtually controlled Australia's base metals industries.

A highly complex and fundamental reorganisation of the Australian base metal industry took place in late 1914 and 1915 after Hughes, then federal Attorney-General, legislated to gain permanent control over these vital resources for Anglo-Australian interests.[31]

Intense political pressure was applied to companies with German connections and/or ownership. One result of the manoeuvring that followed was the purchase of a majority interest by the newly formed Broken Hill Associated Smelters (BHAS) in the Port Pirie smelter in 1915.[32] Through the new combine control of lead smelting, technology, sales and marketing passed into Australian hands.

The principal copper producers also combined to form an association which sold all copper surplus to Australian domestic requirements to the British Munitions Department. The reorganisation included acquisition of the previously German-owned Port Kembla refining plant by an Australian combine, and a new manufacturing plant to produce a range of products, many of them crucial to the war effort.

Zinc production was similarly reorganised. With Hughes's help a zinc producers' association was formed in 1916, which established a refinery at Risdon in Tasmania. Again, all output surplus to Australian requirements was contracted to the British Government for the duration of the war and ten years thereafter in an arrangement which, like its wheat and wool counterparts, proved highly profitable for Australian business interests. As a result of the various government-inspired changes local production of refined lead, copper and zinc rose from 96 341 tons to 210 778 tons between 1914 and 1918.[33]

So far as base metal industries are concerned, the most important long-term changes caused by the war were the permanent shift of ownership and control from foreign to Australian companies, and the creation of substantial local ore-processing capacity.

Commonwealth government intervention in the interests of private enterprise and capital was crucial. The main corporate benefactor was the Collins House Group (CHG), a powerful association of companies headed by financiers like W. S. Robinson, W. L. Baillieu and F. C. Howard. In 1914 the CHG already controlled the richest silver-lead-zinc mines at Broken Hill. By assiduously cultivating Hughes, the group had, by 1918, gained the ascendancy over their rivals and gained effective monopoly control of the Australian base metals industry.

Hughes's favourable treatment of corporate interests like BHP and the CHG upset the Labor Party, unions and workers, especially in the context of the highly divisive argument about who had reaped the economic benefits of the war at whose cost. In the period immediately after the First World War, the CHG's monopoly position at Broken Hill, together with stockpiles already paid for under the imperial purchase agreements, put it in a very strong position to resist workers' demands. For nineteen months during 1919/20

Broken Hill mineworkers were locked out, while shareholders' dividends were still paid.

Being both a precious metal and directly related to the nation's currency and money supply, gold was in a category of its own. At the outbreak of war Australia was still one of the world's largest producers. Gold production, worth £8.7 million in 1914, fell to £5 million by 1918 and continued to drop. Why did this happen in an industry that, on the face of it, should have thrived under wartime conditions?

Much of the answer lies in government actions. In July 1915 gold exports were embargoed, except under the most stringent government-controlled conditions. The embargo, the suspension of convertibility, and the abolition of the gold standard throughout the British Empire until 1925, plus large and rapid rises in costs, were the main reasons for the industry's decline. Despite strenuous opposition from miners and bankers, wartime profits from gold exports flowed to the Commonwealth government as a contribution to war costs. Gold retained in Australia also underpinned the security of the note issue, the increase of which is discussed shortly. Faced with escalating costs, the gold industry entered a slump from which it never really recovered.

Manufacturing

Responses to the war varied across the secondary sector. Most Australian manufacturing industries were not well placed to shift into large-scale war production or import-replacement industries needing complex technology and/or techniques. Measured in overall quantitative terms the war apparently made little difference to the secondary sector which still accounted for only 14 or 15 per cent of GDP by the 1920s. In contrast, qualitative changes were significant, especially for longer term growth prospects.

There are two main interpretations of the war's effects on Australian manufacturing. W. A. Sinclair argues:

> the outbreak of the First World War in 1914 came as an
> interruption to the unfolding process of economic development [as
> a result of which] the chain of capital inflow, public construction,
> population increase and housebuilding was reversed at its source
> . . . [T]he renewal of economic expansion in the 1920s was much
> more the resumption of a process interrupted by war than an effect
> of the War itself.[34]

In the only detailed study of Australian manufacturing development during the First World War to date, Colin Forster took a different line. He concluded:

[t]he net result was a change in the pattern of production so that the war can be regarded as a definite transition period, as a step upward, from a simple to a more mature economy . . . it set the stage for the further diversification and general development of secondary industry which took place in the '20s. The war was the priming charge which set off the chain of events which changed Australia into a mature industrial economy.[35]

Despite their differences, both historians agree that the secondary sector altered during the war. Some changes were temporary, their effects vanishing once the war was over, others became permanent. Unlike the Second World War, the war of 1914–18 did not dramatically transform the manufacturing sector. Assessment is difficult because detailed studies are lacking. Nevertheless, the evidence currently to hand suggests that, as Forster argued, the war influenced the pace and nature of development of Australian manufacturing in a fashion that prepared the way for its later development and maturation. Careful qualitative examination shows that war-related changes generated new production patterns which eventually enabled a greater contribution by postwar secondary industry to national economic growth. It is hard to be more exact. The database is neither comprehensive nor reliable, and any figures should be treated with great caution.[36]

Australian manufacturers supplied the AIF's simpler needs which made up three-quarters of the total Australian army expenditure. Most of the remainder came from Britain, thereby increasing Australia's balance of payments deficit. During the war a £6 million deficit in the first half of 1914 rose to £34 million by 1914/15, and to £65 million by the following year. About £20 million of that was, in effect, a transfer of Australia's war finance overseas. Although the situation improved between 1916 and 1918 as imports fell, the deficit remained at about £25 million.[37]

The war's net effect on some industries was extremely beneficial. Local textile industries, isolated from British import competition, diversified product ranges even though plant and machinery shortages limited expansion. Woollen mills, hosiery and knitting factories thrived on lucrative government contracts. Between 1910 and 1919/20 the textile industry showed the largest rate of increase in product (6.6 per cent per annum) of any Australian manufacturing industry.[38] In late 1918 textiles and clothing were poised to retain a significant proportion of the domestic market, given adequate tariff protection.

Factories making small arms, leather goods, chemicals, and simple metal products also gained substantially from war-generated demand and lack of imports. Few, if any of these industries could compete with British imports under normal circumstances. Measured in terms of productivity, the wartime performance of Australian manufacturing industry was poor, as it was throughout the forty-year time span that includes both world wars. During the First World War real product growth came mainly from increased employment levels.[39] Nevertheless, by 1919, local manufactures included four hundred items not made in prewar Australia.[40]

Ship-building and repairing, industries with major linkage effects into metal and engineering industries, boomed between 1917 and 1920. Other industries to benefit included glass, paints, drugs and medicines, scientific, surgical and optical instruments, musical instruments, confectionery, food and drink. Some were boosted by the so-called 'luxury ban' of 1917 which purported to ban imported luxury goods in the interests of the war effort. It was in reality a protectionist device targeting selected local industries, like motor car body building.

The war created natural protective barriers behind which Australian manufacturing sheltered and grew, albeit slowly and unevenly. 'Natural protection' and overseas price rises relative to local prices improved Australian manufacturers' competitiveness by about 50 per cent between 1914 and 1919.[41] That situation was quickly reversed in the 1920s as large wage increases were awarded just as British and American goods re-entered the market at prices well below their local product equivalents.

With few Australian secondary industries competitive in open markets, powerful pressure for postwar tariff protection was exerted on government by manufacturing interests. The Hughes Government responded in 1921 with the highly protectionist Greene tariff, the stated intention of which was to 'protect industries born during the war . . . encourage others that are desirable, and diversify and extend existing ones'.[42] Natural protection was reinforced by 'protection all round' to shelter industries created or stimulated by wartime conditions.

Effective levels of protection given by the Greene tariff are hard to evaluate, but it did allow Australian manufacturing to consolidate wartime gains, retain domestic market share and provide substantial urban employment. Together with the newly established Tariff Board, the Greene tariff marked a highly significant and deliberate move to greater protectionism and regulation in 1921. Unfortunately, the move also helped to perpetuate some of the less desirable features that have tended to characterise Australian manufacturing to the present day.[43]

The war's main effects on secondary industry may be summarised under four headings: the early consolidation of a relatively diverse iron and steel industry; the transfer into Australian

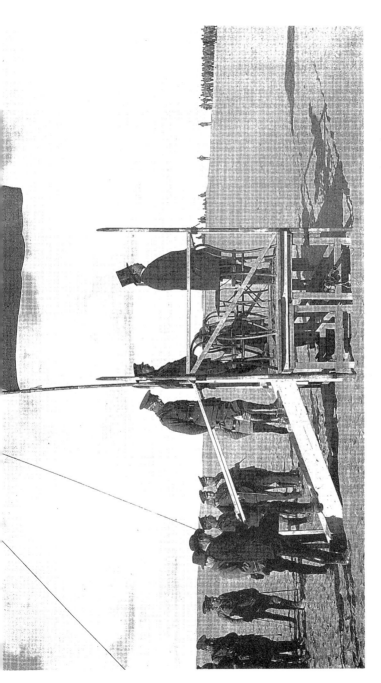

Sir George Reid, Australian High Commissioner in London, addresses a portion of the 1st Australian Division in the Egyptian desert near the Pyramids, 30 December 1914. Behind Reid, with his head bent, is the commander of the AIF, General William Bridges. On the far left is Major Thomas Blamey, who in 1918 became Chief of Staff of the Australian corps under Monash and later, during the Second World War, Australia's most senior military commander. (Australian War Memorial negative no. G1603)

The topography of Anzac. This shows the terrain over which Australian troops fought during the attack of 6 August 1915. (Australian War Memorial negative no. G1810a–b)

Infantrymen and Light Horsemen in the trenches at Gallipoli, May 1915. The Light Horseman smoking in the background and the private in the foreground are father and son. (Australian War Memorial negative no. C667)

Australian troops newly arrived in Flanders from Egypt, 1916. They have just been issued with their steel helmets, a feature of life on the artillery-dominated Western front. (Australian War Memorial negative no. EZ3)

Apprehension has replaced hearty cheerfulness, as the 53rd Battalion waits in the trenches at Fromelles, a few minutes before going 'over the top' on 19 July 1916. (Australian War Memorial negative no. H16396)

Above The aftermath of bombardment, Pozières. This is what remained of the village some months after the battle — a classic illustration of the pulverising destruction inflicted by artillery on the Western front. (Australian War Memorial negative no. E532)

Below Derelict tanks, third battle of Ypres. Although tanks were eventually to revolutionise warfare, they were easily disabled in the conditions on the Western front in 1917. (Australian War Memorial negative no. E1409)

Right Winter on the Somme.
This photograph shows the
reserve line in November 1916
with infantry of the 1st
Australian Division in 'rest'.
Troops were withdrawn to this
reserve line for a few days
before a second term of duty in
the frontline, where conditions
were almost intolerable.
(Australian War Memorial
negative no. E575)

Below Australians in a dugout at
Ypres. This photograph conveys
a strong sense of the mateship
that the sharing of the hardships
of the Western front generated
among troops. (Australian War
Memorial negative no. E1223)

On the Western front artillery was the pre-eminent weapon of terror and destruction. The British poet, Wilfred Owen, wrote of the:

'Great gun towering t'ward Heaven, about to curse . . .
But when thy spell be cast complete and whole,
May God curse thee, and cut thee from our soul!'

(Australian War Memorial negative no. E691)

Barbed wire on the Hindenburg line. Another great enemy of the infantryman was barbed wire, which artillery bombardment often failed to destroy. (Australian War Memorial negative no. E3583)

Troops advancing in the battle of Proyart, 23 August 1918. This
photography, which is reminiscent of popular images of the Second World
War, illustrates how, in 1918, the war in France became open warfare.
(Australian War Memorial negative no. E3051)

The Light Horse taking part in a successful raid on a Turkish party
developing new water bores at Jifjafa in the central Sinai, April 1916. The
war in the Middle East was, in contrast to the Western front in France, a
war of movement in which the Light Horse could play a role much more
in tune with traditional notions of the Australian bushman. (Australian War
Memorial negative no. A221)

THE FOOD BRIGANDS.

SHADE OF NED KELLY—" Well, Well! I never got as low as that, and they
hung me."   *(Queensland " Worker,")*

In this cartoon the enemies of Australian society are depicted as the war
profiteers and and price fixers. (Reproduced in *Labor Call*,
16 September 1915)

Published in *Labor Call* on 23 September 1915, this image illustrates how conscription had become, even at this early stage of the war, a symbol of much wider class confrontation. The figure in court dress, representing the established classes, confronts not only the angry worker but also the devilish genie of industrialisation which has been let out of the bottle.

The Crisis.

Three Cheers for the Basket.

GRANNY: "Now, William, the way to go 'straight' is to break faith with the people who elected you. Drop 'em here, and you may kiss yer proud old Granny!"

Published by the *Australian Worker* on the day the government announced the abandonment of the prices referendum, this cartoon shows Hughes being enticed into betraying the electors by 'Granny', the *Sydney Morning Herald*. (*Labor Call*, 18 November 1915)

A recruiting march in progress through NSW. One method of encouraging recruitment in Australia was for a small group of volunteers to start marching from a country town to a capital city, attracting other recruits on its way like a snowball. (*Sydney Mail*)

A wounded soldier farewells new recruits. This photograph, published in the *Sydney Mail*, reveals the way in which wounded returned servicemen were used in efforts to stimulate recruiting. There is a clear sense of the wounded man handing on the baton of service to the new contingent of volunteers.

One of the arguments evoked by those dedicated to maximising the war effort was the vulnerability of Australia to German domination in the event of Britain losing the war. The caption for this cartoon read:

"'The only way the war can be stopped is to refuse to fight or to make things for the war'—*Wisdom from a Melbourne Socialist meeting.*

THE SOCIALIST UNDER THE LEFT BOOT: 'There you are! We refused to fight, and refused to make things for the war, and it's stopped all right'." (*Bulletin,* 18 November 1915)

FINIS.

A LESSON IN GENDERS.
THE SMALL BOY: *"Masculine, feminine—an' I forget the other, Miss!"*
THE AUSTRALIAN GIRL: *"Shirker!"*

A lesson in gender. The propaganda against the 'shirker' made a direct correlation between willingness to volunteer and masculinity. As this cartoon shows, a 'shirker' was denied his claim to being masculine and was equated with neuter. The fact that it was an 'Australian girl' depicted as denouncing the 'shirker' reflects the role many women played in hounding men to volunteer. (*Bulletin,* 3 February 1916)

SHAMELESS.

'Shameless.' The campaign denouncing the shirker however, at times became confused in its message about masculinity. In this classic Norman Lindsay cartoon, 'Shameless', who has stayed at home, has retained his healthy body and the attention of at least one girl on the beach, while the returned soldiers are emasculated by their wounds and reduced to dependency on women. (*Bulletin*, 21 March 1918)

THEIR TROUBLES—TO-DAY!

This cartoon, from the *Bulletin* of 2 May 1918, reveals many elements of war-time propaganda. The Germans are depicted as animalistic pillagers and rapists, violators of women and defilers of Christian values. The 'shirker' is a lay-about spiv, indifferent to the war, frequenting sporting venues, playing two-up, yet— paradoxically—still getting the girl.

Soldiers voting on the second conscription referendum. Hughes attached great political significance to securing a 'Yes' vote from the AIF. (Australian War Memorial negative no. E1440)

Voluntary aid detachments marching through Melbourne, 24 May 1918. Working in conjunction with the Red Cross, the VADs consisted of men and women who helped in arranging for the comfort of sick and wounded soldiers. More than 10 000 women volunteered for this service. (Australian War Memorial negative no. H2000)

Raising money for the 'War Chest'. This scene of a very crowded Martin Place, Sydney, shows the prodigious efforts that went into raising money for the provision of comforts for soldiers. (*Sydney Mail*)

"ARREST THAT SCOUNDREL."

A reflection on Hughes' authoritarianism and his propensity to see the whole of Australia as insubordinate. (*Bulletin*, 3 January 1918)

A wounded soldier comes home. (*Sydney Mail*)

BILLIWOG

LONDON'S LATEST CRAZE

ALMOST HUMAN

BABIES CRY FOR IT

DIRECTIONS FOR USE

Blow up with wind until head expands, then release hole in face, whereupon Billy will emit loud noises until he goes flat...........

NO WAR IS COMPLETE WITHOUT ONE

'The Billywog'. In this classic David Low cartoon, Hughes is depicted as a puppet-like toy. The directions for use: 'Blow up with wind until head expands, then release hole in face, whereupon Billy will emit loud noises until he goes flat . . .' (*The Billy Book*, National Library of Australia)

Hughes comes home, 1919. Profoundly divisive though he was on the domestic political scene, Hughes retained and reciprocated the affection of many in the AIF, to whom he was known as 'The Little Digger'. (Hughes Collection, National Library of Australia)

hands of base metals industries, and the creation of local processing capacity; consolidation, diversification, and some economies of scale in 'old' industries like metal processing, textiles, clothing and footwear; and accelerated development in some 'new' industries like engineering, chemicals and energy.

The combined effects were extremely influential in shaping the pattern of economic growth in the 1920s and 1930s. Of particular note was a general movement from the capital-intensive primary sector to the labour-intensive secondary sector that slowed the rate of economic growth. Table 4.5 shows the shifts in major areas of production between 1911/13 and between 1921/22–1923/24. Developments in agriculture and mining may be viewed as continuations of prewar trends, accelerated by the war. In contrast, it is arguable that manufacturing growth was directly attributable to the war.

Table 4.5   Production changes 1911–13 to 1921/2–1923/4

	(Averages in £ million)	
	1911–13	1921–2 to 1923–4
Agriculture	46	59
Pastoral	51	43
Dairying	19	24
Forestry	6	6
Mining	23	14
Manufactures	50	66
Total Production	195	212

Source: D.B. Copland, 'Australia in the World War: Economic Apects', J. Holland Rose et al. (eds) The Cambridge History of the British Empire, vol. 7, pt. 1, Cambridge University Press, 1933, p. 601.

Finance

Three main problems confronted the Commonwealth government during the war: how to pay for it, how to balance civilian and military demands on the economy, and how to maintain and fund external trade. Improved finance, more specifically revenue, was the key, but it required institutional change. At the turn of the century, and for some years thereafter, Australia's money supply was issued by the trading banks, the Queensland Treasury and the State mints. As a consequence the fledgling Commonwealth government gained no financial benefit from the process of creating, sustaining and managing the nation's money supply. Change was slow, but in 1910 the Commonwealth took control of the note issue with, by 1911, a proviso that the treasury must keep gold reserves equal to 25 per cent of the notes issued. Even so, monopoly of the money supply required the elimination of private holdings of gold and sterling.

The immense difficulties connected with funding the war drew two main responses from the Commonwealth government. The first involved its concentration of certain powers, and although the Constitution allowed it wide taxation and borrowing powers, these remained dormant until the war provided justification to activate them. As per annum defence spending increased twelvefold, financial problems became acute. Using special wartime legislation, the Commonwealth then moved decisively to transfer some key economic powers away from the States. Banks' gold holdings were requisitioned, and notes replaced gold in interbank settlements. Other measures which impacted more directly on the banking public included abolishing the gold standard, prohibiting gold exports, and effectively suspending the convertibility of notes into gold.

At that time Australia had no central bank, but the enhanced role and greater responsibilities of the Commonwealth government required new forms of organisation and institutions to implement new measures. As a result the Commonwealth Bank, originally conceived as merely another savings and trading bank, became increasingly important. From its inception in 1912, the bank had transacted the Commonwealth's financial business but had had no other special function until the war forced major changes to the note issue and government loan procedures. Both areas were crucial elements of the bank's later assumption of a central banking role, the need for which had been emphasised by new developments connected with improved money markets. The most important new functions of the bank included distributing the expanded note issue, taking responsibility for large borrowing programs, financing Australian international trade, and organising the ten domestic war loans campaigns.[44]

Centralising the money supply substantially increased revenue[45] by shifting the balance of power in favour of the Commonwealth. The note issue was increased sixfold from £9.5 million (with a gold reserve of £4.1 million or 43 per cent) in 1914 to £60 million (with a gold reserve of £23.6 million or 41.5 per cent) in 1920.[46] Over the same period bank credit grew by about 70 per cent. Such rapid expansion of the money supply was inevitably linked to severe inflationary pressures and thus to wage and price issues.

Inflation

Like Britain and the United States, Australia suffered from inflation during and immediately after the First World War. By today's standards it was not particularly bad, and reached double digits only in 1915, but the severity as judged by contemporary standards had major financial and political implications.

Money wages grew irregularly during the First World War, but because of the rapid inflation, lagged well behind price rises. In Melbourne between mid-1914 and mid-1915 meat doubled in price, bread prices went up 50 per cent, flour 87 per cent and butter 63 per cent. These jumps in staple food prices affected most adversely the working classes whose wages left little leeway for increased spending, even on necessities. Social discontent grew and along with it pressure for higher wages and price controls.[47] Drought, trade disruptions, and large-scale transfer of resources to the war effort added to the problem. Figure 4.1 shows how prices and wages diverged, and why price control became such a hot issue.

With the States reluctant to surrender their powers the Commonwealth could do little to remedy the situation. Even the 1914 Royal Commission of enquiry into prices of foodstuffs and other necessities had no price-fixing powers. In the wages area union pressure for new arbitration procedures eventually forced changes. The new centralised and comprehensive allocative and regulatory framework included extension of the basic wage concept to most workers by 1918, introduction of quarterly cost of living adjustments (wage indexation) from 1922 onwards, and a complex system of margins for skilled workers. Enhanced powers for the Commonwealth Court (at the expense of State bodies) were also directly linked to widespread wartime discontent with the existing arbitration system.

The disproportionately heavy impact of inflation on the working classes fuelled labour's already deep sense of being exploited for the benefit of other better off and/or more powerful interests. Wage-earners, their families, pensioners and others on fixed incomes bore a large share of the real costs of the inflationary bout while other groups were less affected. Table 4.6 demonstrates the effects of the inflation on prices, while Figure 4.1 shows how wages and prices moved relative to one another. Nominal, or money, wages represent the actual amount of money received by workers as wages,

Table 4.6 Price increases in Australia (%)

	Wholesale prices	Retail prices	Cost of living
Percentage increase in:			
(a) last prewar decade	11.8	10.5	23.2
(b) five years of war	68.0	47.5	30.1
(c) from July 1914 to June 1920	166.0	87.1	53.0

Source: D.B. Copland, 'Currency and Prices in Australia', Joseph Fisher Lecture in Commerce no. 9, Adelaide University, 15 June, 1921, G. Hassel and Son, Adelaide, 1921, p. 7.

Figure 4.1   Wages and prices 1913–1920

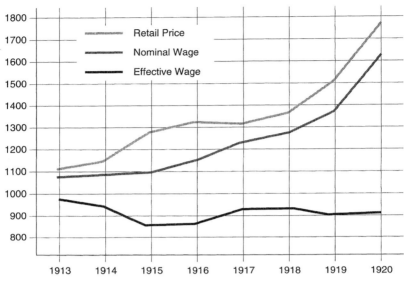

Note: 1911 = 1000

Source: C. Forster, 'Economy, wages and the Establishment of Arbitration', in Stuart Macintyre
and Richard Mitchell (eds) *Foundations of Arbitration: Origins and Effects of State
Compulsory Arbitration, 1890–1914*, Oxford University Press, Melbourne, 1989, p. 203.

whereas the effective, or real, wage is the nominal/money wage
adjusted for changes in the cost of living.[48]

Because this chapter focuses on the war's effects on Australian
economy and society, the precise nature of the causal links between
the money supply and inflation are of little concern. What is relevant
is how the inflationary bout affected wartime production, industrial
relations and the work force, and how they, in turn, influenced the
level and nature of government regulation in the economy.

After the war ended policies were developed to support manufacturing industry, continue long-term population objectives, and
maintain traditionally high living standards by means of a broad
range of regulatory devices and institutions related to tariffs, wage
regulation and industrial relations.[49] The war quite clearly marked
the beginning of a new and different phase of policy-making
directed at questions of distribution rather than efficiency. The shift
depended on the newly acquired powers of the Commonwealth
government vis-a-vis State governments, the accretion of which was
itself a by-product of the need to centralise and extend control over
trade, borrowing, taxation and monetary policy.

War and postwar developments related to wages, prices, living standards, immigration and settlement programs imparted a special and ongoing urgency to issues of social cohesion that surfaced during the war. In one sense Australian prewar public policies had 'constituted a strategy to accommodate the country's economic and social institutions to the expressed needs of the working-class majority'.[50] The postwar policy shifts mentioned above were super-imposed on traditional public policies aimed at the rapid expansion of a (white) Australian population, the protection of living standards and the minimising of social conflict. Another major thrust of public policy continued to emphasise the primary sector as the 'engine' of economic growth.

Industrial relations

As we saw in chapter 2, industrial unrest flared during the war. The reasons for this were complex. They included labour market disruptions caused by recruiting, the apparent loss of control of industrial issues by union leaders, internal divisions within the union movement, conscription, rapidly rising living costs, a general atmosphere of suspicion, and the influence of the IWW.[51] Not all unrest was due to purely economic reasons. The 'alien workers' issue, for instance, which concerned workers who were, or were suspected to be of German or Austro-Hungarian birth, poisoned labour relations in a number of places.

New South Wales accounted for 70 per cent of the total Australian working days lost by strike action in 1914, 76 per cent in 1915, 66 per cent in 1916, 67 per cent in 1917, and 46 per cent in 1918. Across Australia 4 599 658 working days were lost in 1917 along with approximately £2 594 808 in wages. Nationwide, an estimated total of 1945 disputes took place between 1914 and 1918 involving 553 433 workers, 8 533 061 working days, and £4 785 607 in wages.[52] The accompanying loss of production and purchasing power is obvious. The social effects were less obvious, but no less real.

Many of the strikes centred on the NSW coal industry where working conditions and industrial relations were both poor. With coal essential to the war effort, miners' strikes inevitably attracted rapid and decisive government action which further soured industrial relations. The situation deteriorated with reduced shipping, restricted export sales, higher coal prices and a gradual shift to oil fuel all contributing to declining fortunes and endemic unemployment in the industry. Between 1914 and 1918 NSW coal exports dropped from 1 997 565 tons (at 7s8d per ton) to 397 536 tons (at 11s8d per ton).[53] Trade picked up again briefly after the war, but secular (long-term) decline set in in 1920.

The war's worst strike began amongst NSW railway workers in August 1917 over the introduction of timecards. It spread quickly until about 14 per cent of the State's work force were involved. Ports, trade and shipping were paralysed for several weeks with food, fuel and transport the worst affected. As industrial turmoil spread, violence broke out in cities already deeply divided by the conscription debate. With the war effort crippled, the Commonwealth invoked the War Precautions Act, thus taking matters out of the hands of the Arbitration Court. Direct intervention was subsequently used to break the strike by appealing to 'loyalists', often schoolboys or country men, to perform strikers' jobs.[54] Despite violent protests the strike collapsed after six weeks, but there were further implications. 'Not all strikers got their jobs back, and those who did were re-employed on humiliating terms . . . [For those reasons, and] to prevent repetition of such a disaster, the Labor Council determined on the creation of One Big Union.'[55]

During 1917, in the context of government anti-strike actions, the consequent loss of face by union officials, and 'millenarian expectations released by the Russian Revolution'[56] support grew amongst workers for the One Big Union (OBU) concept. Militant OBU supporters aimed at replacing the labour movement's base of craft unions with class-based industrial unionism.[57] In the end opposition from the powerful Australian Workers' Union, craft unions and parliamentarians held the line, and the OBU movement faded into insignificance in the 1920s.

Several changes within the union movement between 1914 and 1918 may be linked either to the war itself, or, less directly, to new arbitration procedures and the enhanced Commonwealth role in industrial relations arising from the war. Between 1914 and 1918 trade union membership rose from 523 271 to 581 755, a remarkable gain given the heavy recruitment of working-class men into the AIF. More careful examination, however, reveals that those figures included a rise in female union membership from 22 600 in 1914 to 50 700 in 1918, which accounted for over half the total increase.[58] The war also speeded up concentration of union membership, a trend that continued after 1918. Between 1911 and 1921 the percentage of union members as a proportion of all employees grew from 27.9 per cent to 51.6 per cent,[59] while the number of unions Australia-wide dropped from 430 to 394 during the war years, that is, there were fewer, but larger, unions.

Commonwealth–State financial relationships

As the war increased the relative size of Commonwealth budgets compared to those of the States, Commonwealth taxation on land, income, entertainment and wartime profits was introduced. Most significant for the long term was the introduction of Commonwealth income tax in 1915. Between 1910 and 1919 State and Commonwealth government receipts from income tax (expressed as equivalent to a proportion of GDP) rose from 0.4 per cent to 3.2 per cent[60] while total tax figures for the same years rose only from 6.08 per cent in 1910 to 7.98 per cent in 1919.[61] Figure 4.2 shows the strong connection between the rapid increases in income tax and the two world wars. Governments justified their actions because, as Holman, the NSW Labor Premier, said, 'to pay for war expenditure

Figure 4.2   Tax collections: income and indirect

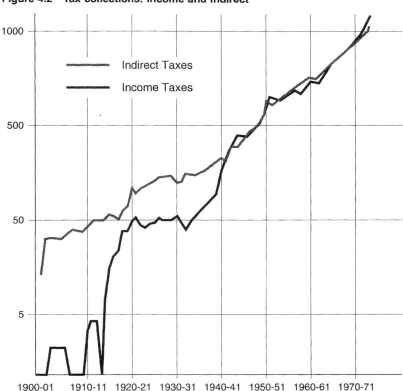

Source: M.W. Butlin, *A Preliminary Annual Database 1900/01 to 1973/74*, Reserve Bank Research Discussion Paper 7701, 1977, facing p. 8.

out of loan money was to eat up the capital of the community. To pay it out of taxation was, as far as possible, to spend only the income of the community.'[62]

Despite Prime Minister Fisher's avowed intention for the war to be funded from domestic sources, the task proved extremely difficult. To 1920 the war cost £374 million (growing to £831 million by 1934) while total government expenditure on the war (1914–18) was £311 million. Some £46 million of that was met from revenue, leaving a deficit of £265 million,[63] of which £194 million was funded domestically, including (a further) £46 million from the increased note issue discussed above. War loans contributed a further £250 million. The remainder had to be borrowed from overseas, but so too did most of the money needed for the States' capital works programs. Therein lay the crux of the disputes between the State and the Commonwealth governments.

Financial problems, especially those affecting States' public works and borrowing programs, have been paid scant attention in discussions about the economic history of Australia during the First World War.[64] Over 70 per cent of Australia's public debt in 1914 was financed in London. Once war broke out, London markets were prepared to finance war obligations, the Commonwealth's highest priority, but not the capital works projects which were the States' principal concern.

Fisher opposed independent action on overseas money markets by State governments on the grounds that competitive borrowing would damage Australia's credit. He proposed instead to raise a common loan in London to fund both the Commonwealth's war needs and the States' public works programs. Important questions of States' rights were at stake, but they eventually conceded in a grudging fashion. Then confronted with the Imperial Government's obdurate response that loans for purposes other than war expenditure would not be condoned, Fisher urgently sought ways to ensure State governments' funding.

Details of Australian–British and Commonwealth–States financial relations during the war are complex. Only three aspects of it are especially relevant here. First, the war increased State governments' financial dependence on the Commonwealth, a move which mirrored similar moves in other spheres of Australian social and economic life. Second, the 1915 agreement between the Commonwealth and five of the State governments 'anticipated, first the voluntary Loan Council of 1924, then the statutory Loan Council, which began to function in 1928 as part of the general settlement of Commonwealth–State finance that has been described as "the greatest constitutional change in the history of the Commonwealth" '.[65]

The third point relates to British treasury antagonism towards 'profligate' Australian interwar borrowing programs. Official attitudes that were to cost the Australian economy and society so dearly a decade or so later stemmed, in part at least, from exasperation with 'importunate Australian appeals for [wartime] assistance under threat of dire consequences . . . and a [consequent] hardening of official attitudes to Australia's "internal extravagance" '.[66] Otto Niemeyer, later to lead the Bank of England economic mission to Australia during the Depression, was then a treasury official.[67]

As we have seen, Australian financial, regulatory and allocative spheres altered as a result of the First World War. Significantly enlarged Federal government powers in the fiscal, monetary and administrative areas at the expense of the States, and the beginnings of the first coherent national institutional framework are some of the more important outcomes. In that way the First World War encouraged the emergence of the kind of institutional frameworks needed to manage the processes of growth and change in twentieth-century Australia.

Overview

This chapter takes a necessarily brief look at movements in the major economic indicators and examines their implications for Australia's economy during and after the war. For the purposes of this particular exercise the most relevant indicators are those measuring national production, income, expenditure, consumption, investment and capital formation. While detailed figures for these indicators are available,[68] a graphic presentation has been preferred here for two reasons. First, graphs make the points in a visual fashion that is relatively clear. Second, the data problems already mentioned also indicate the necessarily general nature of any conclusions at this stage of our knowledge.

Figure 4.3 shows the movements in GDP and GNE (expressed in constant prices). After recovering from the effects of 1914's drought both indicators decline over the war years as economic activity, at best, held steady. When the trend line for GNE less Defence Spending is compared with GNE the vertical gap between the two represents the (substantial) amount of national expenditure devoted to defence purposes. That money was available for neither capital formation nor for (civilian) consumption.

Consumption, investment and capital formation all need to be split into two components, public and private. Figure 4.4 shows the sharp drop in real private consumption as a proportion of GDP during the First World War. The fall resulted from the redistribution

Figure 4.3   GDP and GNE, 1901–1939

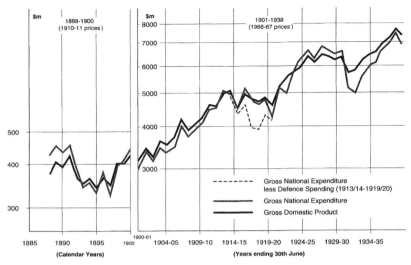

Note: constant 1966/67 prices.

Source: Forster, 'Economy, wages' p. 224, drawing on Butlin, *Preliminary Annual Database*;
N.G. Butlin, 'Australian National Accounts 1788–1983', Source Paper no. 6, 1985, and
data supplied by the Economic History Department, RSSS, ANU.

of resources away from the private sector to the public sector, and
the consequently diminished (private) purchasing power. Increased
real public consumption reflects the other side of that shift of
resources into defence-related activities. Some defence-related consumption may be directly linked to large-scale postwar government
debts incurred for soldier settlement and other repatriation expenses,
and thereby to the increased public sector share of Australian debt
between the wars.

Figure 4.5 which illustrates the war's effect on the rate of growth
of capital formation confirms that resources diverted from real private
consumption were not used for capital formation. The main effects
of delayed capital formation were to put great pressure on both
private and public sectors in the postwar years to 'catch up' with
postponed business, industrial and residential investment (private),
and railways, roads, bridges, water, sewerage and other infrastructure
projects (public). Not until 1923 in the case of private capital
formation, 1924 in the case of public capital formation, were the
respective 1914 figures (in constant prices) exceeded. The magnitude
of that pent-up demand, coupled with public expectations, was central
to the much-maligned 1920s public borrowing programs. Demands

Figure 4.4   Real public and private consumption (as % of GDP)

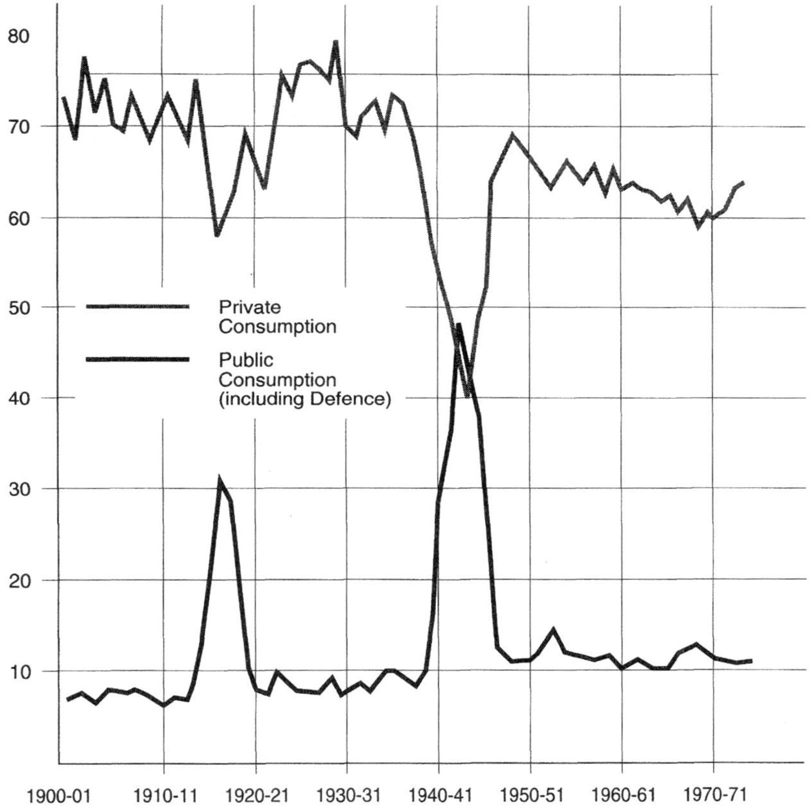

Note: constant 1966/67 prices.

Source: M.W. Butlin, *Preliminary Annual Database*, facing p. 7.

generated by postwar public policies of soldier settlement, war housing and immigration added further to borrowing pressures.

There was little provision for the depreciation of public or private sector assets during the war and not much investment in new capacity. Once hostilities ceased, pent-up demand for urban infrastructure, industrial development, housing and services fuelled a competitive borrowing spree by the States between 1919 and 1927. Public sector debt levels rose rapidly as a result. Table 4.7 shows the magnitude of the capital inflows in terms of investment expenditure on fixed capital.

The retarding effects of the war on investment, one of the principal reasons for decreased capital formation, are shown in

Figure 4.5   Capital stock: public and private by type of asset

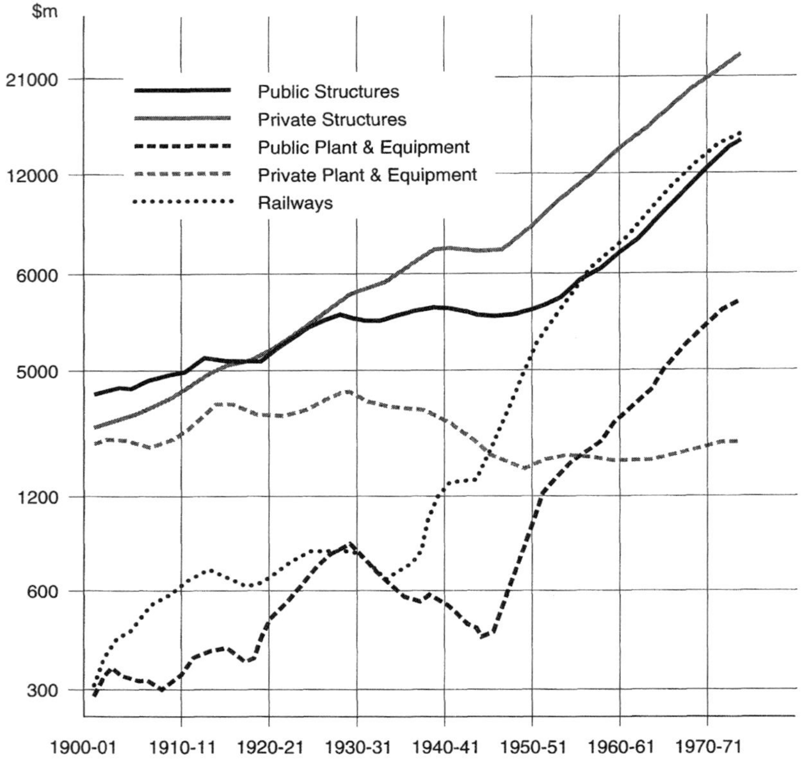

$m

21000

12000

6000

5000

1200

600

300

—————— Public Structures
—————— Private Structures
– – – – – – Public Plant & Equipment
– – – – – – Private Plant & Equipment
············· Railways

1900-01   1910-11   1920-21   1930-31   1940-41   1950-51   1960-61   1970-71

Note: constant 1966/67 prices $m.

Source: M. W. Butlin, Preliminary Annual Database, facing p. 11.

Table 4.7   Foreign investment (net apparent capital inflow as a percentage of total gross fixed capital expenditure)

Period	Capital inflow
1901–14	1.8
1920–30	19.6
1931–39	7.7

Source: Maddock and McLean (eds), Australian Economy, p. 25.

Figure 4.6   Real public and private fixed investment as a proportion of real GDP

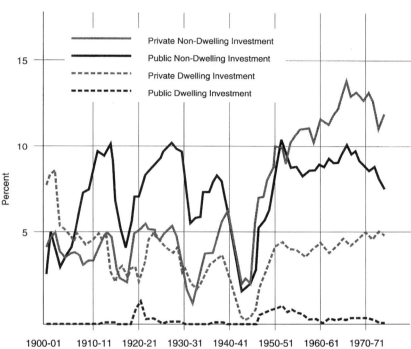

Note: constant 1966/67 prices, %.

Source: M. W. Butlin, *Preliminary Annual Database*, facing p. 9.

Figure 4.6. In view of the high level of postwar demand for infrastructure, and its impact on foreign borrowing, the slow rate of wartime growth in public non-dwelling investment should be noted.

Conclusion

As the preceding discussion has shown, the First World War did not dramatically transform the Australian economy. While forces directly or indirectly attributable to the war reshaped the postwar economy in a number of ways, the situation is not clear-cut. As Colin White has said, 'the war, although in many ways a turning point, reinforced past attitudes, institutions, and even policies'.[69]

Despite the severity of the shock it imparted to the Australian economy, when it is measured in terms of GDP per capita, the war had less impact than the 1890s or interwar depressions. However, it accelerated certain aspects of change relevant to long-term economic growth. In particular, the combined effects of the war on policy making, on aspects of industry, trade, employment, banking and finance, on public and private sector and Commonwealth and State government relations, and on regulatory and allocative frameworks influenced the patterns and processes of growth during the interwar years. In that way the First World War may be seen as helping to create the conditions needed for the development of a recognisably modern industrial economy in Australia during and after the Second World War.

Notes

1 Including tariffs, wages, industrial relations, taxation and/or other government actions which affect resource allocation within and between groups in society.

2 Gross Domestic Product (GDP), at market prices, is a measure of the total flow of goods and services produced by the economy over a specified time period, normally a year, or a quarter. G. Bannock, R. E. Baxter and E. Davis, *The Penguin Dictionary of Economics*, 4th ed., Penguin, Ringwood, 1987, p. 181.

3 K. Anderson, 'Tariffs and the Manufacturing Sector' in R. Maddock and I. McLean (eds), *The Australian Economy in the Long Run*, Cambridge University Press, Melbourne, 1987, p. 168.

4 About 5.4 million by 1921.

5 Avner Offer, *The First World War: An Agrarian Interpretation*, Clarendon Press, Oxford, 1989.

6 Maddock and McLean, *Australian Economy*, p. 19.

7 ibid. p. 35, citing several other sources.

8 ibid. p. 35.

9 N.G. Butlin, 'Bicentennial Perspective of Australian Economic Growth', *Working Papers in Economic History*, no. 72, ANU, Canberra, August 1986.

10 Capital is the stock of goods which are used in production and which have themselves been produced. It includes the real physical elements in all investment contexts. Money should be viewed as a means of expressing a claim. Fixed capital consists of durable goods such as infrastructure, buildings, plant and machinery. Capital formation is net investment in fixed assets: that is, additions to the stock of real capital, in this case of a nation (Bannock, Baxter and Rees, *Penguin Dictionary*, p. 61). Gross domestic capital formation (GDCF), is commonly used to measure one important aspect of national economic growth and development.

11 Manufacturing's share of gross domestic capital formation grew from 8.6 per cent in 1891–1900 to 13.6 per cent in 1901–10. During the same time investment in secondary enterprises more than doubled in

value. P. Cochrane, *Industrialization and Dependence*, University of Queensland Press, St Lucia, 1980, p. 2.

12 M. Keating, 'Australian Work Force and Employment, 1910–11 to 1960–61', *Australian Economic History Review*, vol. 7, no. 2, 1967, p. 162.

13 I am indebted to Dr Diane Hutchinson for this point.

14 *Census Bulletin* no. 18, 1921, p. 12.

15 C. H. Wickens, Commonwealth of Australia, *Census of 1921*, vol. 2, Statistician's Report, Government Printer, Melbourne, n.d., p. 40.

16 D. B. Copland, *Australia in the World Crisis 1929–1933*, Cambridge University Press, London, 1934, p. 16.

17 In 1914/15 70 per cent of female employees worked in tertiary sector jobs, compared with 27.7 per cent in the secondary sector (Keating, 'Australian Work Force', p. 160). These figures, of course, refer only to the paid work force, the consequent distortions and implications of which are analysed in M. Waring, *Counting for Nothing*, Allen and Unwin/Port Nicholas Press, Wellington, 1989. Questions of gender inequality in the work force and pay levels are discussed in more detail in G. Patmore, *Australian Labour History*, Longman Cheshire, Melbourne, 1991, pp. 169–72.

18 As at 30 June 1914, Commonwealth debts totalled £19.2 million compared with States' debts totalling £317.6 million over two-thirds of which had been raised on the London market. C. White, *Mastering Risk*, Oxford University Press, Melbourne, 1992, p. 205.

19 See, for instance, B. Attard, 'Politics, Finance and Anglo-Australian Relations: Australian Borrowing in London, 1914–1920', *Australian Journal of Politics and History*, vol. 35, no. 2, 1989, pp. 142–57.

20 Anderson, 'Tariffs', p. 180.

21 B. Dyster and D. Meredith, *Australia in the International Economy*, Cambridge University Press, Melbourne, 1990, p. 52.

22 Like several other wartime policy initiatives, this foray into 'state socialism' did not survive long. By 1922 the special conditions created by the war had disappeared and the Commonwealth Shipping Line registered the first of a series of losses resulting in the forced sale of its ships in 1928. Nevertheless, the CSL had served Australia well during the war. Despite their relatively small capacity the ships had provided a means by which the virtual monopoly of British shipping in the Australian market could be broken. In that way wartime freight rates were kept down and services improved in a way which would not have occurred without the competition provided by the CSL.

23 For details see A. Barnard, 'Wool Brokers and the Marketing Pattern 1914–20', *Australian Economic History Review*, vol. 11, no. 1, March 1971.

24 K. Tsokhas, *Money, Markets and Empire*, Melbourne University Press, Melbourne, 1990, p. 28.

25 *The Official Yearbook of New South Wales 1928/1929*, Sydney, 1930, p. 565.

26 Tsokhas, *Money*, p. 33.

27 Between the 1911 and the 1921 censuses the 'Industrial Class . . .

displaced the Primary Producing Class for the premier position as
indicated by the number of persons employed . . . [to the extent of]
. . . 124922 or nearly 21%'. C.H. Wickens (Govt Statistician), *Census
Bulletin* no. 18, 1921, p. 12.

28 E. A. Boehm, *Twentieth Century Economic Development in Australia*,
Longman Cheshire, Melbourne, 1979, p. 91. The figures are A$,
expressed in current terms, i.e. not corrected for inflation over time.

29 C. Grimshaw, 'Australian Nationalism and the Imperial Connection
1900–1914', *Australian Journal of Politics and History*, vol. 3, no. 1,
1957, pp. 172–3.

30 Linkage effects refers to the effects of the particular industry under
consideration on other industries which either contribute inputs to it
(backward linkages) or use its outputs as inputs into their own processes (forward linkages).

31 For a detailed account see F. Carrigan, 'The Imperial struggle for
control of the Broken Hill base-metal industry, 1914–1915', in E. L.
Wheelwright and K. Buckley (eds), *Essays in the Political Economy
of Australian Capitalism*, Vol. 5, Australia and New Zealand Book
Company, Sydney, 1983, pp. 164–186.

32 North Broken Hill, Broken Hill South and the Zinc Corporation, all
part of the Collins House Group, combined to own BHAS coopera-
tively. All three were part of the Collins House Group. P. Richardson,
'The origins and development of the Collins House Group, 1915–
1951', *Australian Economic History Review*, Vol. 27, No. 1, 1987,
p. 8.

33 Copland, *Australia in the World Crisis*, p. 570.

34 W. A. Sinclair, *The Process of Economic Development in Australia*,
Cheshire, Melbourne, 1976, pp. 172, 174. Sinclair argues his case in
more detail in 'Capital Formation', in C. Forster (ed), *Australian
Economic Development in the Twentieth Century*, George Allen &
Unwin/Australasian Publishing Company, Sydney, 1964, pp. 11–65.
His argument is the subject of some criticism in K. Rowley, 'Sinclair's
Bankrupt History', *Intervention*, vol. 9. 1977, pp. 87–91, particularly,
p. 90.

35 C. Forster, 'Australian Manufacturing and the War of 1914–18', *Economic Record*, vol. 29, 1953, pp. 211–30. Quotes from pp. 211, 230.
Forster takes his argument further in 'Economies of Scale and Australian Manufacturing', in Forster, *Australian Economic Development*,
pp. 123–68.

36 For example, M. W. Butlin, *A Preliminary Annual Database 1900/01
to 1973/74*, Reserve Bank Research Discussion Paper 7701, 1977,
pp. 2–4. Butlin rates the reliability of a range of data and indicators
from 1 to 3 (in decreasing degrees of reliability) 'with [rating] 3 being
reserved for data from the War years . . .'. p. 2.

37 Dyster and Meredith, *Australia in the International Economy*,
pp. 91–6.

38 B. D. Haig, 'Manufacturing Output and Productivity 1910 to 1948/9',
Australian Economic History Review, vol. 15, no. 2, 1975, p. 143.
Increases in other industries ranged between nil and 4 per cent. Metals

and engineering were the next group, clearly (c. 50 per cent) ahead of the remaining groups.

39 ibid. p. 149.

40 Ernest Scott, *Australia During the War*, vol. XI, of *The Official History of Australia in the War of 1914–1918*, Angus & Robertson, 1936, p. 549 gives details.

41 D. Pope, 'Australian Capital Inflow, Sectional Prices and the Terms of Trade: 1870–1939', *Australian Economic Papers*, vol. 25, no. 46, June 1986, p. 34.

42 Quoted from *Commonwealth Parliamentary Debates,* 1920, in D. Pope, 'Population and Australian economic development 1900–30', in Maddock and McLean, *Australian Economy*, p. 53.

43 N. Butlin, A. Barnard and J. J. Pincus, *Government and Capitalism*, Allen and Unwin, Sydney, 1982, p. 89.

44 For more details see White, *Mastering Risk*, pp. 205–6.

45 C. G. Fane, 'The development of monetary institutions in Australia from federation to the Second World War', *Centre for Economic Policy Research Discussion Papers*, no. 227, ANU, Canberra, 1990, p. 7.

46 Scott, *Australia During the War*, p. 503.

47 ibid. pp. 633–4.

48 The first is expressed in current terms, the second in constant terms, i.e. corrected for inflation/deflation over time. Constant terms allows comparisons to be made far more readily.

49 For a full discussion of the increasing role of government in the economic sphere, see Butlin, Barnard and Pincus, *Government and Capitalism*, pp. 49–107.

50 Stuart Macintyre, *The Oxford History of Australia*, vol. 4, *1901–1942: The Succeeding Age*, Oxford University Press, Melbourne, 1986, p. 27.

51 Scott, *Australia During the War,* p. 683.

52 ibid. p. 665.

53 ibid. p. 679n.

54 Direct Commonwealth intervention also took place in the 1916 colliery dispute and the 1919 seamen's dispute.

55 J. Hagen and K. Turner, *A History of the Labor Party in New South Wales*, Longman Cheshire, Melbourne, 1991, p. 73. With a class-based creed closely related to the ideology of the IWW, the OBU was vehemently anti-conscriptionist. It was particularly strong in Broken Hill.

56 B. Kennedy, *Silver, Sin and Sixpenny Ale*, Melbourne University Press, Melbourne, 1978, p. 159.

57 Australian unions were traditionally based on a particular craft or occupation such as metal-working or mining. The OBU sought to replace that structure with a single union incorporating the entire working class.

58 Wray Vamplew (ed.), *Australians. Historical Statistics*, Fairfax, Syme & Weldon, Broadway, NSW, 1987, p. 164.

59 Macintyre, *1901–1942*, p. 34.

60 Pincus in Maddock and McLean, *Australian Economy*, p. 297.
61 Vamplew, *Australians*, p. 256.
62 Gordon Greenwood, *Australia: A Social and Political History*, Angus & Robertson, Sydney, 1955, pp. 277, 277n.
63 Scott, *Australia During the War*, p. 495; C. G. Fane, 'The development of monetary institutions in Australia from federation to the second world war', Centre for Economic Policy Research Discussion Paper No. 227, ANU, Canberra, 1990, p. 7. The size of the deficit explains Hughes's concerted attempts at the Paris Peace Conference of 1919 to get Germany to cover Australian war costs.
64 Attard, 'Politics, finance', pp. 142–63 is a notable exception.
65 ibid. p. 150.
66 ibid. p. 156.
67 Sir Otto Niemeyer was sent to Australia in 1930 to review the nation's ability to service the very high level of existing external debt and intended future borrowings required for public sector policy and projects. He held highly conservative, economically orthodox views which were the driving force behind the deflationary policies adopted by Australian governments during the Depression. Those policies included cuts in wages, pensions and public works at a time of extremely high unemployment and accompanying widespread hardship throughout Australian economy and society. Niemeyer believed strongly that Australia's profligacy, funded by overseas borrowings, must be reined in to allow the primary sector to resume its 'proper' trading role as supplier of food and raw materials to Britain in exchange for manufactured goods and technology.
68 For example, N.G. Butlin, 'Select comparative statistics 1900–1940: Australia and Britain, Canada, Japan, New Zealand and USA', *Source Papers in Economic History*, no. 4, ANU, Canberra, 1984; 'Australian National Accounts 1788–1983', *Source Papers in Economic History*, no. 6, ANU, Canberra, 1985.
69 White, *Mastering Risk*, p. 187.

5 Australia in the world

David Lowe

In October 1919, Lieutenant Commander J. G. Latham, a member
of the Australian delegation to the recent Paris Peace Conference,
evaluated Australia's involvement in the war and the determining
of the peace. He said: 'The benefits and advantages are of the same
general character as in the case of an infant attaining his majority.
Australia has now an opportunity of taking a greater share in the
moulding of her own destiny.'[1]

This chapter considers the impact of the First World War on
Australia's position in world affairs. It examines whether, as Latham
claimed, the war created opportunities for the expression of Australian interests in imperial or international forums, or whether
Australian leaders struggled to have their voices heard in a
Eurocentric war and peace. In turn, it raises questions about
Australians' attitudes towards changes in imperial relations, and
whether, as a result of the war, Australians were willing to pursue
overseas policies in a more independent fashion than had hitherto
been the case.

This chapter focuses on two perspectives on Australian involvement in international affairs, namely Australia's distinctive interests,
and Australia's relationships with Britain and the other Dominions.
Although it could be maintained that many Australian interests
bridged both categories, there was a tension between the two, which
requires us to ask whether Australians' reliance on the imperial
defence network promoted or detracted from Australia's interests.

Although Australian soldiers were caught up in battles waged
in Europe and the Middle East during the First World War, some
commentators have emphasised the importance of other Australian

concerns, much closer to home. According to Neville Meaney, 'Australians, by the time of World War I, had their own sophisticated perspective on international diplomacy' and looked to the end of the war to bring them opportunities to mobilise imperial and local resources for defence in the Pacific.[2] Concern with security in the Pacific, which had been a preoccupation of many Australians in the late nineteenth century, may have receded from the public mind in the face of a war centred in Europe, but, according to Meaney, Australian leaders were not about to let it be brushed aside altogether. It was not until the end of the war, however, that Australia's voice on this question was heard loudly.

It was, more accurately Hughes's voice. His was the dominant influence shaping Australian foreign policy at this time, and the notable feature of many histories of this period is the prominence they give to him. Sometimes published accounts also reflect a mythology about Hughes's ability to badger the leaders of the world powers into submission. Donald Horne has encapsulated the Hughes legend:

> It was not only what he achieved (or seemed to have achieved)
> that turned W.M. Hughes into the Little Digger. It was the way he
> went about it . . . To the Diggers he was full of spunk and able to
> stand up to authority . . . Billy Hughes was a cheeky little bugger,
> and a real battler . . . [In Paris] this image of the indomitable little
> man added to the image of a national hero who personified
> victory, and a folk hero personifying the suppressed fantasies of
> the people.[3]

This chapter contends that such celebrations of Billy Hughes can be misleading. Australia's emergence on the diplomatic scene was a spectacular one, thanks to Hughes, but it should not automatically be taken as a sign of burgeoning nationalism, of forcing change upon imperial organisation, or of marking the birth of an independent Australian foreign policy.

Another important theme which emerges from several of the major works on this period is that Australia's frustrations and achievements in international relations can be appreciated only by understanding the curious relationship that existed between its diplomacy and that of the other Dominions. Although Hughes and his cabinet tended to equate imperial concerns with British ones, they were fortunate that on many important matters of international relations they enjoyed the support of Canadian, South African and New Zealand leaders. Indeed, whether attempting to assert Australian interests in the Pacific or fashioning the crucial Australian–British relationship, the contributions of other Dominions could be critical.

Regional interests and world war

Although Australia of the early 1900s is renowned for the infancy of its political institutions and for its cultural 'Britishness', it was not without distinctively Australian policies. One vital concern was with the geopolitics of the Pacific and with Australia's security. Australian interest in the South Pacific had been fuelled prior to federation by a variety of influences which will be familiar to students of modern European imperialism. Trading interests, church missions, a demand for indentured labour, security fears, and foreign competition all shaped the Australian colonies' early relations with the islands of the South Pacific.[4] During the first fourteen years after federation several of the country's leaders, in particular Alfred Deakin (prime minister of three cabinets), were determined to forge a distinctly Australian consciousness of the need for clear defence and foreign policies in the Pacific.

Two other early tenets of faith, a dictation test for prospective immigrants in order to ensure a White Australia, and a national customs tariff on imports which allowed for preferences to be directed towards favoured trading partners, reflected and defined a popular orientation towards the British Empire which would endure throughout the first half of the century.

In 1901 Deakin publicly claimed that Australia's Immigration Restriction Act, the cornerstone of a White Australia Policy, was aimed particularly at the Japanese. Not surprisingly, his comments drew vocal resentment from Japan. This ill-feeling had an impact in a wider sphere of international relations when an Anglo-Japanese Treaty of Alliance was struck in 1902, committing each party to come to the aid of the other in defence of their Far Eastern interests, should either party be attacked by more than one power. This treaty, striking, as it did, notes of discord with Australia's immigration policy made for diplomatic awkwardness within an Anglo-Australian-Japanese triangle. However, the Australian legislation was not seriously revised; nor was the Anglo-Japanese alliance which, with subsequent renewals, became a constant in the British Empire's strategic outlook for the next twenty years.

Australian concerns about Japan entered a new era from May 1905 when the Japanese Navy won a crushing victory over its Russian counterpart at the battle of Tsushima. Japan's ascendancy seemed all the more worrying to Australians given the wider changes in the global balance of power caused also by the concurrent rapid growth of the German and American navies. In 1905 Australia had only minimal means of protection from attack by sea, and no independent navy, the early governments having chosen instead to contribute annual sums of £200 000 to the Royal Navy which used the funds to maintain an auxiliary Pacific fleet. After the Russo-Japanese war, Deakin championed a number of measures designed to improve Australia's defences, from harbour defences and the creation of an independent Australian navy, to compulsory military training and the encouragement of closer American involvement in the security of the western Pacific. Efforts were even made to appease the Japanese by modifying the White Australia Policy. Instead of a dictation test for prospective immigrants in 'any European language', the criterion changed in 1905 to 'any prescribed language'.

Crucially, the escalation of Australian anxieties called into question the effectiveness of British pledges of protection, especially in circumstances when the capital ships of the Royal Navy might all be elsewhere than the Pacific. The Anglo-Japanese alliance was designed to relieve any fears of Asian aggression in such a contingency, but the Australians were not reassured. Yet they did not feel able to oppose the ten-year renewal of the Anglo-Japanese alliance in 1911, for fear that they might have to meet a hefty defence burden in order to maintain an imperial Pacific fleet.[5]

In attempting to demolish what he calls the 'myth' that Australia had no foreign policy prior to the Second World War, Meaney has strayed towards exaggeration in his comment that since the end of the nineteenth century, 'Australia's defence and foreign policy has been dominated by one idea—the search for security in the Pacific'. There is, nevertheless, a strong sense of Australian policy makers undergoing a process of education during the decade preceding the First World War in what Meaney calls the 'implacable geopolitics' of local security issues.[6] It was a process which cannot be easily equated with traditional notions of nationalism, for most Australians conceived of local and imperial perspectives as complementary, but it does demonstrate an emerging 'Australianness' in the way Australian leaders conceived of their interests overseas.

There is no space here to debate fully whether the concept of 'national interests', as used by international relations theorists, really encompasses the interests of diverse groups within Australia in the first decades of this century. Australian leaders certainly behaved as though objectives such as a White Australia and defence in the Pacific were constants which transcended class and political boundaries. As Meaney suggests, they also demonstrated a preparedness to guard these interests jealously (hence, the inadequacy of early historical orthodoxy which attributed to Australia 'few distinctive national policies in foreign affairs and almost no independent voice, other than in trade, until World War II').[7]

Initially, the war brought both opportunities and potential dangers for Australian regional interests, resulting from the dismantling of Germany's empire in the South Pacific. In 1914 this empire included, south of the equator, Kaiser Wilhelm's Land, or the northern half of New Guinea, the adjacent Bismarck Archipelago, Nauru, and Samoa; and north of the equator, the Chinese port of Kiaochow, and the Caroline, Mariana, Palau, and Marshall island groups. The Germans were forced to surrender all of these territories to Allied forces in the early months of the war, presenting the Australians with opportunities to extend their own influence in the Pacific, but also creating the danger of other powers, especially Japan, attempting to move into the vacuum of surrendered German possessions.

Within four months of the declaration of war in Europe, Australian, New Zealand and Japanese forces had occupied all of the German colonies in the south-west Pacific. British officials and Australia's Prime Minister, Andrew Fisher, envisaged the occupation of German-held islands north of the equator, but a shortage of warships delayed plans, and by the time the Australians were prepared to venture further north they discovered that the Japanese had done their job for them, with British endorsement.

At first, Fisher seemed resigned to the Japanese occupation of the north Pacific islands, although he became nervous about future Japanese intentions after their territorial and other demands on China during the first half of 1915. Hughes, who succeeded Fisher as prime minister in October that year, was more concerned about the strategic implications of Japan's influence spreading throughout the Pacific. Visiting London in 1916, Hughes pointed out the difficulties in reconciling the British policy of treating Japan as a friendly ally with Australia's determination to curb the spread of Japanese influence and to deny Japanese immigrants entry to Australia. Officials in London, however, maintained that such a reconciliation was possible.

It is important to note that, during his stay in Britain during the second quarter of 1916, Hughes established a reputation as a fearless and outspoken lion figure who championed imperial causes. The weakness of British Prime Minister Asquith's political leadership in Britain, and the inevitable media concentration on events at the front, afforded Hughes the chance to play the imperial maverick, a role which he adopted with relish. He stomped about the British countryside whipping up support for a greater war effort, and caught the attention of the British press to the extent that there are indications of his being urged by the influential press baron, Lord Northcliffe, to stay on in London as a member of Cabinet.[8]

His popularity helped him to secure a place on the team of representatives of the British Empire to an allied economic conference in Paris in June. Here he again enjoyed the limelight of an international stage and revealed his strong views on the need to step up the allied economic blockade on Germany. The conference resolutions very much reflected Hughes's determination to disable Germany and ensure the British Empire's economic prosperity in the aftermath of the war. Not surprisingly, both aims stood to benefit Australia. Only if Germany were forced to pay for all the costs of the war would Australia, which had not suffered direct physical damage, be able to claim full reparations. And if Germany were economically crippled, then Britain would have to trade more exclusively with the Dominions. At the time, however, a number of foreign leaders expressed reservations about the restricted markets Hughes envisaged, and the resolutions of the economic conference were, in any case, overtaken by developments in 1917 such as Russia's collapse, the United States' entry into the war, and deepening economic exhaustion in Europe.

Hughes's diplomatic ventures of 1916 did not alter the British treatment of Australia's concerns in the Pacific. As the war became a draining and protracted affair, the British found the promise of Japanese naval assistance in the Pacific, and in 1917 even in the Mediterranean, increasingly important. As Hughes became aware of this during his 1916 visit to London, he grudgingly acknowledged the division of the Pacific into wartime spheres of Japanese and Australasian influence, the equator being the dividing line.

Some historians have seen Hughes's reaction in 1916 and his confirmation of this in February 1917 as his recognising a situation which then existed rather than acquiescing in a permanent delineation of influence.[9] This distinction affects how we judge the propriety of Hughes's insistence at the end of the war on Australian or British control over former German territories north of the equator. It does not, however, alter the striking impotence of the Australian Government in the context of Anglo-Japanese diplomacy. In an effort to allay Hughes's suspicions of Japanese motives and to avoid confrontations with the excitable Australian leader, British officials tried to keep their Australian counterparts uninformed or misinformed about the full scope of Anglo-Japanese relations. They partly managed to hide their navy's scepticism over the value of Japanese naval assistance, and their misgivings about the prices being paid for Japanese help, in China and the north Pacific; but intelligence in Australia produced independent assessments which entertained grave suspicions about Japan's postwar ambitions. However, in the face of British insistence on the value of the Japanese alliance, and the spectre of a vague but frightening possibility that, if not appeased, the Japanese might seek to pursue their ambitions in alliance with Germany, the Australians resolved to keep their apprehensions quiet—for the duration of the war.[10]

It was a sign of Hughes's mounting frustration with London over Pacific security that he could not quite wait until the end of the war. In May 1918 he called for an 'Australasian Monroe Doctrine in the South Pacific',[11] involving control over a belt of islands to the north of Australia. He did this on the occasion when he and other Dominion leaders gathered in London to participate in drafting the British Empire's briefs on matters to be discussed at the forthcoming peace conference in Paris. The circumstances leading to Australia's representation, both separately and as a member of an imperial panel at the Paris peace conference which opened on 18 January 1919, will be discussed at a later point. What needs to be noted now is that Hughes grasped with relish the unprecedented opportunities to establish Australia's claims to what he considered to be the rightful spoils of war. His means to exert some influence lay in his access to the Imperial War Cabinet, the Empire's delegation to Paris, the Council of Ten at the peace conference (two representatives each from the United States, Britain, France, Italy and Japan), which presided over the most crucial issues discussed in Paris, and the large press contingent following these policy-making bodies.

Hughes and the Paris Peace Conference

There are several detailed accounts by Australians of Hughes's performance at Paris, and many anecdotes in the personal memoirs of those who attended. These accounts put Hughes in the spotlight, but most of the personal memoirs by Europeans and Americans touch only fleetingly on Hughes's role as they cover the broad canvas of conference discussions.[12] The monumental five-volume history of the peace conference (and one volume of documents) by H. V. Temperley, which comprises over 2700 pages, relegates the Dominions to 33 pages in the final volume. A more recent study of international politics during the war consigns Australia to a similar fate.[13] Otherwise, the Australian contribution to the peace process has appeared in works examining the evolution of the British Empire/Commonwealth, an enduring theme which will be considered in detail later. Most descriptions convey the colour in Hughes's argumentative character, and his determination to be heard by the great powers.

To complement these accounts there is an amusing series of cartoons by David Low, the New Zealand-born cartoonist of British and international politics, depicting the diminutive and deaf Hughes as raucous, single-minded, and demanding. Perhaps the peak of Low's satire was his penning of a 'Billiwog', a puppet-like doll reputedly popular in London, which could be blown up until its head expanded and then released, causing Billy to 'emit loud noises'. Low's cartoons and Hughes's adventuresome memoirs alone probably generated much of the mythology about his 'David versus Goliath' successes against European statesmen.[14]

The three most detailed Australian studies[15] suggest that of the Australians who attended the conference, Hughes was certainly the dominant figure. They also indicate that there were moments when two of his advisers, Robert Garran, the federal Solicitor-General, and John Latham, a lawyer with a naval reserve commission, made a significant contribution to Australian negotiating positions.[16] The deputy leader of Hughes's new Nationalist Party, Joseph Cook, came to Paris, but was ignored by Hughes to the point of humiliation.

Without philosophical sophistication, Hughes pressed Australia's claims in the peace settlement primarily on the basis of Australia's contribution to the war—'I speak for 60 000 dead'—and its being on the side of the victors who were entitled to extract rewards. This approach led Hughes into conflict with American President Woodrow Wilson. The President's liberal internationalist ideals were embodied in the 'Fourteen Points' which provided the basic principles for the peace settlements. The 'points' which most disturbed the Australian prime minister were those which foreshadowed the removal of all economic barriers to international trade, and called for the establishment of a League of Nations, an international organisation to adjudicate on matters of international tension, including colonial affairs, and to elicit from its members collective action against aggression. This, and Wilson's tendency towards leniency in determining Germany's reparations bill, were anathema to Hughes's approach to peacemaking.

Today, political scientists would label Hughes as a stringent 'realist', for he appeared to assume that competition and conflict between states was inevitable, and that the first duty of a state was to ensure its own security. He accordingly dismissed talk of internationalism and of possible improvements in international relations. In the words of W. J. Hudson, Hughes viewed war as 'being rather like a risky stock market play in which the winner should profit and the loser suffer'.[17]

The mandate question

Hughes's antipathy towards Wilson's ideals was manifested clearly over the question of German New Guinea. From an early date Hughes had been determined to see Australia annex this territory at the end of the war. Wilson, however, proposed the granting of mandates over former German colonies to responsible powers which would be answerable for their administration to the League of Nations. These mandates would be constituted on the basis of an 'open door' principle, which would guarantee free trade and prevent restrictive immigration laws. Upon learning of the British agreement to Wilson's terms, Hughes raged about the Imperial War Cabinet being a 'sham', and wrote to the acting Australian Prime Minister, W. A. Watt, that 'the only way to get the terms of peace Australia is entitled to is to continue emphatic protest'.[18] (In fact, on this occasion, and on others, the Australian Cabinet were embarrassed by Hughes's confrontationist style, although they generally agreed with the substance of his arguments.)

Given the size of the peace conference, and its preoccupation with European and Middle Eastern matters, it was fortunate for Hughes that other Dominions also felt strongly about the future of certain German colonies. Had he not been able to find allies in W. F. Massey, New Zealand's Prime Minister, and Louis Botha and Jan Smuts, South Africa's Prime Minister and Defence Minister respectively, his lone voice, however insistent, may not have carried the same weight before the Council of Ten. Massey sought direct control over German Samoa for New Zealand, and the South Africans claimed the same right over German South–West Africa. Ironically enough, the Japanese delegation would also lobby in the same vein for direct control over German interests in China and the occupied islands of the north Pacific.

The Council of Ten began to discuss the question of the German colonies on 23 January 1919, and allowed the Dominion leaders to present their cases. Hughes argued for Australia's annexation of New Guinea and the adjacent islands in terms of defence. Given the emphasis in the fifth of Wilson's fourteen points on the need for consideration of 'the interests of the peoples concerned' when deciding colonial claims, Hughes's concentration on the strategic issue was insensitive. Only in subsequent discussions did he suggest that Australian control would bring better living conditions to New Guinea natives. Even then he was often flippant. On one occasion he explained that Australian authorities would never hinder natives' access to missionaries, because, as he was reported to have said, 'I understand that these poor people are very short of food, and for some time past they have not had enough missionaries'.[19]

The British delegates joined the Dominions in their refusal to leave the vague concept of a mandate for the League to define, but Hughes was the most confrontational in conference sessions. Had his naked hostility towards Wilson not been encompassed within a wider umbrella of Dominion expressions of interest, it is possible that the other imperial delegates would have distanced themselves from his outbursts. Other Dominion statesmen gave more thought to the future of a grand English-speaking alliance than to Australia's Pacific concerns. Smuts and Canadian Prime Minister Sir Robert Borden, the Dominion leaders whose diplomatic experience and intellectual endeavours afforded them a certain seniority in Paris, were powerful advocates of a new and close relationship between the Empire and the United States. They were loath to see disputes between the Dominions and the US spoil their hopes. It is symptomatic, therefore, that one of the harshest assessments of Hughes's diplomacy in Paris has come from a historian of Anglo-American relations at the conference. According to Seth Tillman, Hughes was 'a noisome demagogue', and the 'bête noire of Anglo-American relations', who earned the contempt of British and American statesmen.[20]

Given the determination by British, French and Dominion leaders not to relinquish control over conquered colonial and Middle Eastern territories, there was little chance that the terms of the League of Nations mandates would reflect Wilson's hopes for a real transfer of power over colonies to the League. The problem of the German colonies was resolved outside the Council meetings with the drafting by Latham, Smuts and Sir Maurice Hankey, Secretary to the British Cabinet, of a three-class mandate system. This was accepted by Wilson, and acquiesced in by Hughes when he realised that he had little support for continuing the fight for annexation and that his essential objectives were met in the creation of 'C-class' mandates in South–West Africa and the Pacific. New Guinea and Samoa would be administered as 'integral portions' of Australia and New Zealand respectively, which enabled them control over the crucial spheres of trade and immigration. The corollary was that Japan won mandates over former German possessions north of the equator. Hughes was disappointed that the C-class mandate initially stopped short of the Bismarck Archipelago to the north and east of New Guinea, but not even his roaring at Lloyd George in Welsh would convince the British Prime Minister to stretch the patience of Wilson any further.[21] This problem and residual anxieties over whether the constituted League of Nations would confirm Australia's role as the mandated power were removed when the League formally conferred on Australia a 'Mandate for the German Possessions in the Pacific Ocean situated south of the Equator other than German Samoa and Nauru' in December 1920.

The racial equality clause in the League covenant

Much of Hughes's vigour on Pacific issues and Australian security seemed to be fired by a belief that some tremendous confrontation between Japan and Australia was inevitable, given the pressure of population on Japan's resources and the logic of expansion as that nation grew stronger. In Paris he faced what he thought to be a Japanese assault on White Australia and protected trading when the Japanese delegation attempted to secure in the Covenant of the League of Nations an assertion of racial equality. Hughes knew very well that any compromise on the White Australia Policy was tantamount to domestic political suicide. He therefore insisted that any such clause carry the explicit rider that it could not interfere with a nation's exclusive control over its immigration laws.

In his opposition to the Japanese proposal Hughes was more isolated than on the mandate question. He brought to bear all his powers of obstinacy and manipulation of the press, but ultimately he was saved by his *bête noire,* Wilson. As chair of the League of Nations Commission, the body which drafted the final shape of the League, Wilson blocked the inclusion of a racial equality clause. He was probably influenced by recent racial tension on the west coast of the United States, but the prospect of an inflammatory reaction from Hughes, had the vote succeeded, may also have been a factor in his reckoning.[22]

What sort of victories were these then, for Australian interests? A Japanese attack on the sacrosanct White Australia Policy had not succeeded, and Australia's regional 'empire' had grown, qualified by an annoying accountability to the League of Nations. There were clear benefits, strategically, commercially, and in the preservation of White Australia, from extensive control over the whole of eastern New Guinea (the western half remaining part of the Dutch Empire), but these were gained at the price of the Japanese securing prizes in China and the Pacific, north of the equator. The creation of C-class mandates was therefore a mixed blessing. On the one hand, the system provided for continued Japanese influence in the north Pacific; on the other, it prevented them from fortifying their mandated territories, thus relieving the Australians of the need to do likewise south of the equator.

In hindsight, it is difficult to conceive alternatives for Hughes. One strategy which Latham favoured as serving Australian interests better in the long term, was support for a mandate along Wilson's lines, accompanied by American-backed neutralisation of the Pacific, both sides of the equator. Latham assumed, probably correctly, that Wilson's determination to see the Pacific mandates administered under close supervision by the League stemmed from his own fears of Japanese expansion. Most historians have justified Hughes's policy on the ground that there were many uncertainties about the future role of the United States in world affairs (although with hindsight, the historian should not exaggerate Hughes's perspicacity on the basis of the subsequent retreat of the United States into isolation in the 1920s and 30s).[23]

One feature of Hughes's foreign policies in 1918–19 was his fundamental antagonism towards the whole concept of the League of Nations. In the Imperial War Cabinet at the end of 1918 he led the attack on the League and its underlying principle of collective security, which required nations to respond to the League's call for collective action against any state which was named as an aggressor. Hughes believed this concept was an undesirable infringement on the freedom of nations to determine their own actions in international affairs, a view that was shared by influential British politicians such as Winston Churchill and Foreign Secretary Lord Balfour. Lloyd George and the French leader, Georges Clemenceau, also placed more faith in the establishment of effective alliances with the Americans.[24]

Hughes would have preferred the League to have developed as a consultative organ only, and, in common with the rest of the Australian Cabinet, he harboured grave misgivings about the future potential for the League to effect changes in immigration laws. Of concern also was the ability of the British Navy to come to Australia's aid in time of need if it was 'part of a polyglot, heterogeneous force attached to the League'.[25] In the shaping of the League, however, Hughes was noisy without being influential, for there were others better placed to express similar concerns, and the only Dominion representative on the League of Nations Commission was Smuts.

One is left with the clear impression that, for Hughes, the end of the war was not a time for optimism and reform in international relations. As the Versailles peace treaty, which embodied the terms of the peace for Germany, indicated, he was not alone in conceiving of the international system in traditional balance-of-power terms. Few politicians, however, approached Hughes's stature as an apostle of naked short-term, self-interested policy. Perhaps the most illuminating insight came from Latham, who summed up his prime minister 'as a representative of the pre-war school of ideas, and as a good specimen of a forceful person who has learnt hardly anything from the debacle of the last six years'.[26]

One of the best attestations to this image of Hughes was his inglorious membership on an investigative British Indemnity Committee set up by the Imperial War Cabinet in December 1918, and on the British delegation to the Reparations Commission at the peace conference. In the former, Hughes argued that the British delegation should insist on Germany paying a colossal figure in war damages, clearly aware that this might then enable Australia to claim a sum which would tackle the £300 million of public debt accumulated during the war.[27] He sidestepped the issue of how Germany might pay the suggested total of £24 000 million. Even though the British War Cabinet was sceptical, Lloyd George retained Hughes to act as a British representative on the Reparations Commission. It suited him for domestic political purposes to have a vocal advocate of a punitive peace in order to appease political opponents who might accuse him of being 'soft' on the Germans.[28]

A pessimistic analysis might conclude that Hughes's most significant role in the economic settling of the peace was to contribute to a climate of retribution which would result in the infamous 'war-guilt' clause in the Treaty of Versailles. This assertion of German responsibility for the outbreak of the war would fuel German resentment in the 1920s and 1930s and provoke calls within that country for extreme action to force the revision of the treaty.

However much one seeks to credit Hughes with policy-making influence, the most enduring impression in accounts of his role in the peace negotiations is that of a representative of a small nation, whose special and regional interests had been swept to one side by wartime diplomacy for four years, battling to halt the process and recover lost ground. Remarkably, his battles were sometimes successful, but even collectively they did not suggest that a turning point in Australia's relations with the world had been reached. Hughes's efforts to assert Australia's regional interests repeatedly ran against the dictates of a Eurocentric war and peace. On most occasions when Hughes succeeded in achieving international recognition of Australian interests, he also had some potent assistance from more influential actors who, for a variety of reasons, shared some of his concerns in the making of the peace.

Australia and the British Empire in international affairs

As the Paris Peace Conference shows, one of the central themes in any study of Australia's role in the world in the first half of the twentieth century is the importance to Australia of membership of the British Empire or Commonwealth (as the self-governing parts of the Empire became known in the 1920s). This is a theme which requires careful exposition because during the First World War and after, the Empire was evolving into a new series of relationships to which were attached new expectations and commitments. These changes occurred in the context of tensions between imperial ties and the more regional concerns of members such as Australia.

Some of the most important statements on imperial relationships emanated from conferences in London hosted by British governments. Originally called colonial conferences, they were known from 1907 as imperial conferences. In constitutional theory, British governments had the right at this time to overrule legislation passed in the Dominions, but there was no thought of exercising such a right by the time the war erupted in Europe. When, in 1917, Canadian and South African leaders called for a special constitutional imperial conference after the war, it was to redress this imbalance between the legal status of being a Dominion and the political reality of perceived equality amongst members of the Commonwealth.

In the years prior to war, the idea of imperial federation had gained some support in Britain and within the Dominions. This envisaged an imperial council, of British and Dominion leaders, which would define common imperial policies. Centralised imperial defence planning was especially attractive to Australian and New Zealand leaders searching for ways to ensure regular consultation on defence strategies and to integrate their own meagre defence forces with British commands. The southern Dominions met strong opposition to this idea, however, from Canadian and South African governments. In these two countries there was a strong sense that Dominion development led towards national independence, not towards centrally coordinated plans—though neither South Africans nor the majority of Canadians sought to disrupt the fabric of the Empire. It was the Irish who tried to tear a hole in the Empire, fighting a war against British authorities for recognition of their republic. In 1921 the republicans were forced into accepting a treaty with the British which included Irish Dominion status, and from this moment the Irish joined the South Africans and Canadians in the drafting and refashioning of Dominion rights.

In Australia there was no support for radical reform in imperial relations. In contrast to Canada and South Africa, where non-British populations were influential, the overwhelming majority of the Australian population derived from British 'stock' and the ties of 'kinship' were felt to be strong. There were also crucial economic advantages from Australia's close relationship with Britain.

The administration of Australian foreign policy

Australian governments therefore were content to rely on London for representation of Australia's overseas interests (at minimal costs to Australia). Most of Australia's international concerns were conveyed to and assessed in Whitehall, where officials' primary means of communication with Australian governments was through the Colonial Office and the Governor-General residing in Australia. Bureaucratic support within Australia for the conduct of foreign relations was, up to the First World War, negligible. The diminutive Department of External Affairs was entombed within the Prime Minister's Department until 1908 and then led a brief and inglorious period of independence until its abolition by Hughes in 1916.

The war years saw few improvements in administrative support for the representation of Australian interests abroad. Although J. R. Poynter claims that the absorption of External Affairs into the Prime Minister's Department was 'mainly a piece of administrative patricide and cannibalism implying no abandonment of function',[29] the merger was significant in that it facilitated the monopolisation of policy making by Hughes. Hughes generally ignored departmental advice. When he travelled to London in 1916, he relied on W. S. Robinson, a businessman, Keith Murdoch, a prominent journalist with influence in the British press, and Robert Garran. His personal entourage in 1918–19 was similarly composed. In short, says Edwards, 'Hughes's style was more presidential than prime-ministerial'.[30]

In spite of Hughes, there were tentative moves towards something approaching a foreign office, or at least a centre for extended defence intelligence, during the years 1916–21. E. L. Piesse, a member of the Australian Intelligence Corps under the Defence Department from 1909, became Director of Military Intelligence in March 1916. Two years later, W. A. Watt (acting as prime minister in Hughes's absence) moved to have Piesse collect information on questions specifically relating to the Far East. In the first half of 1919 Watt then set up a Pacific Branch within the Prime Minister's Department, with Piesse as Director. Piesse soon became far more than merely a collator of information. After a mission to Japan from August 1919 to March 1920, he began to produce lengthy analyses of Australian interests in the Pacific, encompassing such matters as future Japanese intentions, the role of the White Australia Policy, Papua New Guinea, and the New Hebrides.

Australia's new Pacific Branch did not develop beyond 1921. It was marginalised by Hughes who was not comfortable with 'advice' emanating from this source and viewed Piesse's work with suspicion, especially after he returned from Japan daring to suggest modifications to the White Australia Policy and a revised appreciation of Japanese intentions, since he foresaw no Japanese designs on Australia. Piesse ended his frustrated relationship with government and Pacific affairs at the end of 1923, when the new Bruce–Page administration which replaced Hughes did not revive his mandate.

Australia and the League of Nations

It was no coincidence that one of the more important developments in Australian foreign policy making took place in the context of new responsibilities for the Dominions in 1919. All of the Dominions became members of the League of Nations Assembly in their own right (though they retained the imperial habit and the practical advantages of regular meetings amongst themselves and the British delegations). The functioning of the League was far from clear when it first met in Geneva in May 1919—and Australia made an inauspicious start, protesting at its costs—but it soon became clear that the League would not interfere with imperial ties. The same lack of binding commitments on nations to act as a collective police force, which would rob the League of its effectiveness in the prevention and resolution of international disputes, ensured this. As Hudson comments, the League was doubly advantageous to Australia. It did not impinge on Australia's sovereignty and its Dominion status, yet separate representation afforded Australians opportunities to participate in international discussions on world affairs whenever they chose. Many of Australia's first diplomatic representatives overseas, appointed from the late 1930s on, 'cut their teeth' in League assemblies.[31]

A new independence for Australia?

For students of Australian foreign policy, the major problem in assessing the impact of the First World War on Australia's relations with the world is the question of how, if at all, it encouraged a growth of Australian independence. Is there an apparent contradiction between Hughes's assertiveness at the Paris Peace Conference and Australia's reluctance, as we have seen, to take any initiative in changing imperial relations? How do we reconcile the claim of proponents of the Anzac legend that Australian nationhood was born with the landing at Gallipoli, and the continued adherence by Australian leaders to the imperial framework in which foreign policy was made?

Radical historians have been critical of Hughes who, they maintain, failed to maintain any distinctive 'Australian-ness' in his diplomacy, for all his strutting and fuming on the international stage. He has also been condemned by critics such as Stephen Alomes, for diverting Australian nationalism, which in the late nineteenth century supposedly had the potential to be radical, into militarism and a renewed subservience to the Empire.[32] According to Manning Clark, Hughes and his followers were unequivocally 'King and empire men'. Like Australia, the Australian delegation at Paris was shackled to its imperial past. 'They were not advocates for "the Young Tree Green" ', that is for Australian separateness. 'That Australian voice was not heard in Paris.'[33]

To some degree how one resolves the dilemma of Hughes depends upon how one defines independence. According to W. J. Hudson and M. P. Sharp, in their authoritative work, *Australian Independence*, the marks of independence comprise:

> competence to declare war and conclude peace; competence to negotiate and conclude agreements with other independent states; competence to exchange diplomatic representatives with the governments or heads of state of other independent states; competence to join associations of states.[34]

By the end of the war, Australia did have some 'competence' in several of the above areas. But there was, as we have seen, a distinct lack of Australian interest in the idea of formal, constitutional independence, and Australia had a debatable influence in bringing about such reforms in imperial relations as did occur.

For Hughes the issue of formal independence seems to have been less important in 1918–19 than the need to reward Australians for their loyalty in the war and to ensure that Australia had an effective input into the making of imperial foreign policy. As he told Lloyd George;

> we came into this war because we were part of the Empire . . . but of course you may get us into a war tomorrow of which we may not heartily approve, and therefore it is vital that we shall have some opportunity of moulding the foreign policy of this country before it is made.[35]

Hughes did not see loyalty to the Empire as subservience, or as precluding the championing of local interests. The difficulty in expressing exactly what he did want is noted by Hudson and Sharp, who suggest that, 'The Australian interest lay [not in formulae but] rather in a flexible mix of absolute domestic autonomy, something approaching equality in foreign policy formulation, and imperial protection'.[36]

Hughes's attitude was, of course, mirrored in public expressions of imperial enthusiasm which swept Australia during the war. As we have seen earlier, the rhetoric of loyalty to the Empire was well established before the war and would continue to feature in public life into the 1920s and 1930s when it was especially coveted by conservative politicians keen to exploit the Labor Party's opposition to conscription.

Hughes never really questioned whether Australia's membership of the imperial defence network was in its national interest. He never challenged the essential imperial structure but rather the interactions of its component parts. He was able to iron out some of his grievances relating to the tardiness of London's consultations with him on vital issues when he joined the Imperial War Cabinet at the end of July 1918. With Borden's support, he secured the right to bypass the Colonial Office and the Governor-General, thus providing for his direct access to the War Cabinet even when he was not in London. The communications issue, however, was not treated very seriously by the British over the next few years, and it took the Australian appointment of a liaison officer, Richard Casey, in 1924, to improve the interchanges between Melbourne and London.

The best example of a 'flexible mix' of Dominion rights in the making of the peace was their being awarded dual representation at Paris. Dominion representatives were entitled to attend the conference as delegates in their own right and as alternate members of the British delegation. Initially, late in 1918, it appeared that the Dominions and India would have only one place, to be shared in rotation, on a British delegation of five. Hughes pointed out, in typically strong terms, that such a proposal suggested that a nation such as Australia, despite its blood sacrifice, would suffer a lower status at the peace conference than a minor European power such as Sweden. His views, which incidentally did not have the support of the Australian Cabinet, were reinforced by Smuts and Borden, to whom Lloyd George looked for guidance on the issue of Dominion rights. Again, a loose concert among the Dominion representatives was needed to convince the British Government to press (successfully) for amendment to their status.

As with other instances of Dominion solidarity, it is difficult to gauge respective contributions by the prime ministers, but there seems little doubt that Hughes again played an important, if not determining, role in securing separate representation. W. K. Hancock attributes the recognition of the Dominions' individual and political rights to 'an effective combination' in Borden, Smuts and Hughes; 'Borden making the running in the Imperial War Conference, Hughes raising a clamour in the press, Smuts using his position at the centre of power to slip in the right memorandum at the right time'.[37]

In the event, separate representation at Paris brought little real advantage to the Dominions, who continued to voice their primary concerns as Empire delegates. Ironically, separate representation, and its logical corollary, separate membership of the League, may have even contributed to the alienation of the United States as a potential and powerful ally for Australia. Meaney has drawn attention to the American Republican Party's exploitation, in domestic US politics, of the six votes supposedly 'wielded' by the British Empire in the League. Opposed to American membership in the League, the Republicans used their own interpretation of constitutional relations between Britain and the Dominions to fuel suspicions about the spread of the British Empire. This contributed to the US Senate's refusal to ratify the Treaty of Versailles,[38] with the result that the United States was neither a member of the League nor likely to help meet Australia's Pacific security worries in the near future.

In fact, by the mid-1920s Hughes's contribution towards the securing of separate representation at Paris had begun to look misplaced. During the early part of the decade the Canadians, South Africans and Irish used the separate status issue as a stepping stone for further decentralisation in British–Dominion relations. Despite the efforts of the New Zealanders and Stanley Bruce, Hughes's successor as prime minister, to rekindle a vision of imperial unity, resolutions from the postwar imperial conferences explicitly provided for Dominion independence in foreign policy. The prospect of the British paying even less attention to Australian priorities, especially defence priorities, grew more alarming.

Conclusion

One of the honours conferred on Australian soldiers by C. E. W. Bean was the shooting down of the German air ace, Baron von Richthofen or the 'Red Baron', over the French village of Hamel in April 1918. In fact, at the time his aircraft was hit, the 'Red Baron' was being fired upon not only by Australian ground troops but also by British RAF fighters, and a post-mortem found that the baron's wounds could not have been caused by fire from the ground. Despite this, the 'David versus Goliath' legend of Australian gunners bringing down the Red Baron has lingered in subsequent Australian accounts.[39] An analogy with Hughes's verbal battles with 'great men' such as Wilson and Lloyd George at the 1919 peace conference in Paris is tempting, and for those anxious to find evidence of Anzac-like temerity in the realm of diplomacy it has perhaps been irresistible.

Resisting the temptation to over-celebrate Hughes's character can be profitable. Although more research awaits, particularly in the field of inter-Dominion relations and comparative Dominion studies, we can tentatively sketch a more sensitive appreciation of Hughes's diplomacy and Australia's role in international affairs at the end of the war.

It is hardly surprising to find differences of opinions over Hughes's diplomacy during, and especially at the end of, the war. Australian studies such as L. F. Fitzhardinge's definitive biography of Hughes and Peter Spartalis's account of his diplomatic battles naturally incline towards a certain prominence for Hughes. Hughes's own books, and the memoirs of such figures as Lloyd George, accentuate the 'personality' factor in diplomacy, a field in which Hughes will always feature. Underlying Hughes's diplomacy was a basic egoism which has not been ignored, but has been understated by sympathetic historians. His determination to pull all the strings affecting the representation of Australia's interests overseas was manifested clearly in his monopolisation of the infant Australian policy-making machinery and in his dogmatic approach to reforming imperial–Australian policy coordination in an informal, ad hoc fashion. As Edwards has noted, the concentration of responsibility in a Dominion prime minister was something which London also promoted, and the exigencies of wartime consultations made essential.[40] One of the outcomes was that Australian interests were equated with Hughes, and Australia's emergence in the diplomatic world took the shape of Hughes. Another consequence was that although Hughes's diplomacy often complemented the efforts of Borden and Smuts to reshape imperial ties, this was mostly unintentional. Hughes had little sense of vision for the future of either imperial or international relations. He knew very clearly what he did not want: he would not tolerate any interference with the White Australia Policy; he did not want any new international organisation to interfere with the Royal Navy's capacity to assist Australia in a time of crisis; and he would not see obstacles placed in the path of his exclusive and direct communication with London.

Events in the aftermath of the war did little to resolve the tension between local interests and imperial perspectives. At the 1921 Imperial Conference, for example, Hughes was pleased to see the abandonment of Canadian and South African plans for a constitutional redefinition of the Empire. Yet his hopes for closer consultations with London were dashed the following year by the Chanak crisis in the Dardanelles. Hughes found himself pledging Australian support for British troops threatened by Turkish nationalists, while completely uninformed on the likelihood of a major conflagration. At the same time—to confirm Australia's exclusion from decision making—a conference in Washington, at which Australia was only welcome as part of an imperial delegation, was determining ratios of warships to be held by the major powers in the Pacific.

Hughes's reaction to the Washington conference confirmed the tangle of entwined issues in Australia's overseas relations. On the one hand, he welcomed the result as a significant contribution towards peace in the Pacific; but on the other hand, he warned that the 'beginning and end' of Australia's safety lay in partnership with the British Empire.[41]

Under Hughes's conservative successors Australia in the 1920s remained firmly bound to the Empire for its orientation in international affairs. The war had fostered the sense of 'race' patriotism, which underlay Australians' identification with Britain and, as we shall see in the following chapter, had made it possible for the non-Labor forces to appropriate Australian nationalism, equating it with loyalty to Britain and the Empire. This made it far more difficult for those who perceived the dangers of overreliance on the Royal Navy to alert the nation to the need for Australia to take a lead in establishing security in the Pacific.

Australian leaders were therefore destined in the interwar years to devote most of their energies to strengthening the British 'partnership' and to resisting attempts to dilute imperial commitments. For all the furore and high profile of Hughes in London and Paris, the First World War was not an agent of profound change in Australia's perceptions of its role in the world.

Notes

1 J. G. Latham, *The Significance of the Peace Conference from an Australian Point of View*, Melville & Mullen, Sydney, 1920, p. 3.

2 Neville Meaney, *The Search for Security in the Pacific, 1901–14: A History of Australian Defence and Foreign Policy 1901–23*, vol. 1, Sydney University Press, Sydney, 1976, p. 261.

3 Donald Horne, *In Search of Billy Hughes*, Macmillan, South Melbourne, 1979, p. 102.

4 The best general study on this question is Roger Thompson, *Australian Imperialism in the Pacific: The Expansionist Era 1820–1920*, Melbourne University Press, Melbourne, 1980.

5 I. H. Nish, 'Australia and the Anglo-Japanese Alliance, 1902–11', *Australian Journal of Politics and History*, vol. IX, 1963, p. 201–12.

6 Neville Meaney, 'Australia's Foreign Policy: History and Myth', *Australian Outlook*, vol. 23, 1969, p. 173; Meaney, *The Search for Security*, p. 266.

7 T. B. Millar, *Australia in Peace and War: External Relations 1788–1977*, Australian National University Press, Canberra, 1978, p. 21.

8 L. F. Fitzhardinge, *The Little Digger, 1914–1952: William Morris Hughes: A Political Biography*, vol. II, Angus & Robertson, Sydney, 1979, pp. 144–6.

9   Wm Roger Louis, 'Australia and the German Colonies in the Pacific, 1914–1919', *Journal of Modern History*, no. 4, 1966, pp. 407–21, at p. 412. See also Thompson, *Australian Imperialism*, pp. 207–8; Fitzhardinge, *Little Digger*, pp. 168–70; Peter Spartalis, *The Diplomatic Battles of Billy Hughes*, Hale & Iremonger, Sydney, 1983, pp. 26–7, 48–9. For the text of Hughes's letter of February 1917, see Neville Meaney (ed.), *Australia and the World: A Documentary History from the 1870s to the 1970s*, Longman Cheshire, Melbourne, 1985, pp. 241–4.

10 Louis, 'Australia and the German Colonies'; D. K. Dignan, 'Australia and British Relations with Japan, 1914–1921', *Australian Outlook*, vol. 21, no. 2, 1967, pp. 135–50; Robert Thornton, 'Invaluable Ally or Imminent Aggressor? Australia and Japanese Naval Assistance, 1914–18', *Journal of Australian Studies*, no. 12, 1983, pp. 5–20.

11 The Monroe doctrine derived from a speech by US President James Monroe in 1823, wherein he claimed that American continents were to remain free from any form of European annexation, and that any attempt to extend European political systems to the Americas would be considered as a threat to American security.

12 The three most comprehensive accounts of the Paris conference from the Australian perspective are Spartalis, *Diplomatic Battles*, pp. 122–92; Fitzhardinge, *Little Digger*, pp. 370–418; W. J. Hudson, *Billy Hughes in Paris: The Birth of Australian Diplomacy*, Nelson, Melbourne, 1978, pp. 1–80. See also Malcolm Booker, *The Great Professional: A Study of W. M. Hughes*, McGraw Hill Book Co., Sydney, 1980, pp. 249–68. Contrast all of these with personal accounts such as, Lord Hankey, *The Supreme Control at the Paris Peace Conference*, Allen & Unwin, London, 1963; Edward Mandell House and Charles Seymour (eds), *What Really Happened at Paris: The Story of the Peace Conference, 1918–1919, by American Delegates*, Charles Scribner's Sons, New York, 1921; and David Lloyd George, *The Truth About the Peace Treaties*, vol. I, Victor Gollancz, London, 1938.

13 H. W. V. Temperley (ed.), *A History of the Paris Peace Conference*, vols 1–6, Oxford University Press and the Royal Institute of International Affairs, London, 1920–24 (reprinted editions, 1969). See volume 6, pp. 335–67, for the section, 'The British Dominions'; David Stevenson, *The First World War and International Politics*, Oxford University Press, Oxford, 1988, pp. 252–3, 257–8, 272.

14 David Low, *The Billy Book: Hughes Abroad*, New South Wales Bookstall Co., Sydney, 1918; W. M. Hughes, *Policies and Potentates*, Angus & Robertson, Sydney, 1950, pp. 155–67, 185–91, 197–8, 236–49; W. M. Hughes, *The Splendid Adventure: A Review of Empire Relations within and without the Commonwealth of Britannic Nations*, Ernest Benn Ltd, London, 1929, pp. 78–116.

15 Spartalis, *Diplomatic Battles*; Fitzhardinge, *Little Digger*; Hudson, *Billy Hughes*.

16 Spartalis, *Diplomatic Battles*, pp. 122–92; Fitzhardinge, *Little Digger*, pp. 370–418; Hudson, *Billy Hughes*, pp. 1–80.

17 W. J. Hudson, *Australia and the League of Nations*, Sydney University Press, Sydney, 1980, p. 19.

18 In Meaney, *Australia and the World*, pp. 259–60.

19 In Fitzhardinge, *Little Digger*, p. 396.

20 Seth P. Tillman, *Anglo-American Relations at the Paris Peace Conference of 1919*, Princeton University Press, Princeton, 1961, p. 407.

21 Fitzhardinge, *Little Digger*, pp. 390–2.

22 Spartalis, *Diplomatic Battles*, p. 183.

23 Hudson, *Billy Hughes*, pp. 28–9; Louis, 'Australia and the German Colonies', pp. 420–1; L. F. Fitzhardinge, 'W. M. Hughes and the Treaty of Versailles, 1919', *Journal of Commonwealth Political Studies*, vol. 5, 1967, pp. 130–41, at pp. 140–1.

24 George W. Egerton, *Great Britain and the Creation of the League of Nations: Strategy, Politics, and International Organization, 1914–1919*, University of North Carolina Press, Chapel Hill, 1978, pp. 103–8; Michael L. Dockrill and J. Douglas Goold, *Peace without Promise: Britain and the Peace Conferences, 1919–23*, Batsford Academic and Educational Ltd, London, 1981, p. 61.

25 Hudson, *Billy Hughes*, pp. 51–3; Hughes's letter to Watt, 13 Feb. 1919, in Meaney, *Australia and the World*, pp. 281–2.

26 Quoted in Fitzhardinge, *Little Digger*, p. 415.

27 ibid. p. 379.

28 Arno J. Mayer, *Politics and Diplomacy of Peacemaking: Containment and Counterrevolution at Versailles, 1918–1919*, Weidenfeld and Nicolson, London, 1967, pp. 624–5.

29 J. R. Poynter, 'The Yo-Yo Variations: Initiative and Dependence in Australia's External Relations 1918–1923', *Historical Studies*, vol. 14, no. 54, 1979, p. 245.

30 P. G. Edwards, *Prime Ministers and Diplomats; The Making of Australian Foreign Policy, 1901–1949*, Oxford University Press, Melbourne, 1983, p. 32.

31 Hudson, *Australia and the League*, pp. 186–9. See also P. D. Twomey, Australia and the Search for a Stable International Order, 1919–45, PhD thesis, Cambridge University, 1989.

32 Stephen Alomes, *A Nation at Last? The Changing Character of Australian Nationalism 1880–1988*, Angus & Robertson, North Ryde, 1988, pp. 39–60.

33 C. M. H. Clark, *A History of Australia*, vol. VI, *'The Old Dead Tree and the Young Tree Green' 1916–1935 with an epilogue*, Melbourne University Press, Melbourne, 1987, pp. 111–12.

34 W. J. Hudson and M. P. Sharp, *Australian Independence: Colony to Reluctant Kingdom*, Melbourne University Press, Melbourne, 1988, p. 15.

35 Notes of Hughes in the War Cabinet, 14 Aug. 1918, quoted in Hudson, *Billy Hughes*, p. 5.

36 Hudson and Sharp, *Australian Independence*, p. 55.

37 W. K. Hancock, *Smuts: The Sanguine Years 1870–1919*, Cambridge at the University Press, Cambridge, 1962, pp. 496–7; L. F. Fitzhardinge, 'Hughes, Borden, and Dominion Representation at the

Paris Peace Conference', *Canadian Historical Review*, vol. XLIX, no. 2, 1968, pp. 160–9.

38 N. K. Meaney, 'The British Empire in the American Rejection of the Treaty of Versailles', *Australian Journal of Politics and History*, vol. IX, no. 2, 1963, pp. 213–14.

39 C. E. W. Bean, *The A.I.F in France During the Main German Offensive 1918*, vol. V of *The Official History of Australia in the War of 1914–18*, Angus & Robertson, Sydney, 1937, pp. 536–7, 693–701; Floyd Gibbons, *The Red Knight of Germany: Baron von Richthofen, Germany's Great War Airman*, Cassell and Company Ltd, London, 1930, (this edn, 1936), pp. 370–83; Ian Turner, '1914–19' in F. K. Crowley (ed.), *A New History of Australia*, Heinemann, Melbourne, 1974, (reprint 1980), p. 345.

40 Edwards, *Prime Ministers*, pp. 29–65. This theme is a feature of Edwards's book.

41 In Meaney, *Australia and the World*, p. 324.

6   The Anzac legend

Joan Beaumont

Of all the legacies of war none is as subtle and elusive—or as important—as the changes it brings about in people's attitudes. It is this for which the First World War is remembered most clearly in Australia: for the profound private and public grief it caused; for the new sense of national consciousness it created among the Australian population; and most significantly, for the legend of Anzac which it generated. Even three-quarters of a century later the mythology of 1915–18 shapes perceptions of what it is to be Australian.

The stereotype of the First World War soldier (or 'digger') as a superb fighter, something of a larrikin, instinctively egalitarian, distrustful of authority, endlessly resourceful, dryly humorous and above all, loyal to his mates, is deeply entrenched in the popular culture. In the 1990s Anzac Day remains the celebration which more than any other public event epitomises Australia's national day.

How the Anzac legend was created, perpetuated and exploited has therefore been one of the central questions to preoccupy Australian historians of the First World War.

The creation of the legend: C. E. W. Bean and Ellis Ashmead-Bartlett

It is widely agreed that the assumptions about Australian national character which are central to the Anzac legend predated the First World War. The legend was rooted in already well-established national traditions and anxieties. However, the process by which the

Anzac legend developed its particular form began with the Gallipoli campaign of 1915.

Thanks to the liberal attitude of the Allied commander, Hamilton, towards the role of the press in wartime, this campaign was reported by a number of Allied journalists. Among these were C. E. W. Bean, the official Australian war correspondent, and Ellis Ashmead-Bartlett, who represented the British press. Both men watched the landing on 25 April 1915, Bean going ashore with the troops at 9.30 a.m. that day and Bartlett observing the events from a battleship offshore. Their subsequent reports of this and the later months of the Gallipoli campaign sowed the seeds of the Anzac legend.[1]

Ashmead-Bartlett's glowing account of the landing was the first to reach Australian newspapers, on 8 May 1915. In a much-quoted passage Bartlett enthused:

> The Australians . . . rose to the occasion. Not waiting for orders, or for the boats to reach the beach, they sprang into the sea, and, forming a sort of rough line, rushed at the enemy trenches . . . The courage displayed by . . . wounded Australians will never be forgotten . . . In fact, I have never seen anything like these wounded Australians in war before . . . They were happy because they knew that they had been tried for the first time and had not been found wanting . . . There has been no finer feat in this war than this sudden landing in the dark and the storming of the heights.[2]

Bean's corresponding dispatch, which was delayed by bureaucratic complications with the issuing of his press licence, did not reach Australia until 14 May. It was less florid and more detailed than Bartlett's but still it assured the Australian public that their soldiers had proved themselves heroes.

The publication of these press reports set off an extraordinary chain reaction of public euphoria about Gallipoli and the performance of the Australian troops there. Within four days of Bean's report being received, the education authorities in New South Wales had reprinted both his and Bartlett's dispatches for use by senior students in state schools. In Victoria, meanwhile, an enthusiastic tribute to Australian soldiers by Hamilton was reproduced by the Government in a manner which allowed it to be framed and to be inserted in an issue of the *School Paper*, a monthly publication read by all state school students. The celebration of Empire Day, on 24 May, gave politicians, church leaders and newspapers further opportunity to eulogise the exploits of the Anzacs. Even the *Bulletin*, once the voice of bitterly anti-imperial radicalism, endorsed Empire Day and described Ashmead-Bartlett's report as 'a stirring story' which 'thrilled Australia with admiration for her soldier sons'.[3]

In the months that followed, the Anzacs continued to be celebrated, their performance being so exploited by the Hughes Government in its efforts to maximise recruitment that it has been argued, as we shall see below, that the state appropriated the legend of Anzac for its own purposes of ideological hegemony. The major agents developing and refining the legend during the war, however, continued to be the individuals who initiated it, Bartlett and, pre-eminently, Bean.

Although Bartlett became by late 1915 a trenchant critic of the way in which the Gallipoli campaign was managed by the Allied high command, he continued to be lavish in his praise of the Australasian troops. (It should be stressed, however self-evident the point, that, whatever the impression conveyed by some Australian writers, the Anzacs included New Zealanders.) Bartlett did this especially on a lecture tour of Australia which he undertook in 1916. Under the pressure of censorship and financial exigencies which meant he had to ensure the tour was a commercial success, Bartlett highlighted the performance of the Anzacs rather than the inadequacies of the Gallipoli campaign. His final contribution to the creation of the legend was the film he took of the Gallipoli campaign, the only footage taken.

Bean's role was incomparably more significant. Early in the war, in October 1914, he was encouraged by the Minister for Defence, Senator George Pearce, to consider writing a history of the conflict. He devoted himself thereafter almost obsessively to this task, accumulating a vast amount of detail about every campaign (his diary and notes eventually filled 283 notebooks) and living in the trenches with the men so that he could understand their experiences.[4] In May 1919, after being appointed official historian, Bean began what turned out to be the monumental task of writing and editing the multi-volumed work. Although he originally thought this would take only five years, it took twenty-three. The first volume of the official history was published in 1921, the last in 1942. Of the fifteen volumes of the history Bean wrote six, and he played a significant editorial role in at least some of the other volumes. He also published in 1946 a one-volume summary of the official history, *Anzac to Amiens*.

In addition to this prodigious effort, Bean was responsible during the war for the publication of *The Anzac Book*, a compilation of poems, anecdotes and writings by soldiers at Gallipoli which propagated an image of the Australian as tough, ironic, stoical, sardonically humorous, the archetypal bushman and committed to his mates. In the opinion of one historian, it was this book, which enjoyed enormous sales and popularity, rather than Bean's dispatches or official histories, which 'decisively established the image of the "Anzac" in the popular imagination'.[5]

Bean also promoted this view of the Anzac on many public-speaking occasions after the war and was the main inspiration during the interwar years for the planning and establishment of the Australian War Memorial. This he envisaged as being not only a memorial but a museum, commemorating and explaining to later generations the role of Australians in the war. One of the most popular tourist attractions in the 1990s, the War Memorial has arguably played an even more significant role than the official histories in shaping popular memories of the war and enshrining the Anzac legend in public life.[6]

The legend

What was the Anzac legend as articulated by Bean? Its central element was the assertion that the Australian soldier was naturally and unusually competent. One of Bean's purposes in writing the official history was, as he said in 1938, to consider 'How did the Australian people—and the Australian character, if there is one—come through the universally recognized test of this, their first great war?'[7] His answer predictably was that they excelled themselves. The AIF, he claimed on another occasion, stood out in military history

> as one of the most famous fighting organisations of all time . . . it
> has been referred to by at least some competent authorities in
> Germany, England, and America as being—at any rate towards the
> end of the War—the most effective of all the forces on the side of
> the Allies.[8]

Equally important in the Anzac legend, however, were the reasons Bean gave for this fighting prowess of Australians. The soldiers of the First AIF, he argued, made superb fighters not because they had been drilled, trained or disciplined, as were the European armies they fought with and against, but because they were the product of a distinctive way of life and social structure.

Two elements of Australian life were especially important to Bean: the first was the bush; the second, what he believed to be the uniquely egalitarian social structure of Australian society. Some years before the First World War Bean had undertaken, in the course of his work as a journalist, a number of trips to the remote parts of New South Wales. From these experiences he had returned deeply impressed by the qualities of the bushman, convinced that he typified all that was best and most distinctive in Australian life. Bean also concluded that the experience of living in the bush made Australians natural warriors. These ideas, which were published in a series of articles in the *Sydney Morning Herald* in 1907 and as two books, *On the Wool Track* (1910) and *The Dreadnought of the Darling* (1911), permeated Bean's official history. The bush, he claimed, with its good food, benign climate and active life gave Australians a better physique than their European counterparts. It also induced in them the qualities that made them natural and brilliant fighters: independence of mind, inquisitiveness, eagerness to learn, resourcefulness, an ability to make decisions and a skill at scrounging, no matter how difficult the circumstances. The Australian from the bush, Bean claimed, was 'bred to a habit of decision, whereas the mind of the city man was more dependent on the wills of those about him'.[9]

The obvious objection to Bean's views about the influence of the bush on the AIF—namely that the majority of Australians, even in 1914, lived not in the bush but in the cities—he accommodated by arguing that the bush set the standards for the town (a theme that was to preoccupy him throughout his life). Even those Australians who were city bred, he asserted, had some experience of bush life through outdoor activities.

The bush was not the only factor Bean emphasised, and arguably it was not as important in his explanation of the AIF's excellence as some commentators have maintained. Bean appeared in later years to modify his views on the influence of the bush on the AIF and many of his most celebrated comments on the subject were more qualified than historians who quote him out of context allow.[10] On a number of occasions Bean praised the performance of Australian troops that were drawn from the city rather than the bush; and far more significant for Bean than any differences between bush- and town-bred Australians were the physical and attitudinal differences between Australian and British soldiers. Deeply attached though he was to Britain, where he had spent much of his childhood and had been educated, Bean was convinced that Australians were the best of Britons, in the sense that the term was then used, to mean the white Anglo-Saxons of the British Empire.

It can therefore be argued that the bush was ultimately not as important an explanatory factor for Bean as another characteristic of Australian life: its democratic egalitarianism and the implications of this for discipline and leadership.

Bean believed Australia was an unusually classless society, where the 'people came nearer than perhaps any other to forming one class without distinction of birth or wealth'[11]—a judgment which ignored the reality of class divisions which the conscription crisis of 1916–17, described in chapter 2, made so manifest. This, and the fact the AIF was a volunteer army, ensured it was a uniquely democratic and egalitarian military institution. Officers generally sprang from the same social background as the men they commanded. In many cases they were promoted on their own merits. Moreover, contrary to tradition in the British Army, they held commissions within the units in which they had previously served.

In addition to this social mobility, egalitarianism displayed itself in the Australian soldier's attitude to discipline. Notorious for his refusal to salute and for being undisciplined while on leave, the Australian soldier, Bean believed, was conditioned by his social background not to obey orders unquestioningly; nor to accept the authority of officers simply on the basis of blind deference to rank. Officers had to earn their men's respect by manifesting competence and leadership: the essential qualities of the latter were courage and skill in battle, reliability, intelligence, strength of will and, above all, concern for the men the officers led.

Given this stress on what later commentators have called the 'informal authority' of Australian officers, Bean believed that there was a preference in the AIF for handling disciplinary breaches informally—not by formal sanctions such as fines or cancellation of leave, but rather by the methods of the bush, the officer and the digger stripping off the insignia of rank and retiring behind the shed to prove who was superior.

As with Bean's discussion of the influence of the bush, his views on egalitarianism have sometimes been depicted too simplistically. Bean did concede that officers could be selected because of their education and manners (criteria which are clearly determined by class), and he acknowledged that men who had held commissions in the militia or cadets before 1915 were immediately made officers in the AIF without serving in the ranks. He also admitted that there were some social distinctions between men and their officers, at least when they were off duty. But these differences, Bean believed, were more like those 'between the prefects or monitors of a big school and their schoolfellows'.[12] Moreover, such social differences as did exist were virtually abandoned when the AIF went into the front line. Most importantly, whatever the reality of different living conditions, pay and so on, in their daily interactions officers behaved as if they believed that all in the AIF were equal. (This, it might be argued, is the essence of the Australian ethic of egalitarianism which continues to operate as a powerful social conditioner in the late twentieth century: however obvious the existence of class, this cannot be overtly acknowledged or exploited in social interaction.)

The final, and vital, element in Bean's account of the AIF was mateship. In one of his most celebrated passages in the official history, he argued:

> [The Australian] was seldom religious in the sense in which the word is generally used. So far as he held a prevailing creed, it was a romantic one inherited from the gold-miner and the bush-man, of which the chief article was that a man should at all times and at any cost stand by his mate. This was and is the one law which the good Australian must never break.[13]

And when musing at the end of his first volume on the Gallipoli campaign as to why it was that the Australians hung on at Anzac after the landing, Bean gave mateship as the explanation. It was not love of a fight, nor hatred of the Turk, nor loyalty to Australia or Britain; not even the desire for fame. The answer

> lay in the mettle of the men themselves. To be the sort of man who would give way when his mates were trusting to his firmness; to be the sort of man who would fail when the line, the whole force, and the allied cause required his endurance; to have made it necessary for another unit to do his own unit's work; to live the rest of his life haunted by the knowledge that he had set his hand to a soldier's task and had lacked the grit to carry it through—that was the prospect which these men could not face. Life was very dear, but life was not worth living unless they could be true to their idea of Australian manhood.[14]

As this second quotation suggests, Bean saw mateship as more than a form of emotional and physical support for Australian soldiers in combat. It had an almost religious quality and was another key to the success of the AIF. In the absence of more formal and traditional discipline, it was mateship—peer-group pressure, the fear of letting others down—that provided *informal* discipline, making Australians perform and function as an effective fighting force.

Bean is widely recognised to have done 'more than anyone to create the dominant Anzac legend'.[15] However, Bean's views may not have been as influential, had they not been echoed in the writings of other commentators, both Australian and British. General Sir John Monash, who acquired almost cult status among many ex-servicemen in the 1920s, wrote, even before the first volume of Bean's official history had been published, his own account of the battles over which he had presided in a book entitled *The Australian Victories in France in 1918*. In this book he, too, developed the themes of the AIF's social mobility, its democratic traditions and the unique advantages egalitarianism provided for discipline. Extolling the system of promotion from the ranks, Monash argued:

There was thus no officer caste, no social distinction in the whole
force . . . the whole Australian Army became automatically graded
into leaders and followers according to the individual merits of
every man, and there grew a wonderful understanding between
them.

According to Monash, the Australian soldier combined a 'curious
blend of a capacity for independent judgment with a readiness to
submit to self-effacement in a common cause'. He was intelligent,
physically superior, adaptable, imaginative and brave—his bravery
being 'founded upon his sense of duty to his unit, comradeship to
his fellows, emulation to uphold his traditions, and a combative
spirit to avenge his hardships and suffering upon the enemy'.
'[E]asy to lead but difficult to drive', the Australian soldier was
'proof that individualism is the best and not the worst foundation
upon which to build up collective discipline'.[16]

Another potent source of mythology about the Australian soldier
during the war was the popular versifier C. J. Dennis. His *Songs of
a Sentimental Bloke* (published in 1915) and *The Tales of Ginger
Mick* (1916) presented an image of an Australian digger who was
essentially a larrikin. But he was a larrikin that was transformed by
the experience of battle into a hero. Moreover, just as Bean depicted
the AIF as being united by a sense of national identity and purpose,
so Dennis depicted Ginger Mick as experiencing through war a shift
of identity and allegiance from his class to the wider Australian
nation. So popular were Dennis's books, each of which sold over
40 000 copies in the first months after publication and both of which
were produced in pocket editions for the trenches, that Dennis
became known as the Anzac Laureate.[17]

Reinforcing the impact of such Australian works was the fact
that accolades for the AIF came also from distinguished British
sources. The poet John Masefield published an account of Gallipoli
in 1916 in which he described the troops involved in the campaign
as: 'the finest body of young men ever brought together in modern
times. For physical beauty and nobility of bearing they surpassed
any men I have ever seen; they walked and looked like the kings
in old poems.'[18] Masefield's comments, in fact, applied not only to
the Australian and New Zealand troops but also to the Royal Naval
Division, a fact that was usually overlooked in Australian readings
of the text. So, too, was the fact that Masefield was, at the time of
writing *Gallipoli*, part of the propaganda machine in the United
Kingdom which was intent on presenting the debacle of 1915 in the
best possible light. It is possible that this motivation also underlay
the praise lavished on Australians in 1915–16 by the British press
and by the British commander of the Anzacs, Birdwood, whose

career prospects were closely linked to the reputation of the Australians he led.

The legend and reality

To what degree were these men consciously engaged in myth-making? To what degree were they reflecting the reality of the AIF and its performance in the war?

In the case of Bean, a number of historians have argued that there was an element of conscious myth-making involved in his reporting of the war from 1915 on. In *The Anzac Book*, for example, it has been argued that Bean acted as an 'exceedingly selective editor'.[19] He excluded from the publication any writings that conveyed the danger, the brutality, the suffering, the fear and cowardice within the AIF, the tension between officers and men, the waste of life and the dehumanising effects of war on the Gallipoli Peninsula. On the other hand, Bean included those entries which promoted the image of the digger he favoured: that is, the Australian soldier as tough, ironic, good-humoured, stoical, casually indifferent to enemy fire, a bushman, and gallant in his sporting recognition of the enemy. The last of these qualities was introduced to *The Anzac Book* by Bean himself, and did not figure in any of the literary contributions from the troops.

Similarly, in the official history of the war Bean tailored his account of the Australian soldier to fit his preconceived notions about the Australian character. Despite his passion for factual accuracy, he has also been criticised for sanitising his account of the war. His official history excluded 'the real and ugly face of battle',[20] omitting some of the less savoury aspects of Australians in conflict, such as the killing of prisoners of war and self-inflicted wounds, even though Bean had himself recorded examples of these practices in the diary he kept in the trenches. Moreover, in order to stress the natural fighting qualities of the Australians, Bean underestimated the role of factors like weaponry, training, logistics and leadership in determining the outcome of the war.[21]

Critics of Bean who have argued this case have themselves been taken to task for an incomplete reading of his work.[22] The debate has threatened at times to descend into an arid campaign of textual analysis, but it will doubtless continue, such is the extraordinary dominance of Bean in the historiography of the First World War and Australian military history. At this stage there is a strong case that Bean shaped his account of the AIF in a way which reflected not only his sympathy for the ordinary soldier as opposed to the generals (his is often called an 'democratic' or 'personalised' military history because of its focus on the front-line infantryman rather than on the high command and staff work)[23] but which also promoted a mythologised image of the AIF.

What, then, of the central elements of the legend he cultivated: the superior fighting capacity of Australians, their mateship and their egalitarianism? How much substance is there in these claims?

Australian historians are fond of trying to 'prove' the claim that the AIF was a very effective fighting force by citing various forms of evidence: the first is the complimentary assessment of Australians by soldiers of other nationalities—or even better, the German enemy. Hamilton, for example, is quoted as writing to the King's private secretary, that the Australians 'although hopeless from our point of view as regards punctilio . . . and although having, to put it mildly, a very good opinion of themselves, yet . . . are indisputably splendid fighting stuff'. There were many similar comments by senior British commanders, and even a revisionist historian such as E. M. Andrews concludes that the praise of Australians by senior British officers, though possibly self-motivated in some cases, was 'too widespread to doubt'.[24]

There is also quotable 'evidence' about the AIF's superiority in the work of foreign military historians. The British historian, M. R. D. Foot, for example is quoted by an Australian author as claiming in 1961 that 'The Anzacs . . . were probably, man for man, the most impressive combatants this century has seen . . . Everyone . . . who saw them in action was struck by their air of mastery over themselves and their surroundings; and their sons showed similar qualities in the second World War.'[25] The fact that Foot cites no evidence to support this claim is, however, overlooked.

Historians have also tried to establish Australians' military superiority quantitatively. In the final months of the war, for example, it has been claimed[26] that the Australian Corps took 29 144 prisoners and 338 guns and liberated 116 towns and villages. This represented 22 per cent of the captures of the entire British Expeditionary Force in this period, when Australians formed only 9 per cent of the BEF in the line. The value of such statistics might be questioned: can we make any valid comparisons of the performances of different units of the Allied forces without being assured that the defences and troops which faced them, the terrain over which they were fighting, and the equipment they had available to them were in all respects comparable?

Australian forces, as we saw in chapter 1, undoubtedly did play a significant role in the campaigns of 1918 which led to the breaking of the German Army. Yet, earlier in the war their performance was much more uneven.[27] Even when this performance improved in 1917–18 this was not simply, or even primarily, the result of any natural fighting ability that Australian soldiers may have had. Natural skill, initiative and resourcefulness were only some of the many elements required for success on the Western Front. The Australian Corps succeeded in 1918 because its soldiers, like those of all other nationalities, had been trained in more sophisticated tactics. The armies of which they were part had developed new technology, new techniques of artillery bombardment, and much better planning and organisation at the command level. Of none of these new skills did Australians, either at the level of the infantry unit or high command, have a monopoly.

As for the reality behind other tenets of the Anzac legend—the cavalier attitude to discipline, the AIF's egalitarianism and mateship—these are difficult to test because of their inherent subjectivity. Australian writing on these subjects has tended to lack rigour, sometimes citing Bean himself as the source of supposedly empirical evidence.[28] Australians have also failed to make the detailed comparisons with other armed forces that might give their conclusions perspective.

The question of promotion of officers from the ranks illustrates this. It is true that the majority of officers in the AIF were, as Monash claims, promoted from the ranks. Indeed, after January 1915 the only means of entering the AIF was by enlistment as a private soldier. By 1918, therefore, Jeffrey Grey estimates, the majority of battalion commanders and company commanders had risen from the ranks. This, however, was not necessarily a reflection of any particular social egalitarianism within the AIF. It was rather a response to the rapid expansion of the AIF from two to five divisions in 1916 and to the crippling losses of junior and non-commissioned officers in the campaigns of 1916–17. Nor was promotion from the ranks, as Monash implied, something distinctively Australian. The British Army, too, came to depend increasingly on short-service commissions from the ranks as the war cut a swathe through its officers.[29]

As for the Australian soldiers' discipline—or more precisely, their lack of it—there is a wealth of evidence that the AIF had a reputation, at least among British officers, for being 'hard-fighting, hard-drinking, and wild-living' when not in the front line.[30] Their casual attitude towards military authority and their dislike of military police was also widely commented on. Supporting this, often anecdotal, evidence are statistics indicating that Australian troops committed a disproportionate number of military offences. Of the 182 cases of being absent without leave in the Fourth Army in December 1916, 130 were Australian. Early in 1917, meanwhile, three Australian divisions recorded roughly twelve times more absent without leave convictions than were proved against the other

22 divisions of the Third Army. These statistics may have been inflated by the fact that some members of the AIF were recurring offenders who were sent back to the line after serving their sentences only to go absent without leave again. The refusal of the Australian Government to follow the British practice of using the death penalty for desertion and the high proportion of front-line troops in the AIF may also have contributed to these figures. Yet, even allowing for this, there seems incontrovertible evidence that Australians had 'an endemic dislike of the military'.[31]

This evidence, however, casts little light on the question which is central to the Anzac legend: was there some nexus between the informality and casualness of Australian attitudes towards military discipline in the rear areas of the battle zone and their supposed competence as fighters? Did their disciplinary offences spring from the same individualism and initiative which was the key to their fighting skills at the battle front? Bill Gammage, in his classic account of the Australian soldiers in the Great War, suggests it was: 'Australian success in battle was largely attributable to that same unrelenting independence which so regularly offended law and authority'.[32] Yet, in the end such hypotheses are incapable of being proven empirically.

So, too, it might be argued, are some of the more extreme claims about the Australian capacity for mateship. Undoubtedly there were strong bonds of friendship and deep emotional ties between soldiers in the AIF. To suggest otherwise is to fly in the face of a mass of personal testimony. But was this mateship peculiarly Australian? This is the implication in the work of T. Inglis Moore and Russel Ward, who trace the mateship of the AIF back to the convict experience and bush days of Australian history.[33]

The sociology of military institutions, however, indicates that all fighting forces, whatever their nationality, develop systems of social support in which groups of soldiers are bonded tightly together by comradeship and the practical need to remain a cohesive unit in combat. Mateship is only the Australian name for an almost universal phenomenon. Canadians, New Zealanders and other armies of the First World War lay claim to similar qualities on the part of their soldiers.

The consensus, therefore, among historians of the AIF is that the Australian force did not have the uniqueness that the proponents of the legend claim, except in one significant respect: that it remained a voluntary force throughout the war. To quote Ken Inglis:

> Comradeship is the cement of any army. Initiative and
> egalitarianism were prized as distinctive virtues among soldiers
> from other democracies fielding citizen armies. Nearly every

ingredient of the Australian tradition was found also in New
Zealand perceptions. All except one, and that one was more prized
among Australians by the end of the war than I think has been
later recognized. In 1915 an army composed entirely of volunteers
was not unusual. By 1918 the Australian force was alone among
armies on either side in remaining so.[34]

The power of the legend

In the end, attempts to establish the basis in reality for the Anzac
legend are not especially productive. What matters is not so much
whether the legend was true as why it was believed by Australians
to be so. Why did it acquire such force and persuasiveness in
Australian culture? As Alistair Thomson says: 'Memory is a
battlefield. We fight within ourselves to make a particular
memory of our experiences, and to repress alternative memories.
We also engage in a public struggle between different versions
of the past.'[35]

The Anzac legend is only one version of the Australian experience of the First World War. Why did it gain such immediate
acceptance? How did it continue to be transmitted from one generation to another? Why did it become the dominant memory of the
war?

These questions themselves raise the problem of the source and
nature of legends within any society. In discussions of Anzac, it
should be said that the term 'legend' is used rather loosely. Dictionary definitions assert that legends are in the first instance
unhistorical or unauthentic, though in time they acquire the status
of being historical. Proponents of Anzac, of course, have claimed
from 1915 on that much of the 'legend' was factual. However, as
we have seen, many of its key elements are essentially subjective
and unverifiable: in this sense Anzac does have the qualities of a
legend, as traditionally defined. Given the political purposes to
which it was later put, Anzac also acquired some of the characteristics of a myth, as this was defined by the anthropologist Bronislaw
Malinowski in 1926, in that it became a story about the past which
served as a 'charter' for the present, justifying later institutions and
keeping them in being.

To what degree do such legends and myths arise spontaneously?
How much are they manufactured or exploited by dominant institutions within society, and especially by the organs of the state, for
purposes of social and political control?

Amongst historians of Anzac, answers to these questions have
been diverse. Often they combine elements of both the spontaneous

growth of the legend and the deliberate cultivation and exploitation of it by the state and the hegemonic class—a fact which reflects that the two processes were in reality intricately intermeshed. There is a general agreement that the Anzac legend found a ready acceptance within Australian society because it drew on already established attitudes and beliefs. To use the words of the contemporary anthropologist Bruce Kapferer, it achieved significance through 'a structure of ideological interpretation already integral to the organization of Australian society'.[36]

Pre-eminent among these attitudes was a commitment to egalitarianism and mateship as the dominant ethic of social interaction within Australia. Russel Ward, in his profoundly influential *The Australian Legend* (1958), followed Bean in depicting the Anzac legend as the apotheosis of the bush legend,[37] that celebration of the 'truly Australian' character that had been popularised in the late nineteenth century by the *Bulletin* and writers such as 'Banjo' Paterson and Henry Lawson. Ward, however, went further than Bean, arguing that there was a continuum between the convicts, the diggers of the gold rushes, and the bushrangers of earlier Australian history: all of these manifested and progressively developed the egalitarian collectivism, mateship, manly independence and disrespect for authority that characterised the Anzacs.

This interpretation has been challenged. Mateship, John Carroll suggests, sprang not from the convicts who were 'if anything egoistical, delinquent types, out for themselves, and showing little inclination or capacity for companionship, or indeed constancy of any form'. The bushrangers and gold diggers likewise, in Carroll's opinion, were an unlikely source for mateship. Rather than egalitarianism and mateship developing from some uniquely Australian experience, it is more probable that they were deeply rooted in the British and Irish working class, and imported to Australia by these 'victims of economic subordination' when they emigrated.[38]

In dispute between these historians, it should be noted, is the source of the egalitarian-mateship ethic, rather than its importance as an influence on Australian society. On the latter there is a consensus. A widespread commitment to an ethic of egalitarianism in pre-1914 Australia provided fertile ground on which the legend of Anzac could fall.

This ground was also fertile, it has been argued, for a number of other reasons: firstly, the timing of the war itself. The conflict occurred shortly after Australia had become a federation and at time when, it has been suggested, Australians were searching for a sense of what it was to be a nation, as opposed to a collection of colonies. The exploits of the Anzacs 'provided a sort of terrible richness to the Australian people in what had essentially been a life of emotional poverty in terms of nationality'.[39]

The celebration of the Anzacs is also thought to have tapped a widespread concern in early twentieth-century Australian society about national eugenics. As noted in earlier chapters, an obsession with racial purity and national wholesomeness,[40] which manifested itself in the racially exclusive immigration policy of White Australia, was linked to a social Darwinian belief that struggle and war were the greatest tests of a nation's virility. The performance of the Australians at Gallipoli confirmed that they were not effete. The British stock had not been corrupted by life in the antipodes.

It has also been suggested that the celebration of Anzac drew on cultural values that were not simply Australian but common to a wider Western tradition. Because of Gallipoli's geographical location, and the fact that the enemy was the Turk, the First World War had overtones of the great Crusades against the infidel in the Middle Ages and of a battle in defence of 'civilisation'. The Anzacs, according to Kapferer,

> established an identity for Australia in the context of the very ideological and ontological roots of the Western Judeo-Christian civilization . . . The journey of the Anzacs to the Dardanelles took them to the source of Western civilization where, in the ideological imagination of the Anzac chroniclers, both of the time and in more popular accounts of today, political democracy began, rational thought took root, and great literature flowered . . . The Anzacs symbolize in their youth the rebirth of the very soul of Western civilization and their embodiment of its fundamental ideals.[41]

This is perhaps overstrained.[42] Yet, allusions to the Greek classical tradition were an element of the Anzac legend from its earliest days, starting with the work of John Masefield and continuing through Australian war literature.[43]

Similarly, there have been linkages from the earliest days of the Anzac legend with Christianity. The first Anzac Day anniversary in 1916 coincided with Easter. The impact of these celebrations was enhanced by their virtually overlapping with 'the traditionally widespread public re-enactment of ancient Christian drama of death and resurrection. The analogies, and the interpretive possibilities which this presented were obvious.' The first celebrants of Anzac Day therefore, R. Ely argues, 'had little trouble *finding* just what to do and say'. Anzac Day was not so much invented as 'effortlessly discovered'.[44]

These linkages between Christian ritual and Anzac were reinforced at the institutional level by the enthusiastic involvement of the Protestant clergy in support for the war effort. As we saw earlier, Protestant churchmen accepted the war as part of God's plan for Australia, as a means by which men would be elevated to a higher plane of moral existence through sacrifice, suffering and devotion to duty. Support for the war became 'an act of high Christian virtue'.[45]

Yet this picture of a natural identification between Christianity and Anzac needs to be qualified. Because of the identification of many Catholics with the anti-conscriptionist cause, Catholic clergy distanced themselves from the public celebration of Anzac. Many scholars of Anzac have also noted an intriguing tension between the secular and sacred in the legend. The major war memorials in Sydney, Melbourne and Canberra rely for their imagery not so much on Christian symbolism but on classical traditions—ancient Greece and the tradition of stoic patriotism.[46] (This, interestingly, is in contrast to New Zealand where there was a greater tolerance of Christian symbols in public monuments.)[47] Moreover, Australian soldiers, the subjects of the legend, were often noted for their irreligion. This manifested itself in their humour and their casual disrespect for the Holy Land in which the Light Horse served. An often-quoted story depicts an Australian Light Horseman, who on being shown the tomb of St Jerome at Bethlehem in 1918 and being told that the oil lamp on the top had been burning for five hundred years, says: 'Well . . . it's high time it had a rest'—and blows it out.[48]

Kapferer has seen this irreligion as self-conscious, a virtually intentional rejection by Australian soldiers of Christianity which seemed to them to be part of the disciplinary framework of the military. For him, as for Ken Inglis, Anzac itself became a secular or civil religion, proof that the dominant religion in modern nation states is nationalism. In this context it is significant that the word 'Anzac' acquired protection in the interwar years under government legislation, to prevent its being used in a commercial or blasphemous manner.

All these interpretations of the Anzac legend operate on some level of generalisation, focusing on cultural and social values common to at least significant sections of Australian society. The power of Anzac, however, must also be understood at the level of the emotions of the private individual. For many Australians the overwhelming response to the First World War was grief. For a number of reasons bereavement for Australians was even more painful than it would naturally have been. Government policy precluded bringing home for burial the bodies of soldiers killed in France and the Middle East. The vast distances and the cost of travel meant that very few Australians could visit the graves of the sons, fathers and husbands whom they had lost in the war. Many did not even know the location of the graves: the terrible injuries inflicted by artillery and the pulverising of bodies in No Man's Land meant that countless thousands of those killed had no known graves. Australians, therefore, sought consolation in private remedies such as spiritualism, attempting to communicate with the dead. The immense popular appeal of Will Longstaff's 1927 painting, *The Menin Gate at Midnight*, which depicts the dead of Ypres rising from the grave, is testimony to the power of this private hope of reunion with the dead.

Publicly this grief expressed itself in the erection of war memorials. These sprang up not only in the capitals but in almost every country town and municipality, sometimes while the war was still continuing. It is clear that in some instances these memorials were linked to the politics of the war: the majority of Australian war memorials, unlike those of New Zealand, list not only the dead but also those who volunteered, a reflection of the fact that, after the defeat of the conscription referenda, it was considered significant to have simply served in the war. Memorials erected during the war were therefore part of public campaigns to stimulate recruitment. That said, war memorials remain a powerful public testimony to private grief. As White says, at the public level war memorials are 'a testament to the undignified clamour for the right to define national identity; but at a private level, where they represent a community's response to war, they are memorials to a trauma that would not go away'.[49]

For communities thus traumatised, the Anzac legend must often have had an instinctive appeal. The fact that it celebrated and glorified the men who had been lost provided some solace to those who remained to grieve.

The transmission of the legend

Families of the men who died and of those who returned became then a means by which the Anzac legend was cultivated and transmitted from one generation to another within Australian society. In many instances this inheritance must have been an ambivalent and complex one. Many families were confronted with the return of a wounded man. For them the legacy of the war was not heroic but rather the pain of men crying out in the night as they relived the terror of artillery bombardment; men struggling to cope with amputations, impairment and disfigurement; men coughing their way to a premature death, thanks to the effects of poison gas. The death toll of the war was not limited to the battle casualties of 1914 to

1918. Throughout the 1920s and 1930s huge numbers of veterans died prematurely. Many suffered mental breakdown; suicides were not uncommon.[50] In this there was little to celebrate. Yet, as Patsy Adam-Smith's introduction to her eulogising account of the Anzacs reveals, even here was a place for the legend:

> We grew up in a wrenching dichotomy of deep pride and bewildering discomfort; we lived in a world of proud April days when we wore our father's medals to school, in moments of thrilling, chilling excitement as the Last Post died away, the bugle silenced, and we stood with bowed heads beneath our family names on the ugly stone memorial in our little town . . . We lived in a world where men were called 'Hoppy', 'Wingy', 'Shifty', 'Gunner', 'Stumpy', 'Deafy', 'Hooky', according to whether they lost a leg, an arm (or part of one), an eye, their hearing, or had a disfigured face drawn by rough surgery into a leer. A world where the smell of suppurating sores (we called them 'running') and Rexona ointment was not unknown and where our parents' friends or relatives graduated from crutches to squeaky 'wooden' legs.[51]

As this indicates, the education system complemented the family as a means of transmitting and shaping memories of the war. As we saw in chapter 3, schoolchildren were actively conscripted to the patriotic cause from the earliest days of the conflict. The education authorities encouraged them to produce a vast range of items to be sent to the troops in Turkey, Palestine and France, and to raise funds for comforts for the armed forces. Children produced flowers, eggs and vegetables; gathered scrap material, old clothes and waste paper; collected books, magazines and other marketable items. They provided food and toiletries to the wounded in hospitals in Australia. They even collected leeches from the swamps and ponds for use in medical treatment of wounded ex-servicemen.

Through all this children were fed a constant diet of literature glorifying the heroism of Australian forces and extolling the virtues of the British Empire.[52] As we have seen, the first accounts of the Anzac landing were widely circulated among schools. The first anniversary of Anzac Day was commemorated by the Education Department of Victoria with a special medallion which students were encouraged to buy. Children were enlisted for public demonstrations of loyalty such as the forming on the Melbourne Cricket Ground of the word 'Anzac'. Honour boards listing former students in the AIF were erected in many schools; textbooks featured stories and poems about the Anzacs and their heroic feats. And every morning at assembly in every Victorian school, children sang, to the tune of 'God Save the King':

God bless our splendid men,
Send them safe home again,
God save our men.
Keep them victorious,
Patient and chivalrous,

They are so dear to us:
God save our men.

In the years after the war this socialisation continued, with the progressive ritualisation of Anzac Day and the perpetuation of the Anzac legend in teaching materials. To quote from a history textbook of 1925:

the courage and steadiness of the Australians proved equal to this exacting trial, and their part [in the landing of 25 April] was performed with a valour that placed them at once among the very best of the Empire's soldiers, able to face the most desperate situation with magnificent bravery.[53]

Anzac Day became a public holiday in all States between 1921 and 1927. Its commemoration varied from place to place in some details but central to the ritual, in schools and elsewhere, were two minutes' silence and the reciting of Laurence Binyon's elegy, 'For the Fallen', which begins, 'They shall grow not old, as we that are left grow old'.

It is debatable how effective was all this effort on the part of the state to inculcate children with its version of the war. According to L. L. Robson, Anzac acquired a semi-religious quality:

school children for nearly two generations were made to feel a sense of awe. Children were not always quite sure why Australians had landed at Gallipoli and fought there and elsewhere, but nevertheless were made to realize that something of the utmost importance had occurred. They were told of the virtues of the soldiers, and especially about the sacrifice of the dead, of their bravery and honourable conduct, and the children were urged to emulate them in those qualities.[54]

But was this a universal experience? Almost certainly children's reactions to Anzac depended on what kind of school they attended, their family's politics and religion, how the particular teachers mediated the messages, and whether the students were girls or boys.[55]

Within the wider adult society the legend was promoted partly through the means of Bean's official history. Long though its many

volumes were, they were written and marketed with the intention
of ensuring that they would be widely read and enjoyed. Commercial travellers from the War Memorial approached individuals
offering to sell them the complete set and public servants were able
to subscribe by having a few shillings deducted from each
fortnight's pay. By 1942, 150 000 copies of the official history had
been sold while Bean's concise version of the war history entitled
Anzac to Amiens, published in 1946, sold 13 250 copies in the next
twenty-three years.[56]

Of course, again the impact of such publications might be
debated. How many people actually read them, even if they had
them on their shelves? Nonetheless, whatever its private usage, the
official history acquired the status of the definitive account of the
First AIF. As we have seen, historians still use it, for want of any
more detailed or effective account, as the source for their descriptions and evidence of the war.[57] Radio programs, newspaper articles
and films likewise also came to rely heavily on it. Even in 1981
the film *Gallipoli* used Bean's account, in his second Gallipoli
volume, as the source for its depiction of the charge of the Light
Horsemen at the Nek.

In this way, a process progressively took place in Australian
society over the decades whereby, to use Alistair Thomson's words,
private memories became 'scrambled and entangled by the legend'.
Even those Australians whose experience and memories of the war
may have been different from that depicted by Bean came to some
degree to internalise the version of events portrayed in the legend.[58]
While the war was continuing it would appear that some Australian
soldiers at Gallipoli and on the Western Front began to model their
behaviour on the complimentary accounts of the AIF's performance
in newspapers and elsewhere. Later, when the Second World War
broke out, many of the younger generation had a sense that they
were the heirs to the Anzac tradition. So far as we can tell from
the oral history of the Second AIF, the name of which quite clearly
reflects the sense of tradition being passed on, many volunteers in
1939–40 felt conscious of the need to model their behaviour on the
legendary qualities of the Anzacs and to live up to the reputation
of their fathers.

The appropriation of the legend

In all of this transmission of the story of Anzac there were elements
of spontaneity and a conscious cultivation of the legend by the state
and other agencies. These elements were also present in the celebration of Anzac within domestic Australian politics. At this level,

however, the conscious manipulation and exploitation of the legend was far more dominant than its organic growth. As the work of radical historians has shown, Hughes and later non-Labor governments appropriated the legend from 1916 on for their own, often cynical, political purposes.

Given the profound divisions in Australian society, there were obvious advantages in promoting Anzac as a focus of national unity. It was a means by which the public's shock and horror at the appalling losses of the war could be assuaged and diverted into channels which did not have the potential to damage the war effort. It is also clear that Prime Minister Hughes and other public agencies were intent on using the glorification of the Anzacs as a means of promoting recruiting. The first celebration of Anzac Day in 1916 was seized upon by recruiting agents, with nine recruiting rallies being held in Sydney to coincide with services on that day. In London, meanwhile, Hughes and his adviser, the journalist Keith Murdoch, orchestrated what one historian has called 'an astute and cynical propaganda exercise'.[59] An impressive service, attended by the King, Queen and the Secretary of State for War, Lord Kitchener, was held at Westminster Abbey, preceded and followed by marches of Australasian troops through the streets of London. This served to mask the disaster of Gallipoli and begin the process whereby Anzac Day was 'taken out of the hands of the opponents of war'.[60]

A central element in this process was the exploitation of returned servicemen and especially the wounded. Peter Cochrane has perceptively noted that Anzac in its formative stages was as much a legend of the wounded as of the dead. Stretcher-bearers, who rescued the wounded at great personal risk, were extolled as the embodiment of the highest form of mateship. The classic illustration of this was John Simpson Kirkpatrick, the private soldier who rescued many wounded at Anzac Cove on the back of his donkey. Although British by extraction and serving less than a month at Gallipoli before he was killed on 19 May 1915, Simpson rapidly became an Australian icon. He was a hero of children's books and his mother and sister were invited to the 1916 Anzac ceremony in London.

In Australia, meanwhile, wounded Anzacs were regularly paraded on the recruiting platforms becoming the 'visual pivot of the "patriotic" cause'. The pro-conscriptionist press in 1916–17 also used the wounded Anzac as 'an instrument of coercion', playing effectively for political purposes on the entwined sentiments of sympathy and obligation.[61]

This appropriation of the legend by politicians and public agencies gained momentum in response to what Hughes and conservatives perceived to be a challenge posed to the social order by returning servicemen. The first Australian soldiers to return from the war arrived in Australia from the Middle East in July 1915. Some had been discharged because of ill health; others were sent home in disgrace for breaches of discipline or for having venereal diseases. It quickly became evident that many of them would not fit back easily into Australian society. Within months ex-servicemen were involved in riots, drunkenness and violence in the streets so regularly that their behaviour had become a cause for press alarm. The lack of job opportunities, despite government promises to give ex-servicemen preference in employment, fuelled the returned soldiers' discontent.

To conservatives, this larrikinism and lack of discipline, which might be tolerated in the battle zone if it were translated into initiative in combat, was deeply threatening at home. Even mateship was considered to have the potential to be 'the spring-board for a new socialist movement', given that socialist writers in the 1890s, such as W. G. Spence and William Lane, had equated socialism with being mates.[62] These fears of conservatives were inflamed when the outbreak of the communist Russian revolution in November 1917 provided radical forces in Australian society with a powerful model for violent change.

The response of the Hughes Government to the radical challenge—its establishment of new surveillance agencies and its increasingly authoritarian suppression of dissent—was considered in chapter 2. Of significance here is the way in which the Government moved to marginalise the radical elements of ex-servicemen opinion. Initially, there sprang up a proliferation of organisations purporting to represent the returned soldier. As with their European counterparts, their inspiration was mixed: there was the need of the wounded and ex-servicemen to find solace in the companionship of those who understood their experiences, to perpetuate the comradeship of war, to care for the families of those who had not returned and to campaign for the benefits which they believed they needed to readjust to civilian life.

A number of these organisations were associated with the politics of the Left, but one that became progressively more conservative, while declaring itself to be above party politics, was the Returned Sailors' and Soldiers' Imperial League of Australia (RSSILA). The Hughes Government, after some vacillation, decided to give this organisation a privileged status.

According to the historian of the RSL (as the RSSILA became), this was because the Government recognised the RSSILA's 'increasing domination of the returned soldier' movement and valued its ability to further repatriation schemes.[63] Marilyn Lake, however, some twenty years later has argued that 'a political compact was negotiated between the government and the RSSILA. In return for defending the "powers that be" from their demobilised forces, the RSSILA would be granted the favour of official recognition'.[64] Representatives of this organisation were authorised to recruit members on the boats returning from the war (as opposed to greeting them on the wharves on their arrival), and eventually the RSL was granted the right, unprecedented for any pressure group before or since, of direct access to the Cabinet. This enabled it to lobby very effectively for ex-servicemen's rights: for pensions, preference in employment over trade unionists and those who had not served in the war, and access to land-settlement schemes. These were the initiatives which the Hughes Government introduced in an effort to defuse the unrest of the demobilised forces.

In all of the RSL's championship of the ex-servicemen's case there was a bedrock of humanitarian concern.[65] Yet, the organisation increasingly became the object of criticism. In the process of defending ex-servicemen's interests, it is claimed, the RSL furthered the appropriation of the Anzac legend for the conservative cause. To quote Alistair Thomson, the political struggle over representation of ex-servicemen was 'intimately connected with the struggle over the memory of the war'.

> The RSL and government committees organized memorial celebrations which offered the status of national heroes to alienated ex-servicemen. The militancy of some working class diggers was channelled into carefully controlled Anzac Day parades. Rituals of remembrance mapped out what could be publicly recalled and silenced alternative memories . . . unemployed ex-servicemen campaigned against the creation of the Melbourne Shrine of Remembrance, arguing that it glorified war and that they wanted a more utilitarian hospital instead. But this and other challenges to the creation of the dominant Anzac legend were defeated, and are now forgotten.[66]

The RSL also went far beyond being the advocate of veterans' privileges to assume a self-appointed role as 'the guardian of Australian security and morality'.[67] It assiduously promoted a conservative view of what it was to be an Australian nationalist. 'True' Anzacs—and by extension 'true Australians'—became defined as those opposed to radicalism and the forces of disorder, especially communism. Loyalty to Australia meant loyalty to the Empire and, in the post–1945 era, to conservative governments who advocated the containment of communism far from Australia's shores in South-East Asia. This deeply conservative bias ensured that the RSL provided many, though by no means all,[68] of the members of the paramilitary organisations that sprang up in Australia in the 1920s and 1930s to counter the 'threat' of communism, if necessary by force.

Thus, it is often claimed, the RSL was instrumental in the process whereby the evolution of a radical Australian nationalism was blunted. As we saw in chapter 5, there was a possibility in the years after 1919 that Australia might capitalise on the new international profile it had gained during the war to play a more independent role in foreign affairs. But it did not. For all the claims of Bean and others that on 25 April 1915 a 'consciousness of Australian nationhood was born',[69] in the interwar years Australia remained deeply dependent on the United Kingdom, resistant to constitutional changes in the Dominions' status and derivative in its foreign policy. The RSL, of course, was not responsible for this. Nor, for that matter, was the war itself. Imperial loyalty was inherent in Australian nationalism well before 1914, as indeed was racism. To quote White:

> 'conservative' nationalism emerged quite naturally from 'radical' nationalism, the *Bulletin* of 1920 was a logical development from the *Bulletin* of 1890. There is no need to find in war a decisive break in the tradition: the racism, misogyny, egalitarianism, larrikinism, exclusiveness, potential violence and selective mateship of the legend were all constant, albeit a little more middle-aged, and as much part of a conservative as radical ideology.[70]

It should also be remembered that the alignment of nationalism with the Right was not something distinctive to Australian politics. It was rather a phenomenon which occurred in many other countries across the world in the interwar years, most notably Fascist Italy and Nazi Germany.[71] Nonetheless the war, as we have seen, created a climate in which the rhetoric of loyalty became dominant in public discourse, and the RSL, closely aligned with the state, became a significant agency confirming this.

The RSL also played a contentious role in elevating the returned soldier to a privileged position in Australian society at the expense of other groups. One of its central objectives in the interwar years was to defend the right ex-servicemen had won to preference in employment. This it did assiduously and with considerable success, since it was in the Government's interest to demonstrate that ex-servicemen had special privileges, thus defusing any claims that they had 'missed out on their natural right to social mobility' by going to the war. But again the influence of the RSL should not be overstated. An analysis of income in 1933 shows that in practice 'there was very little difference at all between [ex-servicemen's] income and what they might have expected had they not enlisted'.[72]

Still, whatever the qualifications, in many respects the legacy of the war and the Anzac legend was a divisive one.[73] Australians were divided into those who had gone to the war and all those who, for whatever reason, had stayed behind. The latter included a number of significant groups in Australian society: men too young or unfit to volunteer; men who performed military duties at home;[74] Aborigines; ethnic minorities who had migrated to Australia in small numbers before 1939 and in much greater numbers thereafter; and, of course, women. The Anzac legend is fiercely masculine:

> The word [Anzac] is a war cry 'pitiless as a hurled spear' says the war correspondent and official historian, F. M. Cutlack. 'It conveys something vaguely masculine, ruthless, resolute, clean driven home'. The RSL[,] says a leader, is 'that compact and experienced male force that is so essential to the healthy and progressive life of our country'. The sacred day, the twenty-fifth of April, is 'like a great tall pillar'.[75]

Beyond its very masculine language, the Anzac legend had the effect, White argues, of consolidating male dominance or hegemony in Australian society by extending the celebration of masculinity from the bush to the city. Before 1914 masculine values had been associated with the bush, while women remained notionally identified with the city, supposedly the preserve of 'feminine' values, such as refinement, conventional morality and polite society. The legend of the war, however, allowed men in the cities to be identified with masculine values. Ginger Mick, the digger portrayed in the Sydney-based *Smith's Weekly*, and the majority of the RSL were all city dwellers.

The exclusion of women from the Anzac tradition was not total. Through the celebration of the wounded, women gained a role—though it was the traditional one of nurturing and caring—as nurses. Organisations such as the Anzac Fellowship of Women sprang up, giving women the chance to promote the 'spirit of Anzac' through cultural competitions in schools and other activities. This participation in Anzac, however, was derivative and marginal. Women's exclusion from the mainstream of the legend was reinforced when commemoration of Anzac became linked with revelry in the all-male environment of the pub and public bar. It should be noted, however, that until 1960 the pubs were shut for the whole of Anzac Day in three out of the six States.

It should also be noted that the masculinity of the legend was defined in a way that excluded some men—that is men who refused to volunteer. A cartoon in the *Bulletin* on 3 February 1916 depicted two young pupils and their female teacher in a Latin class. The small boy, struggling to remember the third gender, neuter, says: 'Masculine, feminine—an' I forget the other, Miss!' At which the young girl pupil interjects, 'Shirker!' There was no place in this definition of Australian manhood for men who stayed at home.

The perpetuation of the legend

Confirmed as the dominant memory of the war and 'a nationalist rite of the people'[76] during the interwar years, the Anzac legend was given a new source of inspiration by the onset of the Second World War in 1939. Again there was a chance for Australians to prove themselves and to demonstrate the capacity of the national character to handle crisis, hardship and danger. Yet the rather problematic, and in some sense anticlimactic, nature of Australia's involvement in this conflict precluded the euphoria of the First World War. Much of the Australian experience of 1939–45 was defeat or surrender: Greece, Crete, Malaya, Singapore, Java, Ambon, Timor and Rabaul. Nearly 30 per cent of Australian deaths in this war were in captivity.[77] This was an experience starkly in tension with the glorification of triumph against the odds and military prowess central to the Anzac legend. Only Tobruk, El Alamein and Kokoda possibly fitted into this heroic mould.

Yet the legend survived, and its power to shape Australian memories of war is clear in the writings of prisoners of the Japanese. Whatever the tension between their experiences and the mythology of Anzac, they often strained to integrate their experience into the legend. Wilfred Kent-Hughes, for example, wrote during his captivity a long poem in classic epic style, scattered with reference to the Anzacs and devoting five pages to describing Anzac Day in Changi prisoner of war camp. Describing the cemetery, he said:

Old Anzac veterans volunteered to keep
The graves in order, where new Anzacs sleep. [78]

If this might be discounted on the grounds of Kent-Hughes's conservatism (he became a minister in the Menzies Government in the 1950s) and middle-class education, consider the account by an Australian private of Anzac Day 1943 at 75 Kilo camp on the Burma–Thailand railway:

Just before dawn a few shadowy forms gathered on the road. The flickering light from crude kitchen fires in the background lighted to mutual recognition the drawn faces of a number of 1914–18 diggers . . . The still solemnity of this Anzac morning—their day

since 1915—garbed their emaciated forms with imagined uniforms
. . . On quiet word of command, ranks were formed, and with
shoulders squared to carry the proud heritage of former years of
freedom and victory, they marched to the accompaniment of
mental martial music . . . to where a large wooden cross had been
erected. A wreath of timid jungle flowers and ferns were reverently
laid before this simple shrine, in memory, not only of the fallen of
1914–18 and of this last war, but also of the all too many mates,
whose resting places were marked by an almost endless chain of
pitiful little wooden crosses throughout the length of this trail of
tribulation. The hush was broken by the haunting notes of the Last
Post . . . Thus, the immortal spirit and legend of Anzac, born on
grim Gallipolean slopes, transcended the barriers of Jap and jungle,
with its inspiration to courage and sacrifice.[79]

In the post-Second World War years Anzac became the target
of criticism and even derision, as the involvement of Australian
troops—and, moreover, conscripts—in Vietnam created divisions in
Australian society comparable to those of 1916 and 1917. Even
before this, in 1961, a questioning of the tradition was evident in
the performance of *The One Day of the Year* by Alan Seymour. In
this play, which was at first banned in response to violent objections
by the RSL, a conflict rages within an Australian family about the
value of Anzac, which the young radical student attacks as a
combination of drunkenness, illusion, prejudice and ignorance.

For children brought up in this period, therefore, Anzac Day
was not so much the inspiring experience it had been for their
fathers, but possibly, as Bill Gammage put it, 'authoritarian, conventional, didactic, and dull'. He continued:

To Australians who could not remember the war, it was a day,
except for the emotions of their parents, much like other holidays,
admittedly more important than any save Christmas, but not really
of special distinction, and certainly not epitomizing Australian
identity.[80]

Yet at the same time as this was happening, within the academic
community historians were discovering the Anzac tradition for the
first time as a subject of serious study. One of these was Bill
Gammage himself, who as a university student in the 1960s became
fascinated by the men of the First AIF and eventually, in 1974,
published *The Broken Years* which was instrumental in revivifying
the legend.

In the 1970s and 1980s the legend re-emerged in the mainstream
of popular culture, being enshrined in film and television in programs such as *1915*. Thereafter, as successive seventy-fifth

anniversaries of various high points of the First World War occurred, the legend was celebrated in an uncritical and often romantic manner.

Of course, by this stage it was a legend which had abandoned much of Bean's detail and certainly its earlier imperial dimension: it had few, if any, roots in the bereavement of individuals. But it was still a legend which was capable of playing its traditional political role, articulating a view about the nature of Australian identity and historical experience which was intended to promote an illusion of national cohesion.

This was manifest in the speech Prime Minister Paul Keating made at the entombment of Australia's Unknown Soldier on the 75th anniversary of the armistice of the First World War, on 11 November 1993. In this speech Keating depicted the Unknown Soldier as a representative not only of the dead of the First World War but of all 100 000 Australians who died in conflicts during this century. 'He is', Keating said, '*all* of them. And he is one of us.' And the essence of the legend in 1993?

> it is legend not of sweeping military victories so much as triumphs against the odds, of courage and ingenuity in adversity. It is a legend of free and independent spirits whose discipline derived less from military formalities and customs than from the bonds of mateship and the demands of necessity.
>
> It is a *democratic* tradition, the tradition in which Australians have gone to war ever since.

Significantly, Keating, himself of Irish Catholic extraction, addressed the problematic exclusivity of the legend in its traditional form: the Unknown Soldier, he said, was interred not

> to glorify war over peace; or to assert a soldier's character above a civilian's; or one race or one nation or one religion above another; or men above women; or the war in which he fought and died above any other war; or of one generation above any that has or will come later.

Yet in the end, the legend was affirmed as a key to Australian identity: 'We have gained legend: a story of bravery and sacrifice and with it a deeper faith in ourselves and our democracy, and a deeper understanding of what it means to be Australian.'

And there was scarcely a voice heard in dissent.

Notes

1   The best account of Ashmead-Bartlett's role in the creation of the
    Anzac legend is Kevin Fewster, 'Ellis Ashmead-Bartlett and the
    Making of the Anzac Legend', *Journal of Australian Studies*, no. 10,
    1982, pp. 17–30.
2   *Argus,* 8 May 1915.
3   For further detail on the public celebration of the landing, see K. S.
    Inglis, 'The Australians at Gallipoli—I' *Historical Studies*, vol. 14,
    no. 54, 1970, pp. 222–4.
4   On Bean, see the entry by K. S. Inglis in the *Australian Dictionary
    of Biography*, vol. 7, *1891–1939 A–Ch*, Melbourne University Press,
    Melbourne, 1979; the introductions to Kevin Fewster's *Gallipoli Cor-
    respondent: The frontline diary of C.E.W. Bean*, Allen & Unwin,
    Sydney, 1983, and Denis Winter's *Making the Legend: The War
    Writings of C. E. W. Bean*, University of Queensland Press, St Lucia,
    1992; and Dudley McCarthy, *Gallipoli to Somme: The story of C. E.
    W. Bean*, John Ferguson, Sydney, 1983.
5   D. A. Kent, '*The Anzac Book* and the Anzac Legend: C.E.W. Bean as
    Editor and Image-maker', *Historical Studies*, vol. 21, no. 84, April
    1985, pp. 376–90.
6   The most detailed account of the history of the War Memorial is
    Michael McKernan, *Here is their Spirit*, University of Queensland
    Press in association with the Australian War Memorial, St Lucia, 1991.
    Useful also is K. S. Inglis, 'A Sacred Place: The Making of the
    Australian War Memorial', *War & Society*, vol. 3, no. 2, 1985, pp. 99–
    126.
7   'The Writing of the Australian Official History of the Great War—
    Sources, Methods and Some Conclusions', *Journal of the Royal
    Australian Historical Society,* vol. XXIV, pt 2, 1938, p. 91.
8   'Sidelights of the War on Australian Character', *Journal of the Royal
    Australian Historical Society*, vol. XIII, pt 4, 1927, p. 211.
9   ibid. p. 222.
10 John Barrett, 'No Straw Man: C. E. W. Bean and Some Critics',
    Australian Historical Studies, vol. 23, no. 89, 1988, pp. 109–10.
11 C. E. W. Bean, *The Story of Anzac*, vol. I of *The Official History of
    Australia in the War of 1914–1918*, Angus & Robertson, Sydney, 1921,
    p. 5.
12 ibid. p. 550. For discussion of Bean's views see L. L. Robson, 'The
    origin and character of the First A.I.F., 1914–1918: some statistical
    evidence', *Historical Studies*, vol. 15, no. 61, 1973, pp. 746–7.
13 *The Story of Anzac*, vol. 1, p. 6.
14 ibid. p. 607.
15 Alistair Thomson, 'The Anzac Legend: Exploring national myth and
    memory in Australia', in Raphael Samuel and Paul Thompson (eds)
    The Myths We Live By, Routledge, London, 1990, p. 73.
16 *The Australian Victories in France in 1918*, Hutchinson, London,
    1920, pp. 291–3.

17 See K. S. Inglis, 'The Anzac Tradition', *Meanjin Quarterly*, vol. 24, no. 1, 1965, pp. 36–8.

18 John Masefield, *Gallipoli*, Heinemann, London, 1916, p. 19.

19 Kent, *'The Anzac Book'*, pp. 376–90.

20 Alistair Thomson, quoted in Barrett, 'No Straw Man', p. 104.

21 Alistair Thomson, 'Steadfast until Death'? C. E. W. Bean and the Representation of Australian Military Manhood', *Australian Historical Studies*, vol. 23, no. 93, 1989, pp. 462–78.

22 See Barrett, 'No straw man'.

23 In the official histories there are 6550 individual biographical sketches of the soldiers Bean mentions by name.

24 *The Anzac Illusion: Anglo-Australian Relations during World War I*, Cambridge University Press, Melbourne, 1993, p. 52.

25 *Men in Uniform*, quoted in Jane Ross, *The Myth of the Digger: The Australian Soldier in the Two World Wars*, Hale & Iremonger, Sydney, 1985, p. 28.

26 Peter Pedersen, 'The AIF on the Western Front: The Role of Training and Command' in M. McKernan and M. Browne (eds) *Australia: Two Centuries of War and Peace*, Australian War Memorial in association with Allen & Unwin Australia, Canberra, 1988, p. 192.

27 See Andrews, *Anzac Illusion*, pp. 144–9.

28 See, for example, Ross, *Myth of the Digger*, p. 57.

29 Jeffrey Grey, *A Military History of Australia*, Cambridge University Press, Melbourne, 1990, p. 92.

30 Ross, *Myth of the Digger*, p. 142.

31 Bill Gammage: *The Broken Years: Australian Soldiers in the Great War*, Penguin, Ringwood, 1975 (first published 1974), p. 236.

32 ibid. p. 237.

33 'The Meanings of Mateship', *Meanjin Quarterly*, March 1965, pp. 45–54. For a strong argument against the uniqueness to Australia of the egalitarian-mateship ethos see John Carroll, 'Mateship and Egalitarianism: The Failure of the Upper Middle-Class Nerve' in John Carroll (ed.) *Intruders in the Bush: The Australian Quest for Identity*, 2nd edn, Oxford University Press, Melbourne, 1992, pp. 143–53.

34 K. S. Inglis, 'Anzac and the Australian Military Tradition', *Revue Internationale d'Histoire Militaire*, no. 72, 1990, p. 4. An example of a Canadian claim that their forces were characterised by 'native talents and abilities to solve problems and overcome obstacles' is found in Stephen Harris, 'From Subordinate to Ally: The Canadian Corps and National Autonomy', *Revue International d'Histoire Militaire*, no. 54, 1982, p. 125.

35 'The Anzac Legend', p. 73.

36 Bruce Kapferer, *Legends of People: Myths of State: Violence, Intolerance, and Political Culture in Sri Lanka and Australia*, Smithsonian Institution Press, Washington, 1988, p. 146.

37 Russel Ward, *The Australian Legend*, Oxford University Press, Melbourne, 1958.

38 Carroll, 'Mateship and Egalitarianism', pp. 146–8.

39 L. L. Robson, 'The Anzac Tradition', *Journal of History*, vol. IV, no. 2, p. 59.

40 See Richard White, *Inventing Australia: Images and Identity 1688–1980*, George Allen & Unwin, Sydney, 1981, chs 7 and 8.

41 Kapferer, *Legends of People*, p. 127.

42 See Ken Inglis, 'Kapferer on Anzac and Australia', *Social Analysis*, no. 29, 1990, p. 71. Kapferer replied to Inglis's criticisms in the same issue ('Nationalist History and the Poverty of Positivism', pp. 74–85).

43 For a detailed discussion of Australian war literature see Robin Gerster, *Big Noting: The Heroic Theme in Australian War Writing*, Melbourne University Press, Melbourne, 1988.

44 R. Ely, 'The First Anzac Day: Invented or Discovered?', *Journal of Australian Studies*, no. 17, 1985, p. 58.

45 Michael McKernan, *Australian Churches at War: Attitudes and Activities of the Major Churches, 1914–1918*, Catholic Theological Faculty and Australian War Memorial, Sydney and Canberra, 1980, p. 110.

46 Inglis, 'The Anzac Tradition', pp. 42–4.

47 See K. S. Inglis and Jock Phillips, 'War Memorials in Australia and New Zealand: A Comparative Study' in John Rickard and Peter Spearitt (ed.) *Packaging the Past? Public Histories*, Melbourne University Press, Melbourne, 1991, p. 191.

48 Gammage, *Broken Years*, p. 140.

49 'War and Australian Society', in McKernan and Browne, *Australia: Two Centuries*, p. 417.

50 The mortality among returned soldiers in the 1930s was 13 per cent higher than among the rest of the population (ibid. p. 416).

51 Patsy Adam-Smith, *The Anzacs*, Nelson, Melbourne, 1982 (first published 1978), p. 3.

52 See *Young Anzacs: The Contribution of Victorian Schools to the Gallipoli Campaign 1915*, Ministry of Education, Victoria, Melbourne, 1990.

53 Joseph Bryant, *Great Events in Australian History*, Cornstalk Publishing, Sydney, 1925 (1st edition 1924).

54 Robson, 'The Anzac Tradition', p. 9.

55 A thoughtful exploration of this question may be found in Inglis, 'Anzac and the Australian Military Tradition', pp. 10–12.

56 K. S. Inglis, 'C. E. W. Bean, Australian Historian', John Murtagh Macrassan Lecture, University of Queensland Press, 1969, pp. 25–6.

57 See, for example, Geoffrey Serle, 'The Digger Tradition and Australian Nationalism', *Meanjin Quarterly*, vol. 24, no. 2, 1965, p. 153 where Serle quotes Bean to demonstrate that the AIF was 'far more democratic than most [armies]'. W. F. Mandle (*Going it Alone*, Penguin Books, Ringwood, Victoria, 1980, first published 1978) similarly relies on Bean for 'evidence' of Australian behaviour and qualities.

58 Thomson, 'The Anzac Legend', p. 77.

59 Peter Charlton, *Pozières: Australians on the Somme, 1916*, Methuen Haynes, Sydney, 1986, p. 66.

60 E. M. Andrews, '25 April 1916: The first Anzac day in Australia and Britain, *Journal of the Australian War Memorial*, no. 23, 1993, p. 19.

61 Peter Cochrane, 'Deliverance and renewal: the origins of the Simpson legend', *Journal of the Australian War Memorial*, no. 16, 1990, pp. 19–21.
62 Marilyn Lake, 'The Power of Anzac' in McKernan and Browne, *Australia: Two Centuries*, pp. 199–201.
63 G. L. Kristianson, *The Politics of Patriotism*, ANU Press, Canberra, 1966, p. 12.
64 'The Power of Anzac', p. 206. See also Lake's *The Limits of Hope: Soldier Settlement in Victoria*, Oxford University Press, Melbourne, 1987.
65 For example, see Morna Sturrock, Gilbert Dyett: Architect of the RSL, MA thesis, Monash University, 1992. Legacy, set up to care for the widows and children of deceased AIF soldiers was similarly motivated by a collective ideal.
66 'The Anzac Legend', pp. 75–6.
67 Noel McLachlan, 'Nationalism and the Divisive Digger', *Meanjin Quarterly*, no. 27, 1968, p. 307.
68 For an effective demolition of the notion that there was a one-for-one nexus between the AIF, the RSL and the New Guard see Humphrey McQueen, 'The Social Character of the New Guard', *Arena*, no. 40, 1975, pp. 67–86. However, for the links between ex-servicemen and right-wing violence immediately after the war see Raymond Evans, ' "Some Furious Outbursts of Riot": Returned Soldiers and Queensland's "Red Flag" Disturbances, 1918–1919', *War & Society*, vol. 3, no. 2, 1985, pp. 75–98.
69 C. E. W. Bean, *The Story of Anzac*, vol. II of *The Official History of Australia in the War of 1914–1918*, Angus & Robertson, Sydney, 1924, p. 910.
70 ibid. p. 399.
71 Michael Roe, 'Comment on the Digger Tradition', *Meanjin Quarterly*, no. 3, 1965, pp. 357–8.
72 Richard White, 'War and Australian Society', in McKernan and Browne, *Australia: Two Centuries*, p. 402.
73 See McLachlan, 'Nationalism', pp. 306–7.
74 As John Hirst shows, this included even men who guarded Australian defences during the war. They were refused permission to join the RSL at the end of the war ('Australian Defence and Conscription: A Re-Assessment, Part I', *Australian Historical Studies*, vol. 25, no. 101, 1993, pp. 608–9).
75 Inglis, 'Anzac and the Australian Military Tradition', p, 13.
76 Kapferer, *Legends of People*, p. 147.
77 Wray Vamplew, *Australians: Historical Statistics*, Fairfax, Syme & Weldon Associates, Broadway, NSW, 1987, p. 415.
78 *Slaves of the Samurai*, Melbourne, Oxford University Press, 1946, pp. 87.
79 Australian War Memorial, Private Records 87/183, p. 28.
80 'Anzac' in Carroll (ed.) *Intruders*, p. 64.

Select bibliography

The Official History of Australia in the War of 1914–1918

Bean, C. E. W. *The Story of Anzac: From the Outbreak of the War to the end of the First Phase of the Gallipoli Landing, May 4, 1915*, Angus & Robertson, Sydney, 1921

——*The Story of Anzac. From May 4, 1915 to the Evacuation of the Gallipoli Peninsula*, Angus & Robertson, Sydney, 1924

——*The AIF in France, 1916*, Angus & Robertson, Sydney, 1929

——*The AIF in France, 1917*, Angus & Robertson, Sydney, 1933

——*The AIF in France During the Main German Offensive, 1918*, Angus & Robertson, Sydney, 1937

——*The AIF in France During the Allied Offensive*, Angus & Robertson, Sydney 1942

Bean, C. E. W. and Gullett, H. S. *Photographic Record of the War*, Angus & Robertson, Sydney, 1923

Cutlack, F. M. *The Australian Flying Corps in the Western and Eastern Theatres of War, 1914–1918*, Angus & Robertson, Sydney, 1923

Gullett, H. S. *The AIF in Sinai and Palestine, 1914–1918*, Angus & Robertson, Sydney, 1923

Jose, A. W. *The Royal Australian Navy, 1914–1918*, Angus & Robertson, Sydney, 1928

Mackenzie, S. S. *The Australians at Rabaul. The Capture and Administration of German Possessions in the South Pacific*, Angus & Robertson, Sydney, 1927

Scott, Ernest *Australia During the War*, Angus & Robertson, Sydney, 1936

Other books and articles

Alcock, J. 'Reasons for the rejection of conscription—1916–17', *Agora*, vol. 7, no. 5, 1973, pp. 185–94

Alomes, Stephen *A Nation at Last? The Changing Character of Australian Nationalism 1880–1988*, Angus & Robertson, North Ryde, 1988

Andrews, E. M. '25 April 1916: The first Anzac day in Australia and Britain', *Journal of the Australian War Memorial*, no. 23, 1993, pp. 13–20

——*The Anzac Illusion: Anglo-Australian Relations during World War 1*, Cambridge University Press, Melbourne, 1993

Attard, B. 'Politics, Finance and Anglo-Australian Relations: Australian Borrowing in London, 1914–1920', *Australian Journal of Politics and History*, vol. 35, no. 2, 1989, pp. 142–63

Bacchi, C. J. 'The Nature-Nurture Debate in Australia, 1900–1914', *Historical Studies*, vol. 19, no. 35, 1980, pp. 199–212

Barrett, John 'No Straw Man: C. E. W. Bean and Some Critics', *Australian Historical Studies*, vol. 23, no. 89, 1988, pp. 102–14

Bassett, Jan 'Ready to serve: Australian women in the Great War', *Journal of the Australian War Memorial*, no. 2, 1983, pp. 8–16

——*Guns and Brooches. Australian Army Nursing from the Boer War to the Gulf War*, Oxford University Press, Melbourne, 1992

Bastian, Peter 'The 1916 conscription referendum in New South Wales', *Teaching History*, vol. 5, pt 1, 1971, pp. 25–36

Bertrand, I. 'The Victorian vote in the conscription referendums in 1916 and 1917; the case of the Wannon electorate', *Labour History*, no. 26, 1974

Boehm, E. A. *Twentieth Century Economic Development in Australia*, Longman Cheshire, Melbourne, 1979

Booker, Malcolm *The Great Professional: A Study of W. M. Hughes*, McGraw Hill Book Co., Sydney, 1980

Brugger, Suzanne *Australians and Egypt, 1914–1919*, Melbourne University Press, Melbourne, 1980

Cain, Frank *The Origins of Political Surveillance in Australia*, Angus & Robertson, Sydney, 1983

——*The Wobblies at War: a history of the IWW and the Great War in Australia*, Spectrum Publications, Melbourne, 1993

Charlton, Peter *Pozières: Australians on the Somme, 1916*, Methuen Haynes, Sydney, 1986

Cochrane, P. *Industrialization and Dependence*, University of Queensland Press, St Lucia, 1980

Cochrane, Peter. *Simpson and the Donkey: The Making of a Legend*, Melbourne University Press, Melbourne, 1993

Crew, Jennifer 'Women's wages in Britain and Australia during the First World War', *Labour History*, no. 57, 1989, pp. 27–43

Coward, D. The Impact of War on New South Wales: Some Aspects of Social and Political History, 1914–17, PhD thesis, ANU, 1974

Damousi, Joy 'Marching to different drums: Women's mobilisations 1914–1939' in Kay Saunders and Raymond Evans (eds) *Gender Relations in Australia: Domination and Negotiation*, Harcourt Brace Jovanovich, Sydney, 1992, pp. 350–75

——'Socialist Women and Gendered Space: The Anti-Conscription and

Anti-War Campaigns of 1914—18', *Labour History*, no. 60, 1991, pp. 1–15

Dignan, D. K. 'Australia and British Relations with Japan, 1914–1921', *Australian Outlook*, vol. 21, no. 2, 1967, pp. 135–50

Docker, John 'Can the centre hold? Conceptions of the state 1890–1925' in Sydney Labour History Group, *What Rough Beast? The State and Social Order in Australian History*, George Allen & Unwin, Sydney, 1982, pp. 57–88

Dyster, B. and Meredith, D. *Australia in the International Economy*, Cambridge University Press, Melbourne, 1990

Edwards, P. G. *Prime Ministers and Diplomats; The Making of Australian Foreign Policy, 1901–1949*, Oxford University Press, Melbourne, 1983

Ely, R. 'The First Anzac Day: Invented or Discovered?', *Journal of Australian Studies*, no. 17, 1985, pp. 41–58

Evans, Raymond *Loyalty and Disloyalty: Social Conflict on the Queensland Homefront, 1914–18*, Allen & Unwin, Sydney, 1987

Fane, C. G. 'The development of monetary institutions in Australia from federation to the Second World War', *Centre for Economic Policy Research Discussion Papers*, no. 227, ANU, Canberra, 1990

Fewster Kevin (ed.) *Gallipoli Correspondent: The frontline diary of C.E.W. Bean*, Allen & Unwin, Sydney, 1983

—— 'Ellis Ashmead Bartlett and the Making of the Anzac Legend', *Journal of Australian Studies*, no. 10, 1982, pp. 17–30

—— 'The Operation of State Apparatuses in Times of Crisis: Censorship and Conscription, 1916', *War & Society*, vol. 3, no. 1, 1985, pp. 37–54

Firth, Stewart and Hoorn, Janet 'From Empire Day to Cracker Night' in Peter Spearitt & David Walker (eds) *Australian Popular Culture*, George Allen & Unwin, Sydney, 1979, pp. 17–38

Fischer, Gerhard *Enemy Aliens: Internment and the Homefront Experience in Australia 1914—1920*, University of Queensland Press, St Lucia, 1989

Fitzhardinge, L. F. 'Hughes, Borden, and Dominion Representation at the Paris Peace Conference', *Canadian Historical Review*, vol. XLIX, no. 2, 1968, pp. 160–9

—— 'W. M. Hughes and the Treaty of Versailles, 1919', *Journal of Commonwealth Political Studies*, vol. 5, 1967, pp. 130–41

—— *The Little Digger, 1914–1952: William Morris Hughes: A Political Biography*, vol. II, Angus & Robertson, Sydney, 1979

Forster, C. 'Australian Manufacturing and the War of 1914–18', *Economic Record*, vol. 29, 1953, pp. 211–30

French, Maurice 'The Ambiguity of Empire Day in New South Wales 1901–1921: Imperial Consensus or National Division?', *Australian Journal of Politics and History*, vol. XX1V, no. 1, 1978, pp. 61–74

Gammage, Bill. 'Anzac' in John Carroll (ed.) *Intruders in the Bush: the Australian Quest for Identity*, 2nd edn, Oxford University Press, Melbourne, 1992, pp. 54–66

—— *The Broken Years: Australian Soldiers in the Great War*, Penguin, Ringwood, 1975 (first published 1974)

Gilbert, Alan 'The Conscription Referenda, 1916–17; The impact of the Irish Crisis', *Historical Studies*, vol. 14, no. 53, 1969, pp. 54–72

Gowland, Pat 'The Women's Peace Army' in Elizabeth Windschuttle (ed.) *Women, Class and History: Feminist Perspectives on Australia 1788– 1978*, Fontana/Collins, 1980, pp. 216–34

Grey, Jeffrey *A Military History of Australia*, Cambridge University Press, Melbourne, 1990

Hagen, J. and Turner, K. *A History of the Labor Party in New South Wales*, Longman Cheshire, Melbourne, 1991

Haig, B. D. 'Manufacturing Output and Productivity 1910 to 1948/9', *Australian Economic History Review*, vol. 15, no. 2, 1975, pp. 136–61

Hirst, John 'Australian Defence and Conscription: A Re-Assessment, Part I', *Australian Historical Studies*, vol. 25, no. 101, 1993, pp. 608–27

Hudson, W. J. and Sharp, M. P. *Australian Independence: Colony to Reluctant Kingdom*, Melbourne University Press, Melbourne, 1988

Hudson, W. J. *Billy Hughes in Paris: The Birth of Australian Diplomacy*, Nelson, Melbourne, 1978

Inglis, K. S. 'A Sacred Place: The Making of the Australian War Memorial', *War & Society*, vol. 3, no. 2, 1985, pp. 99–126

——'Anzac and the Australian Military Tradition', *Revue Internationale d'Histoire Militaire*, no. 72, 1990, pp. 1–24

——'Conscription in Peace and War, 1911–1945', in Roy Forward and Bob Reece (eds), *Conscription in Australia*, Queensland University Press, St Lucia, 1968, pp. 22–65

——'The Anzac Tradition', *Meanjin Quarterly*, vol. 24, no. 1, 1965, pp. 25–44

——'The Australians at Gallipoli—I' *Historical Studies*, vol. 14, no. 54, 1970, pp. 219–30; 'The Australians at Gallipoli—II' *Historical Studies*, vol. 14, no. 55, 1970, pp. 361–75

Inglis, K. S. and Phillips, Jock 'War Memorials in Australia and New Zealand: A Comparative Study' in John Rickard and Peter Spearitt (ed.) *Packaging the Past? Public Histories*, Melbourne University Press, Melbourne, 1991, pp. 179–91

Jauncey, L. C. *The Story of Conscription in Australia*, Melbourne, Macmillan, 1968 (first published 1935)

Kapferer, Bruce *Legends of People: Myths of State: Violence, Intolerance, and Political Culture in Sri Lanka and Australia*, Smithsonian Institution Press, Washington, 1988

Keating, M. 'Australian Work Force and Employment, 1910–11 to 1960– 61', *Australian Economic History Review*, vol. VII, no. 2, 1967, pp. 150–71

Kent, D. A. '*The Anzac Book* and the Anzac Legend: C.E.W. Bean as Editor and Image-Maker', *Historical Studies*, vol. 21, no. 84, April 1985, pp. 376–90

Lake, Marilyn 'The Power of Anzac' in M. McKernan and M. Browne *Australia: Two Centuries of War & Peace*, Australian War Memorial in association with Allen & Unwin, Canberra, 1988, pp. 194–22

——*A Divided Society: Tasmania during World War I*, Melbourne University Press, Melbourne, 1975

Louis, Wm Roger 'Australia and the German Colonies in the Pacific, 1914–1919', *Journal of Modern History*, no. 4, 1966, pp. 407–21

Macintyre, Stuart *The Oxford History of Australia*, vol. 4, *1901–1942: The Succeeding Age*, Oxford University Press, Melbourne, 1986

Maddock, R. and McLean I. (eds) *The Australian Economy in the Long Run*, Cambridge University Press, Melbourne, 1987

McCarthy, Dudley *Gallipoli to Somme: The story of C. E. W. Bean*, John Ferguson, Sydney, 1983

McKernan, Michael 'Catholics, conscription and Archbishop Mannix', *Historical Studies*, vol. 17, no. 68, 1977, pp. 299–314

——'Sport, war and society: Australia 1914–18' in Richard Cashman and Michael McKernan (eds) *Sport in History: The Making of Modern Sporting History*, University of Queensland Press, St Lucia, 1979, pp. 1–20

——*Australian Churches at War: Attitudes and Activities of the Major Churches, 1914–1918*, Catholic Theological Faculty and Australian War Memorial, Sydney and Canberra, 1980, pp. 41–58

——*The Australian People and the Great War*, Nelson, Melbourne, 1980

McLachlan, Noel. 'Nationalism and the Divisive Digger', *Meanjin Quarterly*, no. 27, 1968, pp. 302–8

McMullin, Ross *The Light on the Hill: The Australian Labor Party, 1891–1991*, Oxford University Press, Melbourne, 1991

Meaney, Neville *Australia and the World: A Documentary History from the 1870s to the 1970s*, Longman Cheshire, Melbourne, 1985

——*The Search for Security in the Pacific, 1901–14: A History of Australian Defence and Foreign Policy 1901–23*, vol. 1, Sydney University Press, Sydney, 1976

Monash, John *The Australian Victories in France in 1918*, Hutchinson, London, 1920

Murphy, D. J. 'Religion, Race and Conscription in World War I', *Australian Journal of Politics and History*, vol. XX, no. 2, 1974, pp. 155–63

Nish, I. H. 'Australia and the Anglo-Japanese Alliance, 1902–11', *Australian Journal of Politics and History*, vol. IX, 1963, pp. 201–12

O'Farrell, Patrick *The Catholic Church and Community in Australia: A History*, Nelson, Melbourne, 1977

Pearson, A. R. 'Western Australia and the conscription plebiscites of 1916–1917', *RMC Historical Journal*, vol. 3, 1974, pp. 21–6

Pedersen, P. A. 'The AIF on the Western Front: The Role of Training and Command', in M. McKernan and M. Browne (eds) *Australia: Two Centuries of War & Peace*, Australian War Memorial in association with Allen & Unwin Australia, Canberra, 1988, pp. 167–93

Phillips, Walter ' "Six o'clock swill": the introduction of early closing of hotel bars in Australia', *Historical Studies*, vol. 19, no. 75, 1980, pp. 250–66

Reiger, Kerreen M. *The Disenchantment of the Home: Modernizing the Australian Family 1880–1940*, Oxford University Press, Melbourne, 1985

Robertson, John *Anzac and Empire: The Tragedy and Glory of Gallipoli*, Hamlyn, Port Melbourne, 1990

Robson, L. L. 'The origin and character of the First A.I.F., 1914–18: some statistical evidence', *Historical Studies*, vol. 15, no. 61, 1973, pp. 737–49

——*Australia and the Great War*, Macmillan, South Melbourne, 1969

——*The First A.I.F.: A Study of its Recruitment, 1914–1918*, Melbourne University Press, Melbourne, 1982

Santamaria, B. A. *Daniel Mannix: a Biography*, Melbourne University Press, Melbourne, 1984

Serle, Geoffrey *John Monash: A Biography*, Melbourne University Press, Melbourne, 1982

——'The Digger Tradition and Australian Nationalism', *Meanjin Quarterly*, vol. 24, no. 2, 1965, pp. 149–58

Shute, Carmel 'Heroines and Heroes: Sexual Mythology in Australia, 1914–1918', *Hecate*, vol. 1, no. 1, 1975, pp. 6–22

Sinclair, W. A. 'Women and economic change in Melbourne 1871–1921', *Historical Studies*, vol. 20, no. 79, 1982, pp. 278–91

—— *The Process of Economic Development in Australia*, Cheshire, Melbourne, 1976

Smart, Judith. 'Feminists, Food and the Fair Price', *Labour History*, no. 50, May 1986, pp. 113–31

——'The panacea of prohibition: The reaction of the Women's Christian Temperance Union of Victoria to the Great War' in Sabine Willis (ed.) *Women, Faith & Fetes: Essays in the History of Women and the Church in Australia*, Dove Communications, Melbourne, 1977, pp. 162–92

——War and the Concept of a New Social Order, PhD thesis, Monash University, 1992

Smith, F. B. *The Conscription Plebiscites in Australia 1916–1917*, Victorian Historical Association, Melbourne, 1966

Spartalis, Peter *The Diplomatic Battles of Billy Hughes*, Hale & Iremonger, Sydney, 1983

Thompson, Roger *Australian Imperialism in the Pacific: The Expansionist Era 1820–1920*, Melbourne University Press, Melbourne, 1980

Thomson, Alistair 'Steadfast until Death'? C. E. W. Bean and the Representation of Australian Military Manhood', *Australian Historical Studies*, vol. 23, no. 93, 1989, pp. 462–78

—— 'The Anzac Legend: Exploring national myth and memory in Australia', in Raphael Samuel and Paul Thompson (eds) *The Myths We Live By*, Routledge, London, 1990, pp. 73–82

Tsokhas, K. *Money, Markets and Empire*, Melbourne University Press, Melbourne, 1990

Turner, Ian *Industrial Labour and Politics: The Dynamics of the Labour Movement in Eastern Australia, 1900–1921*, Hale & Iremonger, Sydney, 1979 (first published, 1965)

Ward, Russel *The Australian Legend*, Oxford University Press, Melbourne, 1958

White, Richard 'Motives for joining up: Self-sacrifice, self-interest and social class, 1914–18', *Journal of the Australian War Memorial*, no. 9, 1986, pp. 3–16

——'War and Australian Society', in M. McKernan and M. Browne (eds) *Australia: Two Centuries of War & Peace*, Australian War Memorial in association with Allen & Unwin, Canberra, 1988, pp. 391–423

——*Inventing Australia: Images and Identity 1688–1980*, George Allen & Unwin, Sydney, 1981

Winter, Denis (ed.) *Making the Legend: The War Writings of C. E. W. Bean*, University of Queensland Press, St Lucia, 1992

Withers, Glenn 'The 1916–1917 conscription referenda: a cliometric reappraisal', *Historical Studies*, vol. 20, no, 78, 1982, pp. 36–46

Index

Printed in Great Britain by
Amazon.co.uk, Ltd.,
Marston Gate.